TILL THE SUN GROWS COLD

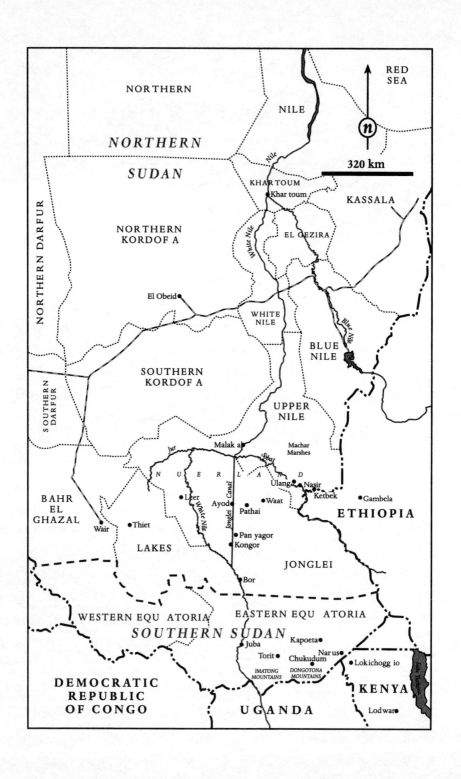

TILL THE SUN
GROWS COLD

Maggie McCune

HEADLINE

First published in 1999
by HEADLINE BOOK PUBLISHING

10 9 8 7 6 5 4 3 2 1

For permission to reprint copyright material the author and publishers
gratefully acknowledge the following:

A.P. Watt on behalf of Michael B. Yeats for an extract from 'A Prayer for My
Daughter' by W.B. Yeats and Macmillan and David Higham Associates for an
extract from 'I am the Great Sun' by Charles Causley from *Collected Poems*; Gibran
National Committee, P.O.Box 116-5487, Beirut, Lebanon, for an extract from 'The
Prophet' by Kahlil Gibran; Essential Music, 47 British Grove, London W4,
PolyGram Music Publishing Ltd by permission of Music Sales Ltd for part of
'Whenever God Shines His Light', words and music by Van Morrison; Faber &
Faber Ltd for an extract from 'Funeral Blues' from 'Twelve Songs' by W.H. Auden
from his *Collected Poems*; Bloodaxe Books Ltd for an extract from 'I Will Live and
Survive' by Irina Ratushinskaya; The Estate of Alice Duer Miller for her poem
'The White Cliffs'; Big Ben Music Ltd for 'The Life that I Have' by Leo Marks.

British Library Cataloguing in Publication Data

McCune, Maggie
Till the sun grows cold
I. Title
823.9'14[F]

ISBN 0 7472 2286 X hardback
ISBN 0 7472 7539 4 softback

Typeset by
Letterpart Limited, Reigate, Surrey

Printed and bound in Great Britain by
Clays Ltd, St Ives plc

Headline Book Publishing
A division of Hodder Headline PLC
338 Euston Road
London NW1 3BH

To Erica, Jennie and Johnny

Look from thy window and see
My passion and my pain;
I lie on the sands below,
And I faint in thy disdain.
Let the night-winds touch thy brow
With the heat of my burning sigh,
And melt thee to hear the vow
Of a love that shall not die
Till the sun grows cold,
And the stars are old,
And the leaves of the Judgment Book unfold.

'Bedouin Song'
Bayard Taylor (1825–78)

Contents

Acknowledgements

My special thanks go to Wendy Holden without whose generosity of time and energy this book might never have been written. To Ben Woolfenden who assisted in the process, and to all those who never lost confidence in my story.

I also wish to thank my family, Erica, Jennie and Johnny. And, of course, Sue, my sister, for listening and for reminding me of my own life.

To Emma's many friends, now my friends: Sally Dudmesh, Bill Hall, Jo Mostyn, Willie Knocker, Liz Hodgkin, Roo Woods, Catherine Bond, Heather Stewart, Bob Koepp, Patta Scott-Villiers, Peter Moszynski and Rory Nugent, all of whom have helped me piece together the jigsaw of Emma's life. And to my friend Catherine Greig.

To the many Sudanese who knew and loved Emma for herself, and especially to Riek, her husband.

On the day she died, Emma was working on a project she had initiated to relieve the suffering of the refugee women and children of southern Sudan. Should anyone wish to make a donation, please make cheques payable to 'Christian Aid' and send to

Emma Fund Horn of Africa Team
Christian Aid
PO Box 100
London
SE1 7RT

Introduction

I knew that my daughter, Emma McCune-Machar, was writing her autobiography when her life was, tragically, cut short on 24 November 1993 in Nairobi, Kenya, at the age of twenty-nine. At the time of her death, she was married to a Sudanese war lord.

As the months and years have passed I have thought about how I could tell her story, working with words from her fragmented and unfinished book called *Wedded to the Cause, Living with the War in the Sudan*. The final chapter of her synopsis reads:

> 'After one year of marriage to Riek Machar I feel that our love for one another has been tested. Instead of pulling us apart the difficulties we have faced have brought us closer together. The circumstances are not ideal and the future is uncertain. The ending of this book has yet to happen. There are many scenarios: to live with the strain of civil war forever, to be killed, to be imprisoned, to be exiled, to be victorious or to live in peace and prosperity.'

Emma kept diaries and wrote letters and these cameos of her life in Africa left me tantalised. She and I had never found the time to sit down and talk about it. So, in the end, I vowed to find out for myself, and to tell others about her free spirit, and about the extraordinary young woman that she was.

As I gained the courage to write it all down, I found myself propelled into action, to pick up the phone, to dial a number, to talk to people, many of whom were total strangers, to ask them when and where their paths had crossed with Emma's, and what impressions she had left.

Inevitably, as the story of Emma's life unfolded, I began to piece together my own story, and the book became a journey of discovery for me, in search of my daughter.

The exercise has been fascinating and rewarding. Every tiny step or chance remark has led me to a closer understanding of my daughter, and of myself. I do believe that each and every one of us has a story to tell, and even the shortest life has immortality.

I began my book with Goethe's powerful words echoing in my head, 'Whatever you can do or dream you can, begin it.'

This I have done, *Till the Sun Grows Cold*.

Maggie McCune

1999

1

It is hard enough to discover where and with whom we truly belong in our lives. But before we die we may have the time and the forethought to decide where in this world we want to rest for eternity. Yet if we haven't had the time to choose the place, despite premonitions of our own death – and then that death comes suddenly – our loved ones, knowing us, must make the decision for us . . .

FOR A LONG TIME NOW I HAVE LIVED ALONE. Near to my house in Surrey there is a church surrounded by an ancient graveyard. A church has stood on this site for at least a thousand years: the walls of the nave are decorated with ghostly twelfth-century frescoes depicting scenes from the life of Christ and the torments of hell. But today is the first day of a new year at the end of the twentieth century.

The setting is quintessentially English. The wintry afternoon light is failing and the graveyard is deserted. Night is falling, dividing everything into black and white. A heavy fall of snow has covered the ground and draped the tombs; an icy and fitful wind is blowing. The rows of gravestones beneath the dark cypress trees circle the church. The headstones, stark against the snow, splashed with yellow lichen, stand upright, or lean at an angle to the universe.

I pause in front of one: the name, the life span, the sad eulogies, the final summing up of a human existence have all been erased by the elemental passing of time. At an adjacent grave someone has planted a miniature Christmas tree. On top is perched the tiny figure of a winged angel made out of pink wool. I turn away, disturbed. What gestures, but ones such as these, futile yet moving, are left to us when we cannot recreate the life of a child who now lies in the darkness, under a blanket of snow?

So from time to time I come here to listen to the resounding silence of the dead, to mourn the losses which we can never recover in this world. Always I am driven to think of my own past, to recollect in tranquillity the things that were never tranquil, to try to understand how they brought us from there to here. In a different world, in a different life, it's possible that my daughter Emma might also have been buried here; and that one day I might have been part of the same earth. But that is futile conjecture. It comes from a life that never happened.

I pull up the collar of my coat against the wind and retrace my footsteps in the snow down the pathway. The shadows are deepening. At home I will warm myself by the fire, make a cup of tea, sit in the silence of the house looking out over the garden which I tend with a passion, and think about the resolutions I should make for the new year which has begun today. But as I walk alone in the freezing night, it is all too easy to believe that my life has no more substance than a shadow; that some truer reality lies here, in the universal company of the dead, in the place of the ghosts.

It was at dawn on a morning in November 1993 that I came by minibus, with a small group of Emma's closest friends, to Wilson Airport, on the outskirts of the Kenyan capital, Nairobi. As we clambered wearily out of the bus and into the mist we were greeted by a young Sudanese man. He was handsome, of medium build, with a charismatic presence. His name was Kwong and he was the aide-de-camp to the man who stood at my side, my son-in-law, Riek Machar Teny-Dhurgon (pronounced Reeak Mashar), a southern Sudanese war lord.

Kwong ushered us reverentially into a single-storey building which was little more than a wooden hut. Inside, a third of the space was a waiting room, furnished simply with dark blue upholstered seats. I sat down here and waited for what began to seem an interminable length of time, deep in controlled and silent thought. Beyond our motionless area, an open-plan office was bustling with activity: a fax machine was spilling out paper and people were rushing to answer telephones. Just inside the entrance, expectant travellers stood amongst baggage of all shapes and sizes: suitcases, boxes, crates and rucksacks strewn across the floor. The walls were covered with maps of the continent in which I unexpectedly found myself.

Wilson is a small but busy airport used by the Red Cross and other aid agencies as a base to ferry food and vital equipment to the remotest corners of East Africa. It is also used by the tour companies who organise exclusive safari expeditions. The passengers gathered together within its spartan terminal at any one time are a contradictory mix of casually dressed aid workers, their faces and clothes tired and sun-creased, and fresh-faced travellers from Europe, smart in their designer safari suits, wide-eyed in anticipation of giraffe lolling across the plains and wildebeest migrating from the Serengeti.

I felt dazed as I watched the pandemonium around me. I looked away, out of the dusty window. It might have been an April dawn in England, though it was already tellingly warm. I was wearing a blue cotton summer dress and carried with me only a small rucksack containing my personal documents, a camera, mosquito net and my washbag. My most cherished item was the BBC's book of poems, *Poetry Please*, which my sister Sue had thrust into my hand just a few days earlier and whose poignant collection of verses had begun to spin around in my head, shining beams of light into every dark crevice of my life.

> *Now more than ever seems it rich to die,*
> *To cease upon the midnight with no pain . . .*
> *Thou wast not born for death, immortal Bird!*
> *No hungry generations tread thee down.*

from 'Ode to a Nightingale' by John Keats

Turning back to the activity inside the hut, my eyes followed our pilot, Heather Stewart, who was running the gauntlet of impatient passengers whilst negotiating the obstacle course of baggage, in an attempt to reach the fax machine. It was her unenviable task, against great odds in this part of the world, to arrange for two light aircraft to fly us from the relative safety of Kenya to the war torn region of southern Sudan that day. Obtaining the necessary passes and visas for our little group was burning up considerable time and patience.

I continued to watch her as she moved about the office. Blonde, trim, in faded blue jeans and a white cotton shirt, charming and gentle, with an infectious enthusiasm for her work, I had already gathered that she could demonstrate a steely assertiveness, should the need arise. I was very grateful to have her on my side.

The owner and chief pilot of her own company, Trackmark, Heather is renowned for her flying ability in this troubled region of Africa. More importantly for our purposes, she was one amongst few who dared to venture into and across such historically hostile territory, transporting aid or agency workers. At extremely short notice, she had agreed to take me and Riek and our largely silent party of fourteen souls to our final destination, using her own light aircraft and another chartered plane.

Waiting patiently in the stiflingly confined space of what effectively doubled as a terminal, and Heather's private office, I sat stock still, willing something to happen as she stoically carried on about her business for some three hours or so, calmly and politely pursuing the official clearance for both flights into the war zone. As well as myself and my son-in-law, our party comprised my sister Sue; my children Erica, Johnny and Jennie, all in their early twenties; Emma's dearest friends Sally Dudmesh and Annabel Ledgard, Patta Scott-Villiers, Emma Marrian, Peter Moszynski and Catherine Bond, and the Reverend Matthews (sic) Mathiang, a larger-than-life Presbyterian minister from Nairobi who watched the entire scene bemusedly, while the rest of us struggled to remain patient.

Sensing at last that something was beginning to happen, my fellow travellers made the final checks on the essential supplies which formed the bulk of our luggage, ensuring that we had sufficient water and provisions to carry us through the next twenty-four hours in a faraway place they knew to be devoid of even the most basic creature comforts. But as I watched them tick off a checklist of emergency rations, food and water were not the most important things on my mind.

Although the morning mist hadn't completely dispersed, the first of the aircraft we would be using, a twin-engined Otter, which looked rather like a Hercules Transporter in miniature, revved its engines and prepared for take off as I stood on the concrete runway, watching. Eight of our party had been chosen to go ahead, including the Rev Matthews, a man who could barely fit his bulk into his tiny aircraft seat. I was to catch the second flight with Riek and my immediate family once they were safely through.

I learned much later that the first flight was designed to act as a sort of decoy for any hostile forces that might be out to get Riek. It would head for Sudan via Lokichoggio, a small town at the Kenyan border, where it would refuel and have all its passengers' documents checked, double-checked and stamped. If anyone suspected Riek was on board, they would be disappointed. Heather would then take us on a different and rather circuitous route via Lodwar, nearer the Ugandan border, two hours later.

As the first plane lifted off and disappeared from sight, it was suggested that we take a short break from the waiting room and try to find a drink somewhere. It was only nine o'clock, but the heat was already intense, and my throat suddenly felt very dry. In one of the many small tin huts lining the airstrip, away from the waiting room and terminal, we found a canteen of sorts and ordered some refreshments. While Riek, ever the politician, used the time to sit talking quietly a few feet away with the Sudanese delegates who seemed to surround him wherever he went, we sat sipping hot, sweet coffee from plastic cups and listened intently to Catherine, a BBC World Service reporter and a close friend of Emma's, as she gave us a potted history of Sudan.

The largest country in Africa, Sudan is, to most Britons, a distant, desert country dimly recalled from school lessons on General Gordon, Lord Kitchener and the defeat of the Dervish army. When the British left Sudan, in 1956, they divided the south into three religious areas. The Upper Nile was handed to the Presbyterian missionaries, Equatoria to the Anglican missionaries, and the Bahr el Ghazal area to the Catholics. But since the end of Anglo-Egyptian rule in 1956, Sudan has been enmeshed in a catastrophic civil war between the Arabic Muslim government – based in the capital Khartoum in the north – and the

Christian rebels, led, in part, by my son-in-law, in the south. In recent years the southern rebels – descendants of cattle-keepers who were taught the Christian faith by the Crusaders and missionaries centuries earlier – had themselves divided and subdivided, causing bitter inter-factional fighting between the two main tribes, the Dinka and the Nuer.

My son-in-law, Riek, is a Nuer, a rebel commander with a breakaway faction of the Sudan People's Liberation Army (SPLA), and descended from an ancient Nuer prophet. A leopard-skin chief, he commands the loyalty of hundreds of thousands of Nuer across vast tracts of swamp and equatorial woodlands in the heart of the Upper Nile region. Despite being formerly united in a common hatred of the arch enemy – the ruling government – the Nuer and the Dinka are historically antagonistic towards each other and need scant excuse to start fighting amongst themselves. They are both tribes with long memories and too many hatchets left unburied. The difference is that in the past they fought with spears. Now they use Kalashnikovs.

Riek's most vociferous adversary in recent years has been John Garang, a Dinka, an American-educated former army officer and leader of the mainstream SPLA. Garang was one of the founder members of the SPLA in 1983, to lead the rebellion against the government, making Riek his most senior commander a year later. Now – after irreconcilable differences – the two men are deadly enemies and it was Garang, rather than the government's forces, from whom Riek had most to fear.

Trying to take in all that Catherine was saying, I found myself overwhelmed by great sadness that such a gentle people, the statuesque race that Emma had chosen to become part of, could kill and fight and maim in the name of either Christianity or Islam. Such a brutal war seemed so out of place in what is still one of the remotest regions on earth, inaccessible to the rest of the world. The deserts, mountains and forests which surround it have acted as a physical barrier against outside influences, and have left it in a past age, where life and death are dictated by the seasons and people live in much the same way as they have done for centuries, eking out a living from the land, grazing their cattle and growing basic crops.

A country rich in natural resources – oil, minerals, timber – and fertile land, it is also the place where the White Nile and the Blue Nile converge to become one mighty river, flowing onwards through a great range of landscapes, cultures and peoples towards Egypt, the Delta and the Mediterranean Sea. The Nile in Sudan is a symbol of how tribal differences might be reconciled, and yet after four generations of war, there is still little prospect of a lasting peace settlement.

I recalled one of Emma's letters home from her first trip to Sudan, in which she described some of the wonder and sadness of Africa, sights that lured her to remain.

'Children jumping in the Nile from high banks, wooden canoes paddled upstream and floated downstream to catch the fish. The islands of water hyacinths. The herons, motionless, adrift. Rising fish, making rings of water . . . A huge upturned satellite dish – an ambitious project financed by the Kuwaiti government to throw southern Sudan into the twentieth century – now sprouted grass and trees from the labyrinth of intricate metalwork. The large saucer-shaped head was drooped in sorrow – a monument to war . . .'

After what seemed like an age, we were at last told that our flight was ready for take off. Settling our account with the waiter in Kenyan shillings, we walked out into the dazzling sunlight to meet the little eight-seater Cessna. In our absence, some seats had been removed from the back of the plane and Emma's sealed wooden coffin with its six brass handles, recently transported from Nairobi Cathedral by the undertakers, had been carefully placed inside and strewn with flowers, handpicked from the myriad bouquets at her funeral service the previous afternoon. Catching sight of the coffin once more, my breath caught in my throat. But then I suddenly felt strangely serene, and at peace. It was comforting to have her there like that with us, to be travelling with her on her final journey back to the country she called home.

The brightly clad Sudanese delegates stood by the plane, waiting quietly to bid farewell to their leader Riek, and to Emma and her family. Moist-eyed women clad in vividly coloured garments and men in sober suits stood waving in the heat haze as Heather opened up the engines one at a time and we sped off down the runway. Within minutes we were airborne, and heading north towards the Sudanese border.

The plane was comfortable though by no means luxurious, with single seats at each window. I sat up at the front next to Heather for most of the journey, Riek sat behind us, catching up with some sleep, his seven-foot frame crammed into his seat uncomfortably. Erica, who had an earache, sat behind me, suffering in silence. Jennie and Johnny catnapped, and Catherine who was at the back sat close to Emma, in silence. I stayed alert and fascinated, talking to Heather from time to time about the landscape below us; silently contemplating my own thoughts in between. But for the circumstances, it would have been an exciting adventure on this my first ever visit to the country which Emma so loved and my inaugural flight in a light aircraft. I couldn't help smiling to myself and glancing back at my daughter's coffin. She had finally got me up in a small plane in to Sudan, as she once said she would, 'by hook or by crook'.

Just over an hour later we landed in Lodwar, a bustling market town close to the Sudanese border. Out of the windows of the plane as we came into land we could see people walking towards us from the little market place nearby, full of stalls selling food, clothes, beds, buckets – all kinds of things. The people seemed to have arrived by any means of transport available to them – donkey, camel, lorry, plane or foot. As in all African markets, empty cardboard aid boxes with the distinctive agency logos acted as makeshift stalls and the traders sold everything from soap, tea and salt, to vegetables – all laid out neatly on display.

Heather suggested that we should get out and stretch our legs while she refuelled the plane, took care of the necessary official procedures and had our documentation checked. We stepped out into the furnace of the day. The hot wind, laden with dust, stung our eyes. The equatorial sun, beating down on our heads, cooked our brains. A small, semi-naked boy – one of many children who crowded around us – pushed to the fore, his arms outstretched to Riek. I pleaded with my son-in-law to ask him to fetch us some straw hats from the market to shield us from the intense heat.

We made our way along a parched and stony path which led to a small Irish missionary station run by nuns, some of whom had been there for twenty-five years. The building was brick, whitewashed inside and outside, with a corrugated tin roof. Sheltered at last from the relentless sun, we were further greatly relieved to be offered chilled drinking water. One of the nuns was a nurse and she tended to Erica's ear, providing some cotton wool and a painkiller to ease her increasing discomfort.

Twenty minutes later Heather appeared to fetch us. Slaking her own thirst quickly, she led us back into the heat once more where Riek stood waiting. He had stayed with the plane throughout and, because he was about to enter the airspace of the country which he partly ruled, he had changed out of his navy blue suit and tie into his trademark combat fatigues, in which he seemed much more at ease. In the confusion of the previous six days, his military boots had not been packed for him and the shiny black brogues he had to wear instead, which squeaked when he walked, seemed more than a little incongruous with his camouflage battledress.

But then so did so much about this calm, velvet-voiced man my daughter had chosen for a husband, I thought. Just before we climbed on board for the final stage of our journey, the small boy I had seen earlier reappeared as if by magic, grinning and holding out four straw hats. What Riek asked for, it seemed, he got.

We fastened our seat belts, and took to the air again, quickly leaving behind the dusty runway flanked by doum palms and banana trees. We had several more hours of flying through the varied landscapes of Eastern Equatoria and the region of Jonglei, before we reached our destination, Riek's home town of Leer.

Suddenly, and without any warning, our little plane began to climb steeply, higher and higher. I had hardly noticed, until my son Johnny turned to Catherine and asked: 'Why are we going so high?'

'To avoid any anti-aircraft fire,' Catherine explained simply. She was just about to explain but Heather, glancing across at me with a concerned expression on her face, interrupted abruptly and changed the subject, pointing out the Dongotona Mountains to our right.

Once we were well across the border and had reached safer airspace, controlled by Riek's men and not Garang's, we descended to fly at our normal altitude. We crossed the small mountain range near Torit and flew over vast tracts of swamp punctuated every now and again by miniature villages peppered with tiny mud huts. As we travelled on and on, I was struck by an overwhelming sense of the vastness of the region, which stretched away on all sides of us, apparently without end. I was reminded of something Emma wrote in her diary, in 1989.

'It was a small twin-engined plane. As we rose above the desert, I could see a wriggling red road below. It was a road I had come to know well. Nothing but sand, scrub, stunted acacia trees. Occasionally a small hummock – otherwise a vast nothingness.'

The swamps below were a strange and fascinating vision, their water luminous beneath the green and glistening surface of reeds and algae. I was mesmerised, thoughts and voices and memories galloping through my mind, keeping time with the tiny shadow of our plane racing across the landscape far below.

After three hours we were within range of Leer, a small pastoral town in the western Upper Nile region of southern Sudan. Leer lies in the heart of Nuer country. Riek was born there; and it remains his family home. It was to this remote and desolate place that we were bringing my beloved Emma, my first born child, and her unborn child, to lay them both to rest in the sun-baked African soil she lived and died for.

My reverie was broken by a movement next to me as Heather fidgeted in her seat and leaned forward over the controls, searching for a first sight of the tiny airstrip which lay below us, somewhere, amidst the swamps, and was notoriously difficult to find. I experienced a flash of panic as I thought: 'What will happen if we can't find the airstrip?'

You need sharp eyes, steady hands and nerves of steel to land a light aircraft on the airstrip at Leer in southern Sudan. You are descending over a featureless swampland with hardly a reference point, only small clusters of mud huts here and there, or an isolated tree. With the landscape below you shimmering in the heat haze, you are straining your eyes for a straight, short and narrow stretch of pale-coloured earth. And – with nowhere else to land within hundreds of miles – you are praying that you find it. Before the panic had time to take hold and squeeze my heart, we suddenly saw, ahead in the distance, the straight stretch of light-coloured earth.

With the expertise and confidence of a veteran, Heather gripped the controls and the plane began to descend towards its target, its engine whining. Within minutes, the trees and the mud huts rose up to meet us. Lining up the plane with the tiny airstrip, she pulled back the throttle and with a jolt we were safely back on the earth.

The scene that now rolled into view, as the plane taxied slowly to a halt amid clouds of dust, was the most extraordinary I have ever witnessed. I can't imagine that anything in my lifetime could possibly surpass it. Peering out of the little passenger window through the settling dust, I could see thousands, literally thousands, of Sudanese men, women and children, in ranks ten or fifteen deep, lining this tiny strip of dirt in the middle of the African bush. I was told later that many of them had walked for days to reach here, and that most had been waiting patiently for up to two days in soaring temperatures, which had by now reached 45° Celsius, 120° Fahrenheit.

With little or no communication with the outside world and news passed on from village to village by messenger, word had come from Nairobi that their leader Riek had been killed along with his wife. Pandemonium had struck; Riek had taken on an almost God-like status to his most devoted followers and they feared the future more than ever without him. Arriving in their droves from across the bush, materialising out of the shimmering heat haze like biblical mirages, they had come now to find out for themselves and to pay homage to the man who had led them for so many years and to the woman he had taken for his wife.

The news that was to greet them when the first plane arrived did nothing to quell their dismay; Riek was alive, they were told, but it was confirmed that his wife, the white woman who had cared so much for them, and who they called 'Emm-Maa', had indeed died. It seemed yet another cruel blow from a God whose harshness to their country left them baffled.

Many of the tall, dark figures who thronged closer and closer held aloft thin wooden poles bearing flags daubed with the red cross of St George, which fluttered in the heat. It was like a medieval scene. They looked for all the world like extras from a film set of the Crusades, draped in their strips of cloth. Others clutched rough wooden crucifixes which proudly proclaimed the Presbyterian Christianity – brought to them centuries before by white missionaries – for which they were now waging a war. From all around came a dreadful clamour, the high-pitched wailing and ululating of the women in time to the thunderous beating of drums made of goat skins and gourds. My heart began pounding rhythmically in my chest, my hands trembled and I watched in wide-eyed astonishment as the sights and the sounds and the heat flooded and filled my brain.

As soon as the propellers had stopped spinning, the door of the plane was yanked open and the raw white humid stillness flattened our hair and clothing. The little advance party from the first plane, who had been awaiting our arrival for an uncomfortable hour, sheltering in the scant patches of shade beneath a few distant trees and long elephant grass, emerged cautiously into the fierce sunlight to greet us formally. As they began to walk silently down the scorched runway towards our aircraft the massed Sudanese took this as a signal to surge forward behind them, desperate for sight of Riek, to confirm that he was truly alive. As soon as Riek's frame filled the doorway of the plane to face them, the crowds lost all control and swarmed in.

Within seconds, they had overtaken the others and surrounded our tiny aircraft with a throbbing wall of bodies and dust, threatening to crush us. The situation was dangerously out of control as hysteria and panic coursed through Riek's people. Retreating hastily back into the aircraft, we caught our breath and tried to quash our own feelings of panic and fear as the clouds of dust billowed in on us. In a vain attempt to calm the situation, Riek tried twice to disembark but each time he was forced back by the multitude. Men and women, mad with grief, were by now literally storming the plane, reaching out to touch us, trying to see Riek, and to catch a glimpse of Emma's coffin through the windows. They were climbing onto the aircraft's flimsy wings, rocking it dangerously and clinging to its wires, while Riek's soldiers and body-guards began to lash out frantically with whips, sticks and batons, forcing the people back.

Overwhelmed by the press of faces at the windows, in the doorway and all around us, our small group of Britons remained huddled together inside, wondering what on earth would happen. Heather's anxiety was particularly acute – we were a very long way from help, and any spare parts, should her aircraft be seriously damaged. Only Riek seemed unfazed, urging the people back from the plane.

As with my appeal for straw hats at Lodwar, Riek's hissed requests for assistance from his followers were suddenly met. Without explanation, a white Land Rover appeared magically before us, incongruously modern in this setting, nudging its way through the wailing crowd before pulling up close to the plane. Riek waited until it was near enough and then jumped down onto its roof in his battledress, his red beret cocked at an angle on his head, and began addressing the crowd through a loud-hailer which someone had thrust into his hand.

Appealing for calm, his richly tonal voice boomed out across the bobbing black heads of the crowd, calming the mood of panic, and gradually the clamour subsided as people began to listen to their leader addressing them in their native tongue. On Riek's hand-signalled instructions, and while he was still speaking, the Land Rover slowly began to move away from the plane towards the small fenced-in compound where he and Emma had built adjacent tukuls or mud huts during their short but extraordinary marriage. To our very great relief the majority of the crowd fell in behind the Land Rover, their banners and crosses forming a fluttering vanguard around the vehicle.

Finally safe to step from the sanctuary of the plane, we did so shakily, helped by the friends and relatives who had watched the whole scene with apprehension and fear. Once we had regained our composure and braced ourselves for what faced us next, Emma's coffin was carefully lifted out by six of Riek's armed soldiers and borne aloft by them amid a persistent crowd of villagers towards Riek's compound.

One giant of a soldier, a Kalashnikov rifle slung over one shoulder, gently picked up a plastic bucket filled with flowers which we had brought from Nairobi and carried it with great reverence on his other shoulder. Clutching the remaining flowers that had by now wilted, we formed a silent but orderly line behind the funeral procession, forcing our leaden limbs to walk us through the searing temperatures to the burial ground. The remaining tribespeople followed on behind.

Walking in step with the Africans in what seemed a long and mournful retinue as the compound came into sight, I looked around and wondered at the strangeness of it all – the peculiar mix of white and black, of civilians and soldiers – flanked by children carrying flowers and men carrying guns. They were all so tall and thin, and walked with the same loose-jointed gait that Emma had. She had always joked that they were the only people she had ever met who dwarfed her five foot eleven inch frame. I pictured her now, walking amongst them in the colourful clothes she so favoured, her glossy dark hair bound up in a brightly coloured scarf, her bangles jangling on her wrist, laughing, smiling, ruffling the heads of the children as she passed.

> *He wedded a wife of richest dower,*
> *Who lived for fashion, as he for power.*
> *She wedded a man unlearned and poor,*
> *And many children played around her door.*

from 'Maud Muller' by John Greenleaf Whittier

The air was hot and still, flies buzzed around our mouths and eyes, the arid red soil crumbled at our feet. A waft of something sweet and sickly assailed my nostrils, already filled with the stench of sweat and the pungent smell of burning cattle dung.

We walked on through the heat towards the oval-shaped half-acre compound which was fenced off with eight-foot high stakes tied tightly together with grasses. Once inside the main entrance, I caught sight of the specially prepared grave, dug to one side of Emma's tukul, a deep vault lined with concrete to prevent human or animal desecration. As each step brought me closer to it, a rhythmic pounding jolted through my body, in time with my heart. I began to feel myself melting into the amazing pageant all around me – the colours and sights and smells, the heat, the thousands of people who each felt something for Emma, who had an equal right to be there and weep at her graveside with me. I was part of something much, much larger, I suddenly realised; I was not an individual any more, but becoming one with an experience which was uniting people of radically different cultures in a single grief. My family and I were truly the outsiders, the pale-faced foreigners in a foreign land, graciously invited to witness an ancient rite of passage that had its roots in the annals of time. For the first time since Emma's death, I began to see that, in a sense, this was not *my* occasion at all, but *ours*.

Clutched in my sweaty hand was a piece of paper, a poem written by Leo Marks for the French Resistance, which I had planned to read at Emma's graveside.

> *The life that I have is all that I have,*
> *And the life that I have is yours.*
> *The love that I have of the life that I have*
> *Is yours and yours and yours.*
>
> *A sleep I shall have*
> *A rest I shall have,*
> *Yet death will be but a pause,*
> *For the peace of my years in the long green grass*
> *Will be yours and yours and yours.*

Although its words still seemed highly appropriate, more so now than ever before as I found myself actually here in the place of the long green grass, it suddenly occurred to me that no words could adequately express the moment and I thrust the crumpled piece of paper back into my rucksack, abandoning the gesture as futile. The sun continued to burn down on us, mesmerising us, making everything dreamlike and surreal.

We entered the burial area and pushed our way through the sweaty throng which had stopped ahead of us and was waiting, silently. We shuffled slowly closer to the grave. The sickly sweet smell I had encountered earlier greeted me once more and its source now lay before me. A cow had been slaughtered in honour of my daughter, its dark red essence congealing and seeping into the dusty earth beside where Emma would be buried, its dead eyes staring up at me, blood bubbling at its nose. Someone behind pushed me forward, indicating that I had to step over it, in accordance with time-honoured traditions that I knew nothing about.

One thousand dark eyes bored into me, watching my face for a reaction. I must have seemed a very strange sight to the people of Leer. A slight, grey-haired Englishwoman, eyes behind sunglasses, face ashen,

I hardly looked capable of bearing the statuesque and beautiful Emma, she of the distinctive laugh and irrepressible energy. Women unknown to me were weeping openly, keening and wailing quietly for my lost child, and yet I felt incapable of tears, as if I were in some sort of trance. It was all I could do to remain upright in the blaze of emotions tearing at my heart. Sally lent me a kanga, a piece of cotton cloth, to wrap around my head, but the pain of my grief could not be shielded from the sun.

An old, thin-faced African, dressed in a long white robe and with a head-dress made of grass, made me jump by flinging himself suddenly to the ground at my feet, crying and howling. Bewildered, I turned to one of Riek's aides, who had appointed himself official interpreter. 'What is he saying?' I asked, deeply disturbed by the sight. The old man threw himself upon me yet again and looked up at me with sad, dark eyes, a look I was coming to know. It told of past sufferings and those still to be endured, of the loss of loved ones, of physical hardship. In those eyes I could see dispossession, hunger and fear.

'He is telling you that he cannot bear the loss of Emma,' the thickly accented voice told me. 'That he can go on living no longer. He is begging you to allow him to be buried with her.' For the first time since I had arrived in Leer, I felt unsettled. The voodooistic nature of the old man's actions disturbed me. Feeling close to breaking point and yet desperate to retain my composure, I pleaded silently to be left alone, and almost instantly, he was pulled away.

We gathered together at the edge of Emma's final resting place under the scant shade of a fig tree. Leaning into each other despite the heat, the friends and family who had travelled so far were finally all reunited, each one of us struggling with our own sadness. The sides of the deep cement vault had been heaped with mounds of loose, dry earth and we awaited the start of what we hoped would be a short and simple service, as we had requested. The Reverend Matthews, plump, shiny and spotlessly attired in a dog collar and dark trousers, a Bible in his hand, suddenly materialised on the roof of the white Land Rover which had been positioned close by the grave. From this vantage point his huge, opulent figure, completely out of context in the impoverished surroundings, began to read prayers, followed by a service of committal.

Focusing on the moment, coping with each second as it arrived, we were surrounded by the throng of human bodies so closely that I felt that we might be pushed into the vault any minute. I could feel breath on my neck, smell the sweat of a hundred people, almost taste the salt of their tears. Accompanied by the sounds of their sobbing and weeping, I watched, dry-eyed, as my daughter's long, thin coffin was slowly lowered by the soldiers into the shadowy rectangle of the grave.

Riek, who – in accordance with his custom and position – had shown little emotion since the day of her death, stood at the head of the grave like a dark sentinel, watching and waiting. Then, without warning, he leapt in one fluid movement into the deep vault, and positioned himself across the coffin, legs astride, to take our bouquets. There was something almost mythological about the scene: a bereaved husband standing in a deep grave, his arms outstretched, reaching for the flowers to place on the coffin of his dead wife and unborn child.

Weeping openly, Annabel threw in a photograph of her new baby, Jessie, born a few months earlier, a son whom Emma had never seen. Emma's brother Johnny and her aunt, Sue, tossed down drooping bunches of blue agapanthus and white lilies. When the cascade of bouquets and personal effects had stopped, Riek stood stock still for a moment, lowered his head and closed his eyes, savouring the last few seconds. He would never again be so close to his beloved Emma, his 'Queen Nefertiti'.

Keeping his tears well in check as ours threatened to overwhelm us, Riek clambered from the grave, mounted the roof of the Land Rover and began to address the crowds through the loud-hailer, as if at some political rally. Introducing us one by one, these strangers who had come to Leer, telling his people who we all were and what relation we bore to Emma, his spirited introductions forced us all to gather ourselves in once more and remain on the edge of control. Shyly, we each nodded to the crowd as Riek's hand pointed to us in turn. Only Erica, with a raging earache and another pain for which there was no cure, could no longer stand it. Sinking, she slumped weeping sitting down on the only thing there was available, the little concrete cross ready to be set in place at the head of Emma's grave. Looking up, I noticed for the first time that the branches of the trees outside the compound were crowded with small boys, like a flock of crows, all gazing down upon the scene in silence.

Almost as mystically as they had arrived in that remote and inhospitable place, the throng of people disappeared after the funeral, dispersing into the bush, melding back into the landscape, becoming one with the earth. Drained of all emotion, the moisture sucked out of us, we were gently led by Riek's men to a red brick building, the Red Cross compound, a few hundred yards away. Pockmarked with bullet holes, its windows broken years ago, the sadly dilapidated haven had miraculously been transformed into a dormitory for its foreign guests. Rows of metal beds covered in mosquito nets awaited us on the verandah, there was water from a single tap to wash with, and a cold beer each from our provisions with which to quench our raging thirst.

I gulped down the amber liquid greedily, and the alcohol flowed through my veins and calmed me. I felt overwhelming relief that the moment I had been dreading so fearfully this past week was finally over. The mêlée had gone and I felt that, for the first time in days, I could breathe again.

Walking round the village to clear my head, I watched as the people gathered together in their own compounds, preparing their evening meal, gathering firewood, or tending to their animals. Other villagers sat chatting as their children played in the dust. I came across a stack of coiled rolls of grass matting – a legacy, I knew, from Emma in her quest to revive old crafts and industries interrupted by the war. At the far end of the village, I came to a river and watched as those who had come so far to pay their last respects to my child, removed their clothes, bundled them up on top of their heads and waded off into the distance as the sun began to set, casting an eerie orange glow. Returning to the compound, I was struck again by the meagreness of the landscape, the constant irritation of heat, dust, mosquitoes and tsetse-flies, and wondered how Emma could ever have survived here.

Later that night, after a meal of goat stew eaten with pancakes dipped in with our fingers, I sat in the shadows on the edge of the compound watching and listening as Riek held court under a vast, luminous full moon and counselled his people well into the night. One by one they would come to him with their problems and speak softly to him in their strange musical language. For ten minutes or so, he would listen intently, and then he would give his judgement. His voice was beautiful and gentle, it came from somewhere deep within him and its resonance reverberated off the walls. I could have sat and listened to it all night but as the exertions of the day and the headiness of the evening overcame me, I finally crept to bed, drifting off to sleep with the dulcet tones of Riek's voice echoing in my ears.

In the restless nights of the months and years that have followed, whenever I can't sleep, I try to recapture that bewitching voice in my head; somehow to record, mentally, the liltingly smooth words in a language I can't understand, but which speaks to my soul of ages past and visions unimagined.

I keep such music in my brain,
No din this side of death can quell,
Glory exulting over pain, and beauty, garlanded in hell . . .
To the world's end I went, and found Death in his carnival of glare;
But in my torment I was crowned, and music dawned above despair . . .

from 'Secret Music' by Siegfried Sassoon

At daybreak the next day, we were all up and ready to go. Heather was extremely anxious to get us safely back into Kenya. If Garang's men had heard about the funeral they would know that Riek was at Leer, and it was too much of a risk to remain a moment longer. Gathering together my few belongings, and trying to prepare myself for the parting, I wandered out into the dawn to be met by hordes of people, many of them relatives of Riek's, silently standing at the entrance to the compound, awaiting our departure.

I was bundled along with the rest of the party towards the dirt airstrip and the plane that would take us forward in time to try to pick up the pieces of our lives. There were soldiers and relatives offering to carry my bags, hands pushing me onwards, people swarming all around me in the early morning mist. Suddenly losing all control, I dropped my things and turned into the crowd, pushing them away with my hands and running back towards the compound as fast as my legs would carry me. I hadn't said goodbye, I wasn't ready, I needed to see Emma alone.

I was so glad I did, to catch a final glimpse. The burial ground was quiet and calm and to my surprise, as if by tribal magic, the open grave had been filled in during the night, the concrete mound topped with soil, smoothed off by a hundred hands and swept. The little cement cross had been carefully set in its place. In the coolness of the early morning, it was my final chance to see Emma at peace.

I had never once doubted my decision to have her buried here, in this place, with these people. I knew it was where she belonged and where her spirit would remain. But at that moment, in that desolate, dusty, God-forsaken place, without even a small garden for her to look out onto, it seemed absolutely unbearable to leave her behind. Alone. I somehow could not accept that her words, her laughter, fearlessness, beauty and vitality had been extinguished forever. She was only twenty-nine years old. She was carrying a child, my first grandchild. It simply wasn't fair.

There would be time enough for me to dwell on the decades of memories, to ponder the unpredictable trajectory of our lives. How fate had somehow transformed an ordinary little English girl who was born in India, grew up in a Yorkshire village, rode a pet donkey, pressed wild flowers and collected sea shells, into the feisty bride of a Sudanese guerrilla leader, involved in a war in a far-off continent; a conflict about which most people in the world have never even heard.

The question came now, under the relentless African sun, as it would come to haunt me again and again: How did we get from there to here?

2

The year was 1942 and the imperial sun was setting in India as war raged across Europe. A uniformed officer of the British Army was coming to the end of a long journey which brought him back from the fighting in Burma to the hill station of Quetta, in the Indian region of Baluchistan, near to the border with Afghanistan. Quetta, now part of Pakistan, is remembered most for the catastrophic earthquake which occurred seven years earlier, killing 20,000 people and all but levelling the British military headquarters.

A S THE OFFICER WALKED ALONG A BUSY STREET, A YOUNG WOMAN APPROACHED HIM. She was pushing a pram. The man and the woman passed by; their eyes met for a split second. He walked on, but was struck with a fleeting impression of a strikingly pretty face, high cheekbones and auburn hair. Then he heard his name called. He turned around. She had stopped, and was smiling at him. Only then did he recognise his wife. They drew together rather awkwardly, with broken phrases of greeting and surprise, into a hesitant embrace.

'Look in the pram,' she said. He bent forward to study the face of a sleeping child for the first time.

I was six months old. I was his daughter.

My father, Alexander George Bruce, first met my mother, Patricia, on a sea voyage when both were passengers on a troop ship sailing from England to Australia via the Far East. He had completed a four-year term as manager of a tea plantation in Upper Assam, before returning to his native Scotland for six months' leave and to see what he could do for the war effort.

It was an idiosyncrasy of the English way of life – the crucial importance of tea drinking – which meant that those working in the industry were granted exemption from military service during the Second World War. But my father had decided not to live out the war in a place where it might be possible to remain oblivious to the fact that there was a world beyond, which was being consumed by death and destruction. Instead he joined a Gurkha regiment and was posted to serve in Burma.

It was while en route to this posting that my mother bewitched him. Australian-born, she came from the demi-monde of the theatrical life and seemed very exotic to the independent, self-sufficient and well-read young Scotsman, who was passionate about country pursuits. She was a bonne vivante, had even posed nude, and spent the previous two years travelling the world in her capacity as a singer with the D'Oyly Carte, including entertaining troops in the Far East. Gregarious and fun-loving, she had left home to escape her own unhappy childhood with a stepfather who drank. Throwing herself into the dizzy world of the theatre and the social circuit, she had become skilled at golf and card games. She met my father when the ship docked at Gibraltar and they were engaged by the time they had reached Malta. My father disembarked at Bombay and she travelled on to Australia, with a promise to join him soon.

Many years later my father confided in me that he had secretly hoped that their liaison might have remained purely a shipboard romance. But just as he was poised to leave India for Burma, my mother arrived, true to her word. Ever the gentleman, my father kept his promise and they were married in the sleepy cantonment town of Dehra Dun, five hours north of Delhi, the gateway to the Garhwal Himalayas. Within a fortnight, my father left for Burma, leaving his new bride behind at the military staff college in Quetta. And so it was that more than a year later he came back, scarcely recognising her, to discover she had borne him a child.

I remember very little about the first four years of my life. I have only snapshot memories of where we lived, as we moved around India from one military base to another, and I was passed from one *ayah* or nanny to the next. My father went back to Burma as a captain of the Tenth Gurkha Rifles and in the spring of 1943, while on continuous patrol for three months, penetrating deep into Japanese-held territory and supervising intelligence-gathering reconnoitres on route marches of over a hundred miles, he was nominated for the Military Cross. His citation read: 'His leadership and professional ability have been most marked throughout the operations and his devotion to duty on these many dangerous patrols is deserving of reward.' Thus it was that a man who had no need to fight because of his profession was awarded one of the highest military medals for gallantry.

When the war was over and after Independence had been declared in India in 1947, we prepared to return to Britain as a family for my first visit to my father's homeland – making a long sea voyage from Bombay's Sassoon Docks. Bombay seemed terribly strange and frightening to such a little girl as me, the air was thick with pollution after the clear atmosphere of Assam and I was quite bewildered by the sheer numbers of people. While we were waiting to set sail my mother dragged me into a cinema to watch the film *The Red Shoes*, which only compounded my misery. I was distraught by the tragic end when the heroine, played by Moira Shearer, fell into the path of a train. The final scene, when she asked for the red ballet shoes with their ribbons to be taken off her feet, remained imprinted on my mind for years.

The voyage did little to cheer me – I suffered from whooping cough and measles and was largely confined to the ship's sanatorium. The only highlight of the trip for me was watching the gully-gully man, an entertainer, perform conjuring tricks with little yellow fluffy chicks. I was transfixed.

Shortly after we docked in England, I was dispatched like a parcel by steam train from London's Euston Station, to visit my paternal grandmother, who lived near Lockerbie in Scotland. My parents remained in London to attend to business. I was five years old, travelling unaccompanied in an unknown land – the first of so many solitary journeys in my life – to meet someone I had never seen before. Even at such a tender age, I began to realise that my mother lacked the most basic maternal instincts.

'Hello, Margaret, my name is Margot,' a smiling woman who introduced herself as my aunt met me on the platform of Dumfries railway station.

'*Namaste,*' I replied dutifully with my palms pressed together and a respectful nod of my head. Bemused at my traditional Indian greeting, she took my hand and drove me to my grandmother's dark, grey stone house, 'Parkend', where, despite my trepidation, I found my grandmother to be kind and full of fun, a real tease despite being recently widowed. My grandfather had been a doctor who had volunteered for war service, much as my father later did, and served in Gallipoli, surviving to write his own reminiscences of that campaign.

Dumfries was an historic and prosperous border town – home of Robbie Burns – and it was there that the granny I never knew I had gave me my first taste of what a normal home life was like, nurturing in me a sense of tradition and family pride. She showed me how to cook and bake, she read to me, spent time with me and played games. I cannot remember my mother ever entertaining me in the same way, or sharing any of her joie de vivre. Only when I was much older do I recall her taking an interest in me – to introduce me to the theatre, opera and ballet that she so loved.

My time with my grandmother and Aunt Margot was very special to me. Margot seemed to me to be a fairy godmother, a pretty woman who was always there to talk to and have fun with. She was Daddy's elder sister, who had mothered both him and their younger brother Stuart, when they were growing up. I tried to be as good as possible, so as not to do anything to make Granny or Aunt Margot send me away, but just as I had started to form my first real emotional bonds with people who appeared to want to return my love, the 'parcel' was dispatched again, this time back to London, to live with my mother for a brief period.

Unable to cope with my constant presence, however, Mummy sent me away again – this time to kindergarten, to mix and play with other children. I remember we had to walk along the pavements in crocodile formation, in pairs, one behind the other, each pair holding on to a strap to keep us together. I would have much preferred to stay at home but my mother simply didn't want me under her feet. I barely remember my father being around, he seemed to be away a great deal. But after five months in England, the three of us set sail again for India, for my father to resume his work on a tea plantation at Doom Dooma in Upper Assam.

Once we were ensconced in one of the comfortable bungalows on the vast plantation in north east India, I entered into one of the happiest phases of my life, made enjoyable mostly by the presence of my new *ayah* Ferami whom I adored and trusted. A rounded, squat woman in her mid-twenties and from the matriarchal Khasi hill tribe, she was devoted to me and I spent more time with her than I ever had with my own mother. In any event, one day my mother simply disappeared; I awoke one morning to find that she had gone.

'Where is Mummy?' I asked my father, more out of curiosity than anything.

'Oh, she had to go away,' he replied, offering no further explanation. She had gone without saying goodbye to me, without leaving me a letter or a present. She had simply vanished. I remember feeling surprise, indignation even, but not much else. In truth I was not bereft – her lack of emotional commitment meant that I could be just as happy with the company of my father and my *ayah*. And by this time, as a pampered little girl in India, there were many forms of entertainment in my life.

I remember going with Lokom, our *mali* or gardener, to the local bazaar to buy coloured tissue paper to make a kite. Kite-flying in India is a great tradition. In the towns and cities, entire families fly brightly coloured kites from every rooftop or open space on the ground; their distinctive diamond shapes dancing in the sky as far as the eye can see. As a child growing up in Assam, it was considered an essential part of my upbringing to join in with this ancient tradition. I can still see Lokom now, squatting on the lawn, hewing pieces of bamboo with a sharp knife to construct the triangular frame. Then he showed me how to boil up sticky rice as a paste to glue the wrapped pieces of tissue around it. We left it to dry in the sun, and the next morning – out with the local coolie, or labourer's, children on top of a small hill – hey presto, the gaily coloured kite actually flew. I was spellbound. But my favourite treat of all was the torch-lit circus which periodically came to town. I would be beside myself with anticipation; half-afraid and half-excited, as I was led into the ring to see mysterious, dark-skinned men, dressed in glittering gold pantaloons and exotically coloured turbans walk effortlessly on hot coals or lie on spiked beds of nails. It was so thrilling.

My father didn't appear to miss my mother at all. He loved fishing and would take me with Ferami on week-long expeditions up the Lohit Valley into the foothills of the Himalayas. He would spend long days on the mighty Brahmaputra River fishing for *mahseer*, a member of the carp family that can reach 100 lbs in weight or more. It is considered one of the most sporting fish in the world, and he would return to base camp triumphant, his bearer struggling to hold up his day's catch. The Brahmaputra in flood is an awe-inspiring sight. When the rains come and the river rises, little can be done to check its power. When the waters recede, they leave behind fertile soil which nurtures a rich harvest of rice, mustard and jute.

My father often rode out on his horse through the tea plantation, checking on the hundreds of coolies who tended the vast acres of lush green bushes that clung to the contours of the undulating hillsides. In the plucking season (the harvest time) the labourers, with wicker baskets strapped to their backs, wended their way between the orderly lines of tea bushes, plucking the topmost leaves. I would follow on my little pony, Peanuts.

'Come on, Rabbit,' Daddy would call out affectionately as I trotted along behind, wearing a broad-brimmed floppy straw hat. He had called me Rabbit ever since I was tiny – I much preferred it to Margaret or Maggie or Miss Bruce – and I loved the fact that no one else but he called me by that name. It was our special secret.

It was a very happy time, despite the absence of my mother, and I never wanted it to end. But soon afterwards and quite without explanation, I was dispatched by my father to the Loreto Catholic Convent and Boarding School 500 miles away in the hill station of Shillong, the capital of Meghalaya, which means literally 'Abode of the Clouds'. The move involved a long and tedious two-day journey by train and then taxi on a snaking road through pinewoods and meadows as we climbed up to the town, known in India as the 'Scotland of the East'. The bumpy, twisting road made me feel sick.

Years later I discovered that the decision to send me to the convent was based largely on the political events at the time. On 30 January

1948, the year after Independence, Mahatma Gandhi was assassinated in New Delhi. Widespread rioting erupted between the Hindu and Muslim communities after the funeral, and many – including my father – feared a blood-bath. Safely locked away in a convent at Shillong, my father felt I would be better protected than on the tea plantation. In the event of a further deterioration in the situation, my passport had apparently been stamped with a visa ready to send me to stay with my mother's family in Australia.

Deposited in Shillong and resigned to the fact that no amount of sulking could persuade my father out of his decision, I decided to make the most of it, and – to my surprise – actually enjoyed myself. An only child who had been rather isolated in Assam, I relished the regular company of other children, a novelty for a single child living in the middle of nowhere. I still missed my father dreadfully, especially the nightly bedtime stories and our tickling games, and I loathed and detested the porridge and rhubarb they served at meals and insisted I eat, but I had new friends and a new place to live and soon Shillong didn't seem so bad after all.

But once again, after just a few months and long before I was able to forge any lasting friendships with either my fellow pupils or the nuns, I was recalled home to the tea plantation, known in Assam as a 'tea garden'. Momentarily, I regretted making a fuss about the boarding school to my father, who, I thought, had now decided to grant my wishes and have me back alone with him. To my very great surprise, when I returned to our bungalow, my mother was waiting to greet me. I had almost forgotten what she looked like after her seven-month absence, as she announced that she had a surprise for me.

'I've been to Australia, Margaret,' she said, 'and look what I've brought you back.' I was thrilled with the stuffed koala bear, but stunned by the baby sister in a cot. I was six years old and I had never felt so cheated in my life.

The next few years held few memorable moments for me, as I was shuttled back and forth between Shillong and the tea garden in Assam. My beloved Ferami was assigned to look after my new baby sister, Suzanne, and as a consequence I was able to spend less and less time with her. Growing fast and racing through all the usual childhood diseases, during the next two years I suffered from poor health, finally contracting malaria and spending many days in the sick bay at school. After a brief visit home to my parents to convalesce, I was packed up and dispatched back to Shillong.

I can still remember the outset of that journey, sitting with my mother on the aeroplane, awaiting take off. My father had accompanied us to the airport but was not travelling with us. Suddenly, he appeared unexpectedly, having boarded the plane in haste. He had, he said, just had word from the doctors who had been treating me.

'Margaret is to go to England,' he informed my mother, and she nodded her understanding. Ruffling my hair fondly, he added: 'Chin up, Rabbit.'

Thus it was that by my ninth birthday, my life had been diverted and I was back in England, only this time to be left behind while my mother and Suzanne – or 'Sue' as she was to be known – returned to India without me. I was probably too young to comprehend any explanation for being abandoned and certainly none was offered, although in retrospect it must have had a great deal to do with my health and the perceived need for fresh English air. I had no choice but to accept the decision and, at my father's request, to try not to cry.

> *Remember me when I am gone away,*
> *Gone far away into the silent land;*
> *When you can no more hold me by the hand.*

from 'Remember' by Christina Rossetti

My new guardians, Mr and Mrs Parker, who ran a boarding house called 'Sea View' in the Victorian seaside town of Worthing, West Sussex, were a very conventional, middle-class couple, whom my mother had encountered – purely accidentally – on a beach. The Parkers had an only child, a daughter called Janet, the same age as me, and took in lodgers to help pay the bills. Janet was blonde with pigtails and, as I discovered on my arrival, attended the same local convent school where I had been enrolled as a day girl. In essence, the Parkers had agreed to take me in primarily to help with Janet's school fees and to be a companion for her.

Thus it was that we two complete strangers came to sleep in adjacent bedrooms and travel to and from school each day on our push-bikes, coming home for lunch and returning in the afternoon for our lessons.

I lived with the Parker family for three years as a paying guest, the bills all signed and paid for by my father in India. Janet was nice enough at first and there was some enjoyment: swimming in the sea throughout the summer months, watching traditional 'Punch and Judy' shows on the five-mile-long Regency sea front. But I remember very little else which entertained me or made me happy on Britain's cold and rainy south coast. I missed India with its warmth and colour; I missed Ferami and my pony; and I longed for the somnolent days of my youth, making paper kites and soaking up the sun.

For three long years, from the age of nine to twelve, I didn't *once* see my own father, mother, or younger sister. There must have been the occasional letter or photograph, but none that I can clearly recall. I made the most of my circumstances and tried to behave myself as best I could, consoling myself with my beloved koala bear and by keeping a scrapbook full of newspaper cuttings about the English royal family. My mother, being Australian and a colonial, had always been passionate about the royals and I suppose I thought that if I became as enthusiastic, she might be a little more pleased with me.

The only highlights during that lonely period were the occasional visits by my aunt Margot, and – I suspect at her suggestion – an offer out of the blue to spend my summer holidays in Blairgowrie in Perthshire, Scotland, with my uncle Stuart, his wife Diana and two young children, none of whom I had ever met. I jumped at the chance to revisit Scotland and be close to my grandmother. It was a sudden respite from the sheer loneliness and those holidays proved to be my only two months of real happiness each year, with picnics in the glens, walks in the heather and swimming in peat-coloured burns, where the water was often so cold, it made your skin tingle.

The presence of my young cousins, Robin and Linda, who were at least six years my junior but with whom I could enjoy childhood pursuits, helped to compensate for the loss of my immediate family. We had great fun playing the simplest games, including 'stepping stones', leaping from boulder to boulder midstream, endeavouring neither to get our feet wet nor to walk along the bank. We climbed trees to examine birds' nests, we fished for brown trout, we gathered field mushrooms and sometimes we even went camping. It was all so different and so relaxed. Those long, lovely summers gave me a sense of belonging and identity, and made me proud to be a Bruce. I felt I had roots after all.

Sometimes during the summer holidays, my uncle Stuart would take me back to visit my grandmother at 'Parkend'. I always loved going to her house, losing myself among the tall hollyhocks and delphiniums of her garden; picking peas and raspberries with her gardener, a tall man who reminded me of Mr McGregor in Beatrix Potter's *Peter Rabbit* stories, and who never minded when I crammed handfuls of freshly picked fruit into my mouth. I loved to sit on a canvas deck chair in the green-painted revolving summer house, watching the butterflies and birds in the garden, or waiting for the plump and jolly lady who collected and delivered the weekly laundry. I can also remember hearing Lizzie, the cook, banging the gong for lunch. This world was a safe world.

But by September it was time for me to return to Worthing, travelling alone as always, to rejoin the Parker household. The train journey from Perth to London was long and lonely with only the guard or a fellow passenger entrusted to keep an eye on me. At Euston I would be met by a distant cousin charged with escorting me across London to Victoria, to board another train for the final leg of my journey.

The first eighteen months of my time with the Parkers were happy enough. I remember seeing snow fall for the first time that winter and rushing out to the back yard. I couldn't understand this manna from heaven; it was like pieces of cotton wool falling from the sky which melted in the palm of my hand. But then, without explanation, Janet began to grow resentful towards me. Cherished books and presents that I had received from Uncle Stuart and Auntie Margot began to disappear and the Parkers began to question my religious beliefs, forcing me to eat their regular Friday fare of jellied eels in a bowl of broth on what should have been my day of fasting.

They laughed at my interest in the royal family, mocking me for keeping my scrapbooks full of photographs and articles. And, for the first time since I had lived there, Mr Parker teased my nightly after-dark fears in which I always checked under my bed and in the wardrobe to make sure that no snakes, jackals or tigers were lurking there, behaviour I now know to be the classic anxiety symptoms of an abandoned child. I was racked with sadness about the change in the Parkers towards me. I had always been on my best behaviour and it didn't seem to me that I could have done anything to upset them. In retrospect I think they simply grew bored of the shy little 'rich' girl in their midst and decided it would be much more fun to make sport of me than leave me be. It felt as if the anchors of my life were being pulled up one by one.

To compound my misery, two events happened which shook me to the core. When I was ten years old, my aunt Margot wrote to say that she had met a doctor called George and was going to marry him. A leading dermatologist, he had been offered a three-year posting in Chicago and they were going to move to America. I felt torn apart. Margot travelled to Worthing to say her goodbyes and to ask me to choose a present from a local shop to remember her by. I chose a 'Benjamin Bunny' bedside lamp, to shine all night and keep the demons away, and then she was gone.

I was still reeling from that news when word came from Scotland that my grandmother had died, the first person to die who was close to me. Mrs Parker told me of her death during my lunch break, before sending me back to school. I was terribly upset and, sitting in class remembering all the happy images of Granny in her warm and cosy kitchen, I accidentally stabbed my thigh with the sharpened end of my lead pencil and made it bleed. Now I really was on my own. I had never felt more abandoned in my life.

It was not long after that that word came from India that my parents and Sue were returning for a brief visit. After such a long separation I was uncertain as to how I should greet them. I wondered what they would be like. Would they be old? Would I even recognise them? Confusion took hold of me as my mind raced with a torrent of emotions. Secretly, I was pleased and relieved at the prospect of possible salvation from the Parkers. I was glad that we were to be reunited as a family, but for how long? Previous experience had taught me never to hope for too much and, from what I gathered, they weren't planning on staying anyway. Putting on my best dress, unplaiting my pigtails and combing out my long dark hair, I braced myself for the reunion with a heavy heart.

> *I will live and survive and be asked . . .*
> *. . . What helped us to live*
> *When there were neither letters nor any news . . .*
> *. . . And the sickening promises made in exchange for betrayal.*

From 'I will live and survive' by Irina Ratushinskaya

We met in the dimly lit front parlour of the Parkers' home, its drab furniture draped in crocheted antimacassars. I sat stiffly on the sofa in the net-curtained window and waited as they were ushered in. Years later Sue told me that her initial urge had been to rush to embrace me, the older sister she barely remembered but had dreamed about. But she was stopped in her tracks by the frosty atmosphere awaiting her: I came across as cold, aloof and resentful to both her and my parents, who greeted me cautiously. Even my father's cheery: 'Hello, Rabbit' – which almost melted my heart and made me run to him – wasn't enough. I had steeled myself from within and I wasn't going to forgive them for abandoning me just yet. Secretly I was consumed with jealousy that Sue had, through no fault of her own, shared a life with my parents which had been denied me. For months after I was reunited with my family, I could not conquer these feelings of rejection. Poor Sue, I was truly horrid to her and yet she worshipped me regardless.

But for now, it was time to pack my few belongings at last and leave the boarding house where I had been so unhappy. I didn't give it, or the Parkers, a second thought. For the next few months, I lived with my family briefly in London, then in Scotland while my father sorted out his mother's affairs, and finally – when my father returned to India – in rented accommodation in the seaside resort of St Leonards-on-Sea, East Sussex. My mother stayed just long enough to arrange for Sue and me to board at the St Leonard's Mayfield Convent of the Holy Child, and then she left for India, leaving me once again with a stranger.

It must have been doubly hard for Sue, being abandoned by her parents in a foreign country and then realising that the sister she had longed to provide her with companionship was against her. To add to her distress, we were placed in separate parts of the school, she in the junior section and me with the older girls, so our paths rarely crossed. But it was a good school and there were some fun times to be had; we swam in the sea before breakfast; the nuns read ghost stories to us at Halloween as we all lay under blankets and eiderdowns; we roasted chestnuts on an open fire and let off fireworks on Guy Fawkes Night. I had my first lessons in tennis, a sport which was to become an enduring passion. During the holidays Sue and I were, as usual, farmed out to various guardians, including an Auntie Bobby in Worthing, and I introduced Sue to summer life in Scotland with Uncle Stuart. It was a great relief to me when Aunt Margot eventually returned from America to live in London in 1956, and thereafter, we spent the remaining school holidays with her and her husband. They never had children and treated us as their own.

By the time I was thirteen, I was so well established as an independent soul, free of my parents' control and influence, that I was acutely embarrassed when my mother surprised us by returning to England. From the earliest age, I had found myself uncomfortable in her presence, and always relieved when the visits were over. Now that I saw so little of her and was able to appraise her from afar, I was even more critical. She was so theatrical, and more than a little eccentric. She had high arched pencilled-in eyebrows and she used to put far too much powder and make-up on her face. To my complete mortification, when she smiled the powder used to crack and fall off her cheeks when she kissed me hello. I sincerely hoped none of my school friends noticed.

Anxious not to have to spend the holidays with my mother, I jumped at the chance to spend them with anyone else, accepting offers from friends. As a consequence, by the time I was seventeen, I was relatively well travelled. I had been all over Britain on various Easter, summer and Christmas breaks, and had even been skiing in Verbier. Sue and I were becoming closer, and I was just starting to meet boys and take an interest in them. All in all, I felt quite content with my lot – until my mother came back onto the scene permanently.

By this time, she and my father were living more or less separate lives and she was bored with her life in India. She took a flat in London in Queen Gate, Kensington and, when I left school, I had no choice but to move in with her. At her suggestion, and because the only options (apart from marriage) open to a young girl back in 1959 were to be a nurse, a cook or a secretary, I completed a nine-month course at a secretarial college in South Molton Street. Several of my former school friends were on the same course and my mother thought it would be good for me to have some sort of qualification. It was the best decision she ever made for me, because it has saved my bacon on so many occasions.

At eighteen, I applied for and was accepted to my first job as a secretary in the education department of ICI. It wasn't work that I particularly enjoyed, but it set me very high standards and I learned a great deal. Living with my mother during that time wasn't easy, however, and her unpredictable nature began to cause me great distress. Sometimes she would be out at parties and dinners day and night and I'd never see her; other times she would spend the days hanging around our flat in her dressing gown, moody and temperamental. I stopped bringing friends back when she ruined two cocktail parties I organised – the first by storming out of her bedroom half-dressed to tell us to keep the noise down, and the second by locking me out of the flat when I went to see my friends off. I had a few casual suitors in those days but I would never have dreamed of inviting them home to meet her.

When my mother surprised me by suggesting that I take six months off work and sail to India to see my father, I jumped at the chance. It was 1961, I hadn't seen him for four years and neither had she. Sue was still in school and I rather imagined my mother was bored of my company and wanted to be alone. She discovered that some old friends from Assam would be travelling to Bombay on the SS *Chusan*, the luxury P&O liner, and she booked me a passage. Thus it was that, aged nineteen, I set sail for India once more, the most enjoyable of all my solitary journeys.

Life on the *Chusan* was quite the most enchanting experience I had ever had. As we sailed through the Bay of Biscay, on to Gibraltar, through the Mediterranean and via the Suez Canal to India, my days and nights were filled with ritzy cocktail parties and dinners, handsome men ready to whisk me onto the dance floor and numerous shipboard romances. I ended up being the runner between one couple, delivering secret love letters like some Shakespearean maid. We drank Pimm's and crème de menthe, we ate lobster and crab, and danced the magical nights away. I met my first ever lesbians, there was a rape attack and a robbery, and it seemed to me that the entire experience was like something straight from the pages of an Agatha Christie novel. I was hypnotised.

By the time I disembarked at Bombay, I was still floating on air. But then reality hit me with the dirt, smells, and dust of a country I hadn't seen for twelve years. The city was humming with activity; its millions of residents appeared to be constantly on the move. The skyline was clogged with silhouettes; Christian churches vied with Hindu temples for space between the myriad buildings. There were beggars everywhere and our party of five had to run the gauntlet and nudge our way through the incredible traffic to get to the Victoria train terminus. Our journey to Calcutta on the Central Railway was hauled by an ancient locomotive and took almost three days and nights because of a derailment the previous day. There had been several fatalities and the train on which I was travelling stopped to pick up the dead and injured.

Conditions on the train were very basic compared to the sumptuousness of the *Chusan*. The ironically named Calcutta Express consisted of carriages which were little more than a string of rusty tin cans thrown together. They were incredibly hot and sticky, offering little respite from the heat; passengers hung from every doorway, window and roof, and we were largely confined to our compartment. We got our meals by placing an order at one railway siding, then collecting them at the next. Invariably they consisted of a chilli omelette and a *chapati*, the unleavened bread of India, handed through the carriage window from the platform below by a man in a turban. All washed down with sweet tea.

At one such stop, a member of our party was so desperate for something more substantial that he handed over some cash to a passing Indian in the hope of securing a bottle of whisky in return. The stranger, delighted with his good fortune, was last seen riding into the bazaar on a rickety bicycle trying to wave as he wobbled on, his white *dhoti* wafting in the breeze as our train pulled out of the station.

By the time we arrived at the grand Victorian Howrah Station in Calcutta very early one hot and dusty morning, we were exhausted. The platform was teeming with people – some jostling for a seat on the next departing train, others touting for business, and of course the ubiquitous beggars. It was noisy, busy and steamy; worse even than Bombay. But the crush, the press and bustle of the railway platform was multiplied one hundred-fold on the mile-long Howrah Bridge, just a few yards away. The traffic on the huge web of girders which crosses the muddy Hooghly River has to be seen to be believed. Cars, trucks, buses, tramcars, rickshaws, scooters, bicycles, ox-carts, people, cows, goats and donkeys all jostle their way across – an estimated three million people are said to cross it every day. With great difficulty, I made my way through the pandemonium and across India's largest city to the airport, so that I could catch an internal flight to Assam.

It seemed an age before the little plane I finally boarded started its descent three hours later and landed safely at Dibrugarh in Upper Assam, touching down on a tiny airstrip constructed from sheets of metal with holes for the grass to grow through. My father was waiting to meet me. I was more than a little shy and somewhat reserved as I stepped forward to greet him after so long a separation, but he grabbed me by the hands and hugged me warmly.

'Welcome home, Rabbit,' he said, and the tears welled in my eyes. He was genuinely thrilled to see me, and proudly introduced me to friends who had come with him to the airport.

Memories of my happy childhood in Assam with my *ayah* flooded back as my father and I sat on the verandah of his bungalow sipping iced gin and tonic. We chatted animatedly as the small creatures of the night came to welcome me. Geckos clung to the wire netting that enclosed the verandah, waiting for the insects attracted by the lights, and fireflies flickered in the warm night air. The large colonial fan whirred overhead, keeping us cool as we caught up on all the years we had lost.

The next five months were my happiest for years as I thrived on all the flattery and attention paid to me by my father and by the many single young men working in Assam. The word had gone out – Alec's daughter had arrived from England – and there was no shortage of admirers. I was attractive enough for my age – slim and dark, with large hazel eyes and, so people said, a pretty smile. I had inherited my mother's high cheekbones and my grandmother's sparkle, and for the first time in years I felt loved and admired. A 'honey-pot', my father used to call me.

Daddy was forever telling me how much I had blossomed during my time with him and there was no doubt that the lifestyle and daily routines suited me very well. I could hardly bear to think of returning one day to the drabness of London and a humdrum existence shared with my mother.

A tea planter's life was extremely gentle in those days. The managers were mostly British, hired from overseas by the tea companies in London, to supervise vast tea estates in far flung corners of the globe. The job was well-paid with the added attraction of a comfortable lifestyle in a warm climate for employees and their families. A working day generally started at six o'clock, with breakfast served at eight o'clock, followed by another three hours' work on the plantation or in the factory, followed by lunch or 'tiffin' at noon and a siesta. The two hours after lunch were golden and silent: nobody stirred, not even the coolies. All were sheltering from the blistering heat of the day. After siesta there was a little more work to do, leaving time for tennis, a round of golf, or a chukka or two of polo before the sun sank. Then the 'sun downer' drinks parties began, followed by dinner and dancing. It was all heavenly.

However much I was enjoying myself, at the back of my mind I knew that one day it would have to end. Six months, my mother had told me, and five had already passed. My father was very supportive of anything I chose to do on my return, although when I told him I really wanted to be a doctor, he laughed.

'How about nursing?' he suggested gently, seeing the hurt look on my face. From then on, my heart was set on a career in nursing and I resolved to sign on at a nursing school immediately on my return to England. My mind was made up. What I hadn't counted on was a man by the name of Julian McCune.

A friend of my father's, thirty-four years old – fourteen years my senior – a devilishly handsome bachelor with something of a playboy reputation, Julian was universally known as 'Bunny' in the days when it was deeply fashionable to have a nickname. Taller than me, debonair and quite glamorous, he wore a yellow check waistcoat when I first set eyes on him at the Jorhat Races, something very daring for the time. Clean shaven, with mousy-coloured hair, a long, angular face and large front teeth, he was utterly charming and completely believable. Irish-born, but raised in Yorkshire, he had recently been posted to work as an engineer in Dibrugarh, supervising the machinery needed to grade and prepare the tea leaves. Passionate about shooting and fishing, he was urbane and witty, the one man every hostess wanted at her cocktail party, not least because he had the unique ability to make a woman feel wonderful.

A month before my departure, Bunny called at my father's bunga-low unexpectedly one evening. There was to be a snipe shooting party, he said, and we were both invited. I joined the shoot gladly, carrying the cartridges and relishing the excitement of the hunt, as we waded through a *beel*, the swampy edges of the river, and the natural habitat for snipe, duck, geese and the jungle *morghi*, ancestor of all domestic fowl.

I glanced at Bunny from time to time and we made polite small talk in the dusk, but – because of the yawning age difference between us – I honestly had no visions of romance. I could see, however, that he was a man of many charms and I was more than intrigued. Later that evening, at dinner, he held court with his fellow diners, telling us of the time he spent a night in jail after accidentally hitting a sacred cow with his car after an excellent curry lunch at the famous Firpos restaurant in Calcutta. Falling into bed after the accident, he was awoken by an angry crowd at the gate and dispersed them by firing his shotgun over their heads. Half-tiddly, half-asleep and standing semi-clothed in the window, at the moment of pulling the trigger, he said, his *dhoti* slipped from his waist and dropped to the floor, leaving him 'starkers'. I looked around the table and watched as everyone listened, bright-eyed and enraptured, while Bunny delivered his punch-line.

In the heady days and nights that followed, with their endless rounds of drinks and dinners, Bunny began to show an increasing interest in me, and although not entirely unexpected after all the flattery of the previous five months, I found myself particularly delighted by his attention. My father, however, was not so pleased. Paternal concern told him that Bunny was not exactly what he had in mind as a suitable companion for his daughter.

As Bunny's keenness became more and more apparent, Daddy's concern grew and he decided to send me away for a few days. A *shikar*, or tiger safari, he said, was something I really should experience before going back to England to start my nursing career. Off I went, with Daddy informing me that he had banned Bunny from following me. But, of course, Bunny secretly caught the very next plane and we spent a blissful few days together on safari, our excitement heightened by the forbidden nature of our liaison. I felt like Juliet with her Romeo.

A week later, Bunny called to see me at my father's bungalow. It was a few days before I was due to fly home and I was packing in my bedroom. Bursting in suddenly and grabbing me from behind, he announced: 'I want you to marry me.' I spun round to face him, astonished. Unworldly and still a virgin, I had an enormous crush on him by then, and was probably on the verge of having a torrid affair behind my father's back, but I honestly never thought it would go any further than that. I was stunned.

Unable to think of anything else, I blurted out: 'I am a Catholic, I want seven children and I've hardly any money,' speaking in an almighty rush. Blushing, I dropped my head; this was most certainly not how I had intended to respond to my first ever offer of marriage.

Bunny put his hands on his hips and looked at me in astonishment. His forehead wrinkled into a frown and I feared he might have changed his mind after my outburst. ''Struth!' he exclaimed, but then his face broke into a huge grin and he pulled me towards him in an embrace. With that next kiss my fate was sealed.

3

'The engagement is announced between Julian, only son of Major L.G. McCune and the late Mrs McCune, of Helen's Bay, Co Down, and Margaret Patricia, elder daughter of Mr and Mrs A.G. Bruce of Doom Dooma, Assam, India.'

The one-paragraph announcement in the 'forthcoming marriages' section of the Daily Telegraph was the first my mother knew of my plans. My father had sent word to London via telegram, but the announcement Bunny had placed was published before she got a chance to read Daddy's message. It was March 1962 and the wedding was set for 3 November in Assam: six months before I was to marry a stranger in a foreign land.

I DECIDED TO RETURN TO ENGLAND TO COLLECT WHAT FEW BELONGINGS I HAD, BUY A WEDDING DRESS, PREPARE A TROUSSEAU AND FACE MY MOTHER. After six heady months of a whirling social life, I somehow felt I needed a spell of reality. When my father saw me off at the airport, his parting words were: 'For goodness' sake, Rabbit, when you come back to get married, don't bring your mother with you.' It was a plea from the heart.

On the journey home alone, I reflected long and hard on my decision to accept Bunny's unexpected offer of marriage. I knew that I found him very attractive, if enigmatic, and loved the idea of spending more time in India, somewhere I felt very much at home. But most of all I accepted that – coming as it did on the eve of my departure – my decision to accept his proposal and spend the rest of my life with someone I barely knew was, perhaps in part, born from a desire to escape from my mother.

She was waiting for me when I flew back alone to Heathrow. Her face was like thunder. She was naturally incensed that she had been deliberately excluded from my plans for the future. As we made our way back into central London, I peered out of the car window into the grey rain and was struck by the colourlessness and chaos of the city. My mind was still far away in the green land of Upper Assam.

Throughout the journey my mother constantly berated me about the decision I had made and wanted to know why she hadn't been told. It wasn't so much that she disapproved of my future husband, she had never met him, but more that she – as my mother – had not been asked her opinion. I felt like screaming at her, berating her for all the years when my opinion had never been sought, when she had made decisions about my life that had caused me the greatest unhappiness. But I couldn't. Instead, I sat looking out of the window, with tears welling up inside me, willing the journey, and her dreadful haranguing, to come to an end.

By the time we had reached her flat, I had to escape. I couldn't face another minute of her ranting. I dumped my bags and ran from the building, heading for a Sunday evening Mass, which I knew was being said in a small Catholic church just around the corner in Kensington High Street. As I crossed the road, feeling so destroyed by her disapproval, I could not have cared one jot if I'd been run over by a bus. It was the first time in my life that I had felt suicidal. When I arrived at the church, breathless and weepy, I needed my mentor, my God. I dropped to my knees and joined in with the prayers as new words started to formulate in my mind.

'Hail Mary, mother of God . . . I vow that I will never, ever do this to any daughter of mine. She may marry the man she wants, when and where she wants, and in any way she likes . . .'

It took all my strength to ignore my mother's increasingly erratic behaviour during the next few months, as she continued to punish me. Partly to get away from her once more, I settled into a secretarial job at an engineering firm in Tottenham Court Road, and started to plan what clothes and provisions I should buy both for the wedding, and for life in the tropics. Bunny sent me some money to buy my engagement ring. I compiled a humble list of wedding presents after window-shopping, wide-eyed and alone, in the West End and I remember thinking that a set of bathroom scales was the most blatantly frivolous thing I had ever asked for in my life.

I excluded my mother from my shopping trips, and most of the preparation for the big day, as she grew increasingly neurotic, culminating in my choice of wedding dress. I knew that my mother had always been, perhaps, a little jealous of my father's side of the family, but I never realised quite how much until I told her I had chosen a very simple wedding dress, at a price of £25, from Harvey Nichols, in order to offset my grandmother Bruce's beautiful lace wedding veil, offered to me by my aunt Margot. From that moment on, my mother set out to ruin the plan.

Decrying my choice of gown, she dragged me off to Moss Bros, to buy a second-hand dress for the princely sum of £8. The one she picked out for me was so elaborate in lace and embroidery that it would have been impossible to wear the full-length heirloom veil with it, and she chose a very short, plain veil for me to wear instead. Seeing her determination, I capitulated without a murmur, hoping just to be able to survive the next few months until I escaped, with no further confrontation. The smirk of victory on her face remains in my memory to this day.

It was not very long before relations between us grew so tense and unpleasant, however, that I felt I had no alternative but to take matters into my own hands. I returned home to the flat one evening to find that she had unpacked my carefully folded trousseau and strewn it around my room. Her interference with my possessions was the straw that broke the camel's back and brought back horrible memories of the Parkers and my missing presents. In a fit of pique I decided to move out to share a flat with some friends. Not in the best frame of mind to try life as a single girl in London, however, and finding myself unable to relate to my new flatmates, I suffered the humiliation of returning to my mother's flat with my tail between my legs. That only made matters worse, and with the mounting tensions there, I knew I had to find another escape route.

The one person who had always come to my rescue in the past was my aunt Margot, and – once again – she offered me a helping hand. I could go and stay with her and George, she said, in their spacious house in Hereford Square, not far from my mother's, and I accepted, knowing that I would, at last, find some peace and tranquillity during my final weeks in England.

I shall never forget the turmoil of emotions – betrayal, rejection and shame – as I walked away from my mother's flat, along Gloucester Road, carrying a large suitcase which contained all my worldly possessions. By the time I arrived on Margot's doorstep I was stifling back the tears. As usual, she was wonderful – firm but kind. She settled me in and didn't ask too many questions. Margot, of all people, knew that I was finally admitting defeat in my relationship with my mother. She had won.

A month later, in October 1962, I set off on my solitary journey to Assam, to marry a man I hardly knew. All our wedding presents and my belongings had been shipped to Calcutta and I followed by plane, clutching the sewing machine my aunt Margot had bought me as a present (and which has remained an old family friend ever since). The whole country was holding its breath as the Cuban Crisis came to a head on the other side of the world, but all I could think about was getting through the next few days.

My intention was to arrive in Calcutta and spend a week with friends of Bunny's before proceeding to Assam a day or two before my wedding. My father had sent me a distressing telegram to inform me that my mother had decided to attend the wedding after all and had arrived in Doom Dooma ahead of me to oversee the final arrangements. My heart sank, but I knew there was nothing I could do. Within a few weeks I would be Mrs Julian McCune. My mind remained focused on that thought, as I flew eastwards across the globe towards India in a BOAC plane to embark on the next phase of my life. But, as with most of my life plans, it seemed, I was to be thwarted. I hadn't anticipated the outbreak of what came to be known as the Cartographic War. China had invaded north-east India. The border between India and China had been established after the Chinese Revolution, at the beginning of the century, as an imaginary line following the

Himalays, the highest watershed in the world. Skirmishes at the border had occurred in 1959, but by September 1962 the Chinese army had advanced in force over India's north-east frontier.

Prime Minister Nehru declared a state of emergency and sent troops in to take back the territory. It was a tense and chaotic time for the expatriates working in Upper Assam, who felt that they had been abandoned by the Indian and British governments. Many fled from the prospect of invasion and its consequences, driving south to Calcutta or forcing their way onto outbound flights, which were meant to be exclusively for women and children.

Calcutta had been intended as a pit stop for me, a quiet week of calm and re-acclimatisation before I flew on to become Bunny's bride. Instead, I arrived to discover that I was stranded, not knowing whether my parents, and Bunny, were alive or dead, prevented from taking a flight to Assam, and unable to contact anyone there. I was caught up in the middle of something over which I had no control. I had no choice but to wait for fate to deal me a hand . . .

For Bunny, too, as I later discovered, the situation was equally frustrating. Unsure whether or not I would be allowed to board my flight, he had awaited my arrival at the small Dibrugarh airport in Assam. When he realised that I was not amongst those few passengers who did disembark from the Fokker aircraft, and hoping that he was not in the process of being jilted, he drove back to my father's plantation, to report my non-appearance.

Communications in those remote areas thirty years ago were at best unreliable, at worst non-existent. There had simply been no way to alert him to the fact that I would not be on that flight. But, since numerous guests had managed to get through before the political crisis had worsened and were fully intent on a wedding, it was decided that the celebrations should go ahead the following day as planned, regardless of the absence of the bride. Typical Bunny. I can just hear him now: 'No reason why we can't all have a jolly good party, just because Maggie didn't make it.' So that is exactly what they did.

A week later on 9 November, the situation had calmed slightly and I finally managed to get a flight into Assam, to be met by Bunny's smiling face, and acid words from my mother who berated me for the problems I had caused.

'You do realise, don't you,' she chided, 'that I have had to go to the very great trouble of organising a second wedding cake.' It was a subject she refused to drop for most of the evening.

Later that night, on the very eve of my wedding, I finally lost my patience with her and we had our first ever war of words. I was hurt and upset that she had come to India in the first instance; I wanted nothing to spoil what should have been the happiest few days of my life, and I was determined not to let her get the better of me on this occasion. Telling her as much on the verandah, while Bunny and Daddy hid in my bathroom drinking gin and tonic, I watched aghast as she stumbled through her response. It was only then and for the first time in my life that I was suddenly struck, as if by a thunderbolt, with the realisation that she was drunk. My mother, the once beautiful, once joyous Australian theatre star and singer, whose light was, perhaps, extinguished by the constraints of married life and motherhood, had – somewhere along the line – turned to alcohol for solace.

From that moment on, her previous moods and tantrums, her erratic behaviour and badly applied make-up, were miraculously explained to me. When she had stayed in her dressing gown all day complaining of the noise I was making, she had merely been nursing a hangover. When she became moody and snappy in the afternoons, it was the drink talking. I couldn't believe that I had never seen it before. And now that I did, my mother suddenly became much less frightening to me.

'You're drunk, you should go to bed!' I exclaimed, and, watching her mouth drop open in astonishment, I turned on my heel and slammed my bedroom door in triumph. There comes a time in every parent's life when they suddenly realise that their child is no longer a child; that they have slipped through their fingers and are gone. This was my moment, and that of my mother. There was no going back.

The following morning, on 10 November 1962, on a blissfully warm and sunny day, I married Bunny in the small missionary church of St Joseph's in Doom Dooma, the only Catholic establishment for several hundred miles. The delayed wedding service was conducted by a Belgian priest, Father Jerrard, whom I had known since I was a child in Assam.

It was a happy day, and I no longer even minded that I was wearing a dress not of my choosing. The church was draped in brightly coloured Indian bunting and the aisle was decked with garlands of orange marigolds, each one a vivid pom-pom. I wore tiny blue shoes as my 'something blue', one of Granny's lace handkerchiefs as my 'something old', and some wax orange blossom flowers of Granny's for my 'something borrowed'. My bridesmaids were three children of friends of my father's. Mummy wore a remarkable hat but behaved herself, my father gave me away and beamed all day and the whole service was over in the blink of an eye.

My wedding present to Bunny was a gold stud for his collar. I had already bought him a set of gold cufflinks with our initials engraved on them. His present to me had been a course at the London Shooting School and a Purdy twelve-bore shotgun, worth a fortune, which I later innocently swapped for a Webley & Scott twenty-eight-bore, because I thought it suited me better.

After the marriage service, we returned to Daddy's bungalow for a reception on the verandah and it was perfect. There was only a small gathering, as most of the official guests had attended the brideless reception a week earlier. Sue didn't come, as she was still at school in Sussex, and Aunt Margot and her husband couldn't make it, but I didn't mind. I was truly content at last and the fairy-tale ending echoed round and round in my head: 'They got married and lived happily ever after.'

The speeches were hilarious, particularly that of the best man Peter Smith, known as 'Smudge', who made great fun of the fact that I was called Rabbit, my husband Bunny and he worked for a firm called James Warren. You can imagine the innuendo that followed.

For our honeymoon, Bunny took me on a fishing trip on the Brahmaputra, where I had spent many happy childhood days with my father. It was a magical few days. The boatman and some servants had gone on ahead and set up camp. We had tents and a proper bed and mattress, and it was there that I lost my virginity. We fished all day and in the evening returned to base camp for drinks and dinner, all beautifully prepared in advance. I managed to catch my largest fish ever, a golden-brown *mahseer* which weighed 15 lbs. It was an excellent fighter, and exciting to land out of the crystal-clear waters that flowed from the snow-clad mountains.

But any expectations I had of settling down to quiet and unbroken domesticity were, however, soon shattered. Within days of being married I was evacuated, because of the renewed threat of a Chinese invasion, and for the next three weeks I was a refugee in Calcutta, waiting nervously for news, with few belongings. In the haste to leave Assam, the servants had accidentally handed me a suitcase packed full of Bunny's clothes, not mine, so I had little more than the clothes I stood up in. And then, out of the blue, as suddenly as it had blown up, the threat was over. The Chinese had halted their advance into India and agreed ceasefire terms. It was safe for me to return to Assam and, within days, Bunny and I were reunited in our bungalow near Dibrugarh and I was able to resume my new role as a *memsahib* in India.

In March 1963 we celebrated my twenty-first birthday at a club evening in Doom Dooma, attended by family and friends. To my very great embarrassment, a group of bachelors, all former admirers, composed and sang a ditty in my honour, calling me the 'Belle of Assam'. It was a lovely evening and we danced in the ballroom, in the shadow of the Himalayan foothills.

I don't think I can say that I was ever truly passionately in love with Bunny, or he with me, but between us in those early days, we developed a warm companionship through mutual love of *shikar*, shooting and fishing, which had once been such an integral part of my childhood spent with my father. Bunny continued to be the life and soul of all parties, while I enjoyed playing the dutiful wife. He worked hard enough and provided me with a very comfortable lifestyle, even though I was often rather lonely. Gradually, though, as I grew in confidence and became accustomed to my new way of life, I started to go out a great deal more, playing tennis and making friends with other wives. I had married a good man, I decided, one who had rescued me from the trap of my mother and a duller life in England, and for that I was truly grateful.

Love's not Time's fool, though rosy lips and cheeks
Within his bending sickle's compass come;
Love alters not with his brief hours and weeks,
But bears it out even to the edge of doom.

from Sonnet CXVI by William Shakespeare

I had never hidden my desire from Bunny to have a large family. Seven children, I had told him on the night he proposed, although I think he took it in good sport. What he may or may not have ever really understood was how deep the need was in me to create a large and happy family, to compensate for my solitary childhood. I would lie awake at night sometimes, imagining the gardens around the bungalow filled with my laughing children and their *ayahs*; taking them fishing for shrimps in the shallows of the Brahmaputra; or out riding on their ponies. I had so much love to give, and I yearned for someone to give it to.

At the age of twenty-one and after six months of marriage, I fell pregnant and Bunny was as delighted as I was. Everything went according to plan and I thrived as the weeks and months passed. I was so looking forward to the arrival of my child, and I made all the preparations with a happy heart. My mother, who had remained in India and in better shape, surprised me by taking a great interest in my pregnancy. It was as if she was somehow trying to make up for her lost years of motherhood by showering all her love and affection on her first, as yet unborn, grandchild. I felt a little uneasy.

Long before my pregnancy and throughout it, the highlight of our week during the 'cold weather' season from November to February was to go fishing with friends and family every Sunday on the Brahmaputra. We would leave the bungalow before daylight, aiming to reach the banks of the river by the time dawn was breaking through the mist rolling down from the foothills of the Himalayas. In our dugouts, laden with food and fishing tackle, we would set off up the river, often forming small convoys, making for the minor tributaries where the fish were plentiful. Our dugouts had outboard motors, which were prone to breaking down, more often than not owing to less than delicate handling by our boatmen. Ideally we would reach a destination by nine or ten o'clock in the morning, just as the sun was beginning to break through and burn away the mist.

In places the Brahmaputra is as wide as the eye can see as it races to meet the holy River Ganges. It has a fast-flowing current which carves out ever-shifting channels in the sandy riverbed. Sometimes these channels are deep; but it is all too easy to run aground unexpectedly, even in a flat-bottomed dugout, juddering to a stop with the propeller spewing out water and sand. When this happened we could try to manoeuvre our way off the sand bank by using tall, thick bamboo canes as poles; or we could lighten the boat by jumping into the river and pushing it off into deeper channels of water. The sandbanks changed position daily according to the whim of the currents and so the lie of the riverbed was often difficult to read. And there were other hidden dangers; the monsoon floods would frequently sweep giant teak trees down the river, some of which might be caught, partially submerged or completely unseen, in the uncharted waters we navigated.

One Sunday, as we were returning late in the afternoon from a day's fishing, Bunny and I had what almost proved to be a fatal accident. I was heavily pregnant: it was only a few weeks before my child was due to be born, but I had gone along for the company and the adventure anyway, not wanting to be left by myself at home. We were travelling down river in convoy with my father and mother, who were following us in a separate boat, when our dugout, moving at some speed, hit a solid, submerged object. In a matter of seconds the boat had capsized and we were all flung into the water. Bunny disappeared from view down river, while the boatman, with seeming indifference to the calamity, calmly hauled himself back onto the upturned boat, on which I still had a tenuous handhold. He seemed perfectly content to sit there and be carried downstream by the current, making no attempt to help me, despite my mother's hysterical screaming from the other boat.

My main concern at that stage was not for myself but for our two dogs – both English Springer Spaniels – who had been in the boat with us and were now trapped under the upturned hull. With growing panic about their fate, I tried to right the boat, whereupon it promptly sank, parting company with all our kit which either sank also, or disappeared into the current. The dogs and the boatman swam for the riverbank.

I followed them, swimming as strongly as the circumstances allowed, but as I neared the shore, the water weighed down my ungainly figure and my wet clothes and carried me away from it and further downstream. Looking up I realised I was being swept towards an enormous upturned teak tree, with jagged roots as big as a house. The water was gushing and swirling through the vast spiked fingers of the roots, creating powerful undercurrents. For the first time in my life I felt a genuine – if strangely objective – fear for my safety, and for the life of my unborn child. I really thought I wasn't going to make it. 'If I don't do something now,' I felt, 'I'll be sucked under and pinioned against the roots of the tree, helpless against the force of the current. And my baby, what about my baby?'

Everything seemed to go into slow motion as adrenaline pumped through my veins and gave me the extra strength I needed to kick my legs as hard as I could to free myself from the overwhelming rush of water. I turned, beating against the current, and managed somehow to reach a floating tree trunk. Kicking and spluttering, trying to keep my head above the gushing water, I forced myself to make one final push towards a calmer stretch of the river, where my father had held his boat steady, and from which my mother was shouting her encouragement.

By the time I reached their boat, and was pulled unceremoniously on board, I was shaking and exhausted. Wrapped in a blanket, shivering with shock and cold, I clutched my swollen tummy and prayed that all would be well. Bunny and our boatman soon clambered aboard, equally shaken, and we managed to grab the dogs by the scruffs of their necks and pull them to safety. With the boat lying very low in the water and the sun dipping beyond the hills, we made our way cautiously down river. It was a race against time to reach the *ghat*, or boathouse, before the light faded. We were long overdue, and those of our party who had set out that morning for different locations were nervously awaiting our return.

All the way home, in the silence of a glorious sunset, its vivid orange and red hues tinting the sky and mirrored in the calmer waters of the river, I relived the drama over and over in my mind. This was my closest brush with death and yet I had felt strangely calm. There was no panic, no terror as I might have expected. Just an incredible surge of power, a need felt deep within me to save myself and my child, as I called out in my mind for help. 'My baby, my baby.'

I had read somewhere that an unborn child can experience many of its mother's emotions and can hear and feel certain sensations. A close friend also told me that Indian mothers believe that a baby in the mother's womb will reflect the talents and activities practised by its mother during her pregnancy. Patting the swelling under my wet garments I wondered how and if my baby would be affected by our brush with death. Had I whispered to my child's soul? By the time we reached the boathouse, on the edge of dark, I felt euphoric and a trifle invincible.

After a thorough checking over by a doctor and two nights' tender loving care in the Longsoal Central Hospital in Barahapjan, a small tea garden hospital near Doom Dooma, I was returned home safe and sound. Five weeks later I went into labour and was rushed back there, to be tended by friends of ours, Dr Bill Burton, the principal medical officer, and his wife Wendy, who was the Matron. The labour was long and painful and I shocked all the Indian nurses by demanding that I be given no painkillers.

'I want to *feel* this baby being born,' I protested and they conceded.

At 4.05 pm on the evening of 3 February 1964, they delivered me of a seven-pound daughter. Holding her in my arms for the first time, my eyes filled with tears of joy as I let the waves of relief and emotion wash over me. She was the most beautiful neat dark-haired baby girl, tiny and vulnerable and yet somehow surprisingly strong. Her eyes were open from the moment of her birth, and she either puckered her forehead with an interested expression, or looked as though she were already deep in thought about some serious matter. I called her my 'little bushbaby' with no idea how prophetic the nickname would become.

Bunny came to visit with flowers and was thrilled at the sight of his daughter.

'Have you decided what we are going to call her?' he asked, as he cradled her in his arms and stroked her head with his fingers. We had already disagreed about names because he wanted his daughter to be named Anna, after a favourite former girlfriend.

But I had long had a name in mind if it was a girl, a name I thought sounded so pretty.

'Emma,' I told him defiantly, smiling up at him in a moment of pure contentment. 'And, Bunny, I have a feeling that one day she is really going to make something of her life.'

4

Emma and I spent seven days in hospital, getting to know each other. She was a good baby and, although I was tired from the constant feeding, I enjoyed the early stages of motherhood. My own mother, banned from coming to see me in hospital in case she caused a scene, sneaked in anyway and was beside herself with joy at the sight of her first grandchild. She just had time to present me with a beautiful christening gown for Emma before she was discovered by a nurse and frogmarched off the premises. Examining the white lace gown she had bought, I had visions of my wedding dress and put it back in its box.

BUNNY CAME TO SEE US EVERY DAY AND WAS AS PROUD AND CHARMING AS EVER. He was staying with Bill and Wendy in their bungalow and the night before I was due to be discharged, I accepted an invitation to join them for supper. Settling Emma down into her carry cot in their spare bedroom, I heard a gentle tapping on the door. It was Ali, Bill and Wendy's head houseboy, a wizened, balding man with kindly eyes. I had known him for many years. Stepping into the room quietly with a smile, he asked:

'Please, Memsahib, may I see the baby?'

Indians love babies and I passed her to him gladly, watching as he held her in his arms. His dark face looked down at her and he murmured softly.

When supper was over, Bunny drove Emma and me back to the hospital. There was some sort of commotion later in the night which woke me, but it soon died down and I thought nothing more of it and went back to sleep. I only found out afterwards that the commotion had heralded the arrival at the hospital of Ali, who was rushed there after being discovered mortally wounded – stabbed through the heart – outside Bill and Wendy's bungalow. The gentle houseboy who had so tenderly cosseted my child only a few hours earlier died later that night. No one ever found out why, or by whom, he had been murdered, but I found it very unnerving that the first stranger to take my daughter in his arms had had his life so suddenly and brutally extinguished within a few hours.

Emma spent the first two-and-a-half years of her life in India, enjoying a happy and blissfully worry-free childhood. She was a free spirit right from the start, relishing the space and the freedom in which to grow. Curious about everything, investigating each unusual flower or leaf she came across, she was always so interested in the world around her. She would stop to study the tiniest everyday object with such joy and triumph in her own discovery that the rest of us looked at whatever had caught her attention with renewed appreciation.

From a very young age, she showed individuality and verve, developing some eccentric habits – refusing to wear clothes (although I insisted on shoes) and adorning herself with ethnic jewellery belonging to her *ayah*. Friends who visited from England and saw her padding around the garden naked, layer upon layer of necklaces decked about her down to her belly button, advised me I should get her accustomed to wearing clothes before I took her back to England on leave.

I loved being with my child, but life at home was rather solitary, so I punctuated it with regular visits to our club, where the local tea-planting community gathered. We would play golf, tennis and polo. Sometimes we would watch an old film. I played some of the best tennis in my life on grass courts during those club afternoons in Assam. My partners were mostly Indian men, Rajputs, the young royals, who were naturals at the game – the Indian women were not sufficiently liberated to participate. While the adults played, the children – watched over by their *ayahs* – enjoyed the sandpit or the swimming pool or the swings. Emma always loved the swings; swinging her legs higher and higher, giggling infectiously and begging to be pushed that little bit further.

My biggest treat, as it had been from the outset, was to go fishing on the Brahmaputra. Bunny and I went every Sunday, with family and friends, almost always returning with great baskets full of silver-scaled fish. The banks of the river were open expanses of sand, similar to a beach, and we enjoyed glorious picnics, splashing in the water with Emma, building sandcastles and teaching her the simple joys of the riverside.

Clad only in a swimsuit, with my favourite hat – a blue and white floppy-brimmed item made for me out of batik cloth by the local *dherzi* or seamstress in the bazaar – I would play happily with my daughter for hours on end, while Bunny splashed in the river with his beloved dogs or went fishing. Emma had a matching little white hat made for her, and together we would while away the hours in those carefree days, taking long rides downstream in a dugout pushed by one of the boatmen in his huge saucer-shaped straw hat.

Emma adored the water although she truly thought she was at the seaside rather than on the banks of a river, because it was so wide. In a school project years later, when she was twelve, she was asked what she recalled of her childhood in India. She wrote:

'I remember Daddy and a friend stood on the bank of the river, but it did seem like the sea to me. Mummy and I were in this boat and the thing I can remember most is Mummy's hat and the man with the long pole also with a big hat.'

I had, by this time, made several good girlfriends, including Gina, an Englishwoman, who had been a fashion model and who was a friend of Bunny's from Calcutta. Along with Wendy Burton, we asked her to be one of Emma's godmothers and she agreed. What was unusual about Gina was that she had married Bhaiya, an Indian maharaja. Tall and powerfully built, Bhaiya was in his forties and a fine international polo player. He had an English public-school education, and perfect manners. His mother, the Dowager Maharanee, was matriarchal, short in stature, rotund, but very beautiful. Not long after Emma was born, Bunny and I received the first of many invitations from Gina to her home, the Palace of Cooch Behar.

The palace was formidable – architecturally symmetrical, with two extensions standing proud of the building. There was a dome, a vast portico and two lakes or 'tanks' in front of the palace, flanking the long gravel drive, which was, in turn, bordered with beautifully tended flower beds filled with waves of scarlet cannas. During those somnolent days, we would go on early morning *shikars* to shoot snipe and duck, tailed by curious villagers all the way, moving like camp followers to watch our progress. Coming home we would row on the tanks in hollowed out wooden skiffs, before adjourning for lunch and a siesta. We played tennis in the late afternoon.

In the evening, after pink gins, we dined in a vast hall, adorned with portraits of Bhaiya's ancestors, mounted hunting trophies of tigers, leopards and buffalo, and vast ornate gilt mirrors which reflected the candlelight. We were waited on by an army of bearers, each one wearing a white frock coat with a Nehru collar, trousers, a red and gold sash at the waist, and white and red braided *pughris* or turbans on their heads. They entered bearing huge gold or silver platters of steaming hot and quite delicious curries, which we would eat with chapatis and all manner of spicy side dishes.

The banquets were the most sumptuous I had ever experienced – twenty or more people seated round a huge polished mahogany table, guests who had been invited from as far away as Calcutta or Delhi. Not far from the palace was a small river, where Bhaiya kept a herd of elephants. I remember once setting off on an elephant to meet a house guest who was arriving at the palace's private airstrip by plane. He emerged from the plane to be greeted by the massed trumpeting of jungle beasts.

It was a charmed and magical time, and one which I wanted Emma to be able to retain a link with. She was baptised in the Sacred Heart missionary church in Dibrugarh on the afternoon of Wednesday 25 March 1964 by a Spanish priest. He raised his eyebrows when I told him that the Maharanee of Cooch Behar was to be her godmother although he softened somewhat when he saw that she was blonde and English. Gina bought Emma a beautiful Indian silver dressing-table set as a present and she and Bhaiya were our honoured guests. The ceremony was simple and afterwards we went back to our bungalow for a 'whoopee' or party. Christened into the Catholic faith, the stage was set for Emma to grow up blessed and with godparents I felt could offer her friendship and spiritual guidance.

Sadly, for Gina and Bhaiya, their charmed life was to end in tragedy. Bhaiya died of a heart attack a few years later at a time of great change in India, when many of the palaces had been confiscated by the government and the status and wealth of the maharajas stripped. Gina was left an impecunious widow and had to leave India. The palace fell into decay and is now deserted, a crumbling ruin, overgrown with creepers. I lost touch with my daughter's godmother forever.

By contrast, our life was simple and uncluttered and I still spent most of my time at the bungalow. Emma filled her days playing with the servants, learning to ride her first tricycle, or plunging fearlessly into the swimming pool, floats on her arms. The gardeners in particular adored her. She would pad around after them, usually naked, watching them dig and plant, sow and weed, with a fascination unusual for a child of her age. Whenever possible she would try and help them, squatting down alongside them, her fingers deep in the fertile soil, although I am afraid more often than not she pulled up the plants they had only just bedded in.

She had a beloved *ayah* called Toto, who looked after her wonderfully, but I also took a very active role in her daily life. Concerned that she should meet and play with other children from an early age, ever conscious of my own lonely childhood, I started a small playgroup for her and six other children of a similar age but different cultures, some European, some Indian. I had no teaching experience other than common sense and a desire to share, but the experiment worked.

Emma transcended the ethnic divides effortlessly; she became a strong-willed and determined toddler, and was popular with the other children. I strove to give her the freedom I had never had, both physically and culturally, and although that meant that she was sometimes rather spoilt, I like to think it also helped her become the remarkable person she came to be.

May she become a flourishing hidden tree
That all her thoughts may like the linnet be . . .
O may she live like some green laurel,
Rooted in one dear perpetual place.

from 'A Prayer for My Daughter' by W. B. Yeats

Ebullient and not at all shy, Emma faced life's hurdles with tenacity. Even at such an early age, she never seemed fazed by adversity or by events which might have sent another child whimpering behind their mother's skirts. Once, when she developed ringworm in her scalp, and the doctor advised that it would be best to shave off all her hair, I arranged for the *nappit*, or barber, to come and he duly arrived by rickshaw. Under the eaves of the bungalow he went to work with a cut-throat razor during a playgroup session. I deliberately asked him to come then so that the other children could watch the transformation, and would not ostracise Emma when they saw her bald. It worked: they accepted it as something normal and Emma did not flinch from being at the centre of attention. The only person who was upset was me – to see her soft brown locks shaved off hurt me greatly.

My parents led quite separate lives from ours but enjoyed being able to see their granddaughter on our weekly fishing expeditions. But when Emma was still quite young, the marital discord that had been bubbling between them for so long finally erupted. Announcing that they would be getting a divorce, my mother prepared to return home to England, to live alone in a house in Teddington, west London, for the rest of her days. My sister Sue was by then training as a nurse at Hillingdon Hospital and promised to keep an eye on her while Daddy and I remained in Assam. As we bid my mother farewell from Dibrugarh airport, I felt nothing but relief that she was leaving my life again. Ours had always been a difficult relationship and I found her presence unsettling.

Not long after Mummy left, Bunny, Emma and I flew to Britain for our first 'leave' since being married. It was an opportunity for us to meet each other's family and friends, whom neither of us had met previously, owing to the fact that we were married abroad. It turned into a hectic three months, travelling to and from County Down in Northern Ireland, in order to spend as much time with Bunny's father as possible. Dr Gordon McCune was a retired GP, a dear and gentle man, coping stoically with paralysis caused by a stroke. He had lived alone as a widower for the previous eleven years. It was a lonely life for him with his only child, Bunny, living overseas. I liked him enormously and was glad that we were finally able to meet. We also travelled to Yorkshire, visiting Bunny's mother's side of the family, to Scotland to meet my relatives and to London to meet Aunt Margot and Uncle George. We returned to Assam in time to celebrate Christmas 1964 in our own bungalow where, I was soon to discover, I was pregnant again. In August the following year, 1965, a sister arrived for Emma. She was equally beautiful, with an extremely determined chin. She was named Erica on Bunny's insistence – after the mother of an old flame.

Quite apart from the needs of a growing family, we were now faced with a worrying situation. India and Pakistan had declared war over Kashmir, the tea industry was 'Indianising', replacing British workers with native staff, and we now had two small children in tow. We had already begun to think about moving on when Bunny was made redundant. Daddy, too, was pensioned off and wanted to leave India. He had been regarded with the warmest affection by his staff, and was given an emotional send-off during which he was presented with a silk scroll tribute, and adorned with garlands of marigolds.

We considered a move to South Africa, where many of our friends had emigrated. But quite apart from the delicate political situation in South Africa and in neighbouring Rhodesia at the time, it posed an insurmountable hurdle to us living there. Neither Bunny nor I had racial prejudices: we had always enjoyed mixing with people of other races, and had hoped to instil the same liberal views in our children. But in South Africa in the mid-1960s, apartheid was the rule of law and we would not even be allowed to have any black people to our house as guests. Faced with such an unpalatable thought, we decided to emigrate to England.

I was sad to be leaving Assam. It held such fond memories for me both as a child and more recently, and I had always considered it 'home'. Bunny, too, had been very happy there, and Daddy was quite bereft. But a new life in England beckoned and I was excited by the challenge.

There was something which disturbed me just before we left India, however. Crating up and shipping home our most precious belongings, we sold off the remainder locally. A colleague of Bunny's came to collect several items he had agreed to purchase, but in the end he never paid us. I made my own enquiries, only to discover that Bunny owed him money, which he'd failed to repay.

It was 1966 when we arrived in England – the year Britain won the World Cup, when the Moors Murderers were headline news, and Harold Wilson was the new Labour Prime Minister. A coal tip at Aberfan in Wales collapsed, killing 116 children, there were numerous nation-wide industrial strikes, and London at the time of the Beatles and the Rolling Stones was dubbed the swinging capital of the world.

To start with we had nowhere to live and no idea what we were going to do. My father retired to his native Scotland, moving into a house he had owned in Dumfries for many years, but which was far too small for all of us. So my marvellous Aunt Margot took us into her house in Hereford Square for three months – babies and all – while Bunny looked for work.

Bunny was very much 'old school' and rarely if ever discussed his personal or business affairs with me. For a while I had no idea how he planned to make a living in England. After knocking on the doors of several old friends but getting nowhere, he eventually decided to go into the security monitoring business, investing £2,000 of his limited savings into a franchise with a company called Photo Scan, who were pioneering the newly designed closed-circuit television monitoring systems. Bunny's territory was to be North Yorkshire and we had a month to move up there and find a home.

Waiting in London while Bunny sorted things out, we had some marvellous times with Aunt Margot and Uncle George. They had been incredibly kind and had taken to the children. Erica, particularly, was a joy to them both and they handled her with consummate ease. Once on a trip out in their car, Erica sat on Uncle George's knee and bounced up and down so violently with excitement that he gave her the nickname 'Madame Yo-Yo'. From that day to this, Erica has been known as 'Yo' to all her family and close friends.

Waving goodbye to London, we finally drove north to Yorkshire on a bitterly cold and bleak February day in 1967. In the first few months of our living there, I often doubted, after the warm climes of India, that I would be able to endure this new life in what now seemed a strange and foreign country to me. I tried to cheer myself up by taking the children to stay in a guest house at Sandsend, near Whitby, but it was so cold and miserable, so utterly depressing, that it was all Bunny could do to stop me packing up and heading straight back to the lush green warmth of Assam. But Yorkshire was to remain our home – in one way or another – for the next twenty-two years. We spent the first few months in temporary rented accommodation near Northallerton which lies east of the A1. Bunny was, by now, travelling many miles throughout the vast Riding of North Yorkshire, promoting Photo Scan, while I found out about schools for the children.

Unbeknown to me, he was also secretly plotting to realise a childhood dream – to live in an old property near Bedale called Cowling Hall. Bunny was absolutely determined that we should all live in the house, especially once he discovered that the current tenants were Army people based at Catterick, and about to be posted elsewhere.

Cowling Hall was a tall, angular Queen Anne house set on a hill. Bunny remembered it well from his childhood years at the nearby Aysgarth Preparatory School, and, in later years, during his courtship, when he went out riding and hunting in the company of the head-master's daughter, Wanda. By the time I met Wanda she was already happily married to the new headmaster of Aysgarth. Their children and ours forged lifelong friendships, as Bunny and I did with Wanda and her friends.

Owned by Sir Claude and Lady Smith-Dodsworth, Cowling was the dower house to Thornton Watlass Hall, and was so strange and unique architecturally that it merited an entry in Pevsner's *Buildings of England*. It was a kind of seventeenth- and eighteenth-century architectural jigsaw, which fitted together and yet didn't quite make sense to the eye. It had a crescent-shaped drive on one side and – I was delighted to find – a large walled garden on the other, complete with a ha-ha, or ditch, at the far end. Beyond, there were open fields where sheep grazed, and the Vale of York spread out into the distance.

Using his innate charm, Bunny persuaded Lady Smith-Dodsworth to let Cowling to us for a peppercorn rent of £6 a week indefinitely, starting with a five year lease. The arrangement was presented to me as a fait accompli. I had no say in it, although my first sight of the house certainly impressed – the façade was very grand. In fact, the house was not really so large as it appeared, because it was effectively only one room deep. We certainly didn't enjoy a luxurious or extravagant lifestyle there, because – even at the best of times – we never had an abundance of money. And, as I was soon to discover, life at the Hall had more than its fair share of drawbacks.

Utterly exposed to the elements, it was the coldest house in which I have ever lived. An essentially tropical creature, I remember carrying butter on a plate to the open fire in the drawing-room to soften it in winter so that we could have toast and honey for tea. But by the time I had returned to the kitchen, which was some distance away, the butter was iron-hard again. The kitchen wing was the oldest part of the house and was supposed to be haunted. The little enthusiasm I had for living there dwindled still further at the prospect of sharing the house with the ghosts of the past. Our two Springer Spaniels sensed something peculiar from the start and refused to go up or down the back stairs. I later discovered that the house had been exorcised and that many of the people, mainly men, who lived within its walls had later died in mysterious or tragic circumstances.

The only consolation I had was that the resident ghost – said to be the spirit of a woman wronged – was believed to favour Roman Catholics. Perhaps because my mind was tuned to matters supernatural, other things haunted me – signs and portents. On wintry days when the wind howled and the mist rose so quickly that it covered the windows in a shroud, I had the intuitive feeling that somewhere, in our future, an unforeseen unhappiness lurked. Not long after we had moved in, and with the Hall still not properly furnished, Bunny arrived home from work one evening to find me sitting at the bottom of the stairs, my head in my hands.

'What's the matter?' he asked.

'It's this house,' I said. 'It *is* haunted. I don't think I can live here.'

No matter how hard I tried, I was finding it increasingly difficult to feel at ease within its walls. He knew how I felt, we had discussed it before, but now he realised I was serious.

He thought for a moment. 'Well, if you feel that strongly about it, I'll cancel the lease.'

That was so typically Bunny – acting compassionately and on impulse with no thought as to where we might live instead or how we would go about it.

I appreciated his offer but the thought of moving yet again suddenly brought me to my senses.

'No, no – you can't do that,' I suddenly decided, rising to my feet. 'Let's give it a try.'

So try we did, and as the days grew longer, lighter and warmer, the house didn't seem quite so bad. With a new coat of paint on the walls and woodwork, and our own belongings filling the bare rooms, I began to feel more comfortable in our new home.

And there were many compensations for its gloom. The surrounding scenery and rolling countryside were wonderful, the children grew up on the simple pleasures offered by English rural life, and I thrived too. So much so, that in due course Emma's second sister, Jennie, was born, in September 1968 (named after Jennie Jerome, Winston Churchill's mother), and then, two years later, in 1970, our son whom I named Johnny despite Bunny's dogged determination to call him Randall. Both children were born in the Victorian splendour of Harrogate General Hospital, a far cry from the little tea garden hospital in Assam. As with the arrival of all his children, Bunny recorded their birth dates, weights and times in his leather-bound Game Book; sandwiched between details of how many pheasants he had 'bagged', and which of his beloved Springer Spaniels had recently given birth to a litter of puppies.

I was determined to make a success of things at Cowling Hall, my first home in England. Bunny also seemed to settle in well to our new way of life. Although he had been living as an expatriate for seventeen years, he could still pursue his love of fishing and shooting in the heart of the North Yorkshire countryside. He knew a number of local families from his schooldays, so we quickly made friends. Naturally there were more constraints and conventions in Yorkshire than there had been in

India, but Bunny adapted well, taking on the pose of a local squire, even though he lacked the estate – or the funds to pay for it. His father died in 1968 and left him several thousand pounds in an inheritance, but I never saw any of it, and Bunny resisted my attempts to urge him to invest in a property somewhere locally, rather than carrying on renting.

He spent money like water and rarely thought of the consequences. Constantly inviting people back for dinner or to stay at a moment's notice, he didn't seem to realise that his generosity and gregarious nature meant that I spent most of my time in the kitchen, plucking pheasants, scaling salmon or cooking up huge meals on an old and temperamental Aga. Weary enough from the strain of having four small children, I hired 'Tompee' – Mrs Thompson, a marvellous local woman – in to help me out, and, during the summer months, Polish au pairs, but otherwise it was mostly left to me.

Bunny's way of making amends was to go to the local cash and carry store and buy up huge amounts of extravagant goods – smoked salmon, prawns, chocolate gateaux – and bring them home triumphantly. They were things we really didn't need, and they simply cluttered up the freezer, but it was his clumsy way of trying to make my life easier.

Then Bunny informed me, almost casually, that he had left his job. An old friend worked in the steel industry in Sheffield and Bunny assured me that he would give him work. Three months later, when that hadn't materialised, Bunny was desperate and began hammering on a few doors. A distant cousin, Peter Russell, an engineering entrepreneur, came to our rescue and offered Bunny a sales job. Peter had not seen Bunny for years, but remembered him as a charismatic charmer, a social animal, and thought that this urbane, self-confident expatriate might be just the person he needed to promote spare parts for agricultural machinery to the county set. I remember being hugely relieved that Bunny was going to have a source of income at last. My scant savings had all been used up, and the money his father had left him seemed to have evaporated.

Unaware of the difficulties their father was facing, the children got on with their lives and blossomed, Emma in particular. Fiercely independent, adventurous and, in some ways, precocious, she went to school in a little World War Two Nissen hut at Catterick Garrison, ten miles away, and loved it. She was forever bringing friends home from school, often inviting them without asking me – a self-confident trait she inherited from her father. One of her passions was to learn to ride and she began with our donkey, Nellie. Emma adored Nellie and would spend long hours with her arms clasped around her neck, even if the consequence was that from time to time, she picked up fleas. I lived in anticipation of the moment when I would catch her furiously scratching her head and I had to get out the special solution purchased shyly from the local chemist.

In time, Bunny bought her a pony called Misty, and then Peanuts, a lively and mischievous chestnut Arab, named after my pony in Assam, who needed a great deal of exercise, and who we eventually had to give to the local riding school. When Emma went on her first Pony Club camp with Misty, she came back exhausted by the rigours of sleeping under canvas and tending to her pony. When I went to collect her she was shattered, but blissful, as any small girl would be having spent an entire week living with, and for, her beloved pony. During the entire week, she hadn't even found the time to brush her teeth, but had loved tending to the animal's needs before her own.

Her younger sister Yo joined her at school and had a much quieter time. A lovely girl, Erica was always rather shy and sensitive. She smothered Jennie and Johnny and lived very much in the shadow of Emma – quite literally, in the end, as Emma's height soared and by the age of twelve she was towering over most of her friends.

'Mummy, they've shoved me at the back in the school photograph again,' Emma bemoaned bitterly one afternoon shortly after coming in from school. It was a constant complaint of hers that she was too tall and didn't like it.

Sitting her down at the table, I held both her hands in mine for a heart to heart.

'Emma, my darling. There is absolutely nothing you can do about it,' I told her, 'so why not just *enjoy* it? There are probably dozens of girls at your school who would love to be as tall and slim as you. People will look up to you all your life, so please make the most of it.'

It was advice that she took to heart and, from that day on, I think she really did enjoy the power her height gave her over other people. Once she had got through the gangly stage and was fully grown, she was a statuesque five feet eleven inches tall and thoroughly enjoyed using it to her advantage.

Through our contact with the girls' school, our circle of friends quickly expanded, and the children joined the Brownies and other clubs. For my part I helped with the local playgroup twice a week in Thornton Watlass village hall; I served 'meals on wheels' to old age pensioners around Bedale, helped with the cricket teas and was elected to the local cancer research committee. I had, by then, changed my faith from Catholicism to Church of England – the only difference from the children's point of view being that I had moved from 'the talking church' to the 'singing' one. It was all much what was expected of me in the country life we had become a part of.

Cowling seemed to be permanently alive with friends, particularly during the summer months, when there was a constant flow of visitors and guests. Despite the effort involved, I loved having a full house and welcomed the space we had to entertain the children. There were games and toys and a dressing-up chest filled with my old clothes for them to wear – including my wedding veil chosen by Mummy which Jennie, ever the showgirl, claimed as her own and wore to almost every occasion, even church.

In the garden there was a seesaw, a sandpit and a wonderful swing roped to a tall sycamore tree which allowed the children to go danger-ously high. Emma, who always loved swings, was particularly fond of this one. There were bikes to ride along the lanes or round and round the tennis court, ponies to trot out, and dogs to walk across the open fields. There'd be conkers and fireworks and Halloween parties. We'd rake up the autumn leaves and have huge bonfires, the smoke permeat-ing the fabric of thick woollen jumpers with its incense, before rising in a tall plume and seeping horizontally into the still evening air for as far as the eye could see. As the house stood high on the hill, it was wonderful for kite-flying in the windy months, and Emma was particularly keen, just as I had been when I was a little girl in India. I can see her now, her face tilted to the heavens, with an expression of pure delight, as a captive red kite dangled and danced at the far end of her string.

Being on a hill had its disadvantages too; there was always a temptation for the children to flirt with danger, hurtling downhill on their bicycles or on sledges in winter, sometimes with disastrous results. All my children have scars to remind them of those carefree days.

Christmas was always special at Cowling. Frost painted the fields and trees white, and icicles hung like sugar sticks from gutters and rooftops. Gramps – as my father was universally and affectionately known by then – joined us from Scotland, and the children would put on little plays for him in front of the fire, dressing up and dancing and singing in tutus and fairy-tale costumes. Every year, on Christmas Eve, the carol singers from Bedale would come, wrapped in scarves and mufflers, their breath pluming out on the air, their footsteps crackling on the snow, under an ice-rimmed moon. They would arrive with much blowing on hands and stamping of feet before shuffling inside to stand round the Christmas tree in our hallway singing for all they were worth. Their fingers still stiff from the cold, we would reward them with schooners of sherry and warm mince pies, as the blaze from our fire reddened their cheeks.

Cowling Hall was also a happy home for another reason – it was the place that I first came into regular contact with my sister Sue. By then working as a night nurse in London, she suffered endless sleepless nights as her body clock acclimatised. I would invite her for weekends in the country to help her unravel. During those Yorkshire days she and I first became close, tentatively almost, and, to our mutual amazement, decided that we really rather liked each other. It was a friendship that has come to mean a great deal in my life, particularly after the death of our mother.

Sue had always been much closer to Mummy than I. For some reason, probably because she spent longer with her in India to begin with, she could always handle her, I think she was emotionally more mature. By the time I was living in Yorkshire, both Mummy and Sue lived in London and saw each other regularly. In 1973, Sue married Martin, a former Royal Marine, in London, and we were all invited – my daughters were to be her bridesmaids and Johnny her pageboy. Travelling down from Yorkshire for the occasion, I saw my mother for the first time in years and introduced her to her grandchildren. She appeared delighted to meet them all at last, but I remember thinking how little she had changed.

Within a year, she was desperately ill with cancer. Sue telephoned me one night in the late summer of 1974 to tell me she was dying and to ask me to come. I travelled to London – my last solitary journey involving my mother – to her bedside in the Charing Cross Hospital. The sight that met me was so shocking and distressing that I had to run from her room. The frail figure of a woman lying in the bed bore no resemblance to the vivacious Australian theatrical star I remembered as a child. Sue had failed to give me adequate warning about how ill she looked. In my shock, I remember wanting to smash every mirror in the place and I pleaded with the nursing staff never to allow Mummy to see her own reflection.

It was a futile request and within days she had slipped away. As I sat through her colourless funeral – attended by a handful of relatives – I wondered where it had all gone wrong. She had looked so vulnerable towards the end, so harmless. Where was the wicked witch I had created in my mind, the woman who had caused me so much pain, for which I had never found it in myself to forgive? In her place, I found a mother who needed her daughter's love and forgiveness as she faced her own death. More than anything, I think I felt overwhelmingly sad that I had never really liked her. After the funeral I realised that the feeling had been mutual – when my mother's will was published, she had left everything she possessed to Sue. I wasn't even mentioned by name: as far as she was concerned I didn't even exist.

At Cowling Hall, life went on. The children had barely known their grandmother and were completely unaffected by her death. Emma was sensitive enough to ask me if I was all right on my return from the funeral, but other than that my mother's demise was largely overlooked.

Bunny and I led virtually separate lives by then – we had just drifted into a sort of polite impasse as I devoted my time to the house and children, and he to work and country pursuits. Apart from mealtimes, our spheres rarely coincided. But Bunny never stinted on his time and affection with the children. He especially had time for Emma, as she was the eldest, while I naturally spent more of my time looking after the youngest, Johnny. Having a boy added a new dimension to family life, as he developed different interests from the girls. To this day my daughters accuse me of spoiling him because he was the only boy, and the youngest of my children. But in reality, with the demands of a growing family, I simply didn't have the time to be as strict as I had previously been. Constantly tired from the exertions of the day, I decided, after Johnny, that four children was quite enough – my grandiose plans for seven melted away.

In time, Emma moved on to our local primary school in Thornton Watlass, before being enrolled at a boarding school, Polam Hall, in Darlington. It was a joint decision between us; she wanted to go there to be with all her friends and I knew her educational chances would be improved at the school. Much as I missed her, she was only a weekly boarder – coming home every weekend – and she flourished. She grew to be taller and even more slender. Independent of spirit, she became increasingly confident academically and was good at sport – badminton and hockey especially – but her best talent was for art. From a very early age, she would paint and draw everything around her. She loved to enter competitions and was constantly sending paintings off to newspaper and television contests.

When the children's television programme *Blue Peter* began to have Christmas appeals for good causes, she would badger everyone – not just the family, but also her friends and teachers – to join in the collections of keys, stamps or milk bottle tops. The ability to motivate and galvanise people into action was an early trait which she nurtured throughout her life. She relished the sense of joint participation between people in order to achieve a common goal. I don't believe she ever understood the concept of failure; and from early on she had strong views on right and wrong.

Emma had a capacity for doing everything with great gusto. She loved to participate and to share, she was never any good at just watching. Coupled with her inherited love of the countryside, from the minute she first saw the West of Yore hunt ride out on a Saturday with all the usual pomp and ceremony – the braying and yelping of the hounds, the stirring cry of the hunting horn and everyone dressed in hunting pink and black – she was determined to take part. A novice to begin with, she became a proper little Thelwell girl, bouncing up and down and inevitably taking some tumbles, delaying the 'cry' and incurring the impatience of the experienced riders on their great strong horses. They soon came to admire her bravery and daring, however, for one aged only ten, and it was after she joined that the Bedale Pony Club had to bring in a special rule limiting future hunt members from joining unless they had reached a certain level of experience.

I was never keen on riding, but I knew that I would have to learn so that I could ride out with my daughter and keep an eye on her. It seemed to me a parental responsibility. So once a week, after the children were all put to bed, I would go to the Catterick Garrison riding school for lessons. Those floodlit evenings in the indoor school provided me both with an escape from running the household and a great personal challenge; the fact of the matter was that I was simply terrified at the prospect.

With persistence, however, I made sufficient progress to be able to join the hunt on a real gent of a horse called Smokey Joe. Emma and I rode to hounds over some rugged countryside, jumping dry stone walls and the becks that criss-crossed the Yorkshire moors, and we both found it exhilarating. If I could find a gap in the walls, or steer my way around a particularly nasty ditch, I was greatly relieved. When I couldn't, I would steel myself to go for the jump, hoping for the best. But I closed my eyes every time. Emma, however, always headed for the most difficult jumps, wide-eyed and fearless.

The last day of my hunting season fell on a soft spring day in March. 'I'm glad I've done it,' I thought to myself, as I glanced across at Emma, her head thrown back, laughing. That day stays forever in my mind. Strolling through the beauty and peacefulness of that late afternoon with my eldest daughter, I heard, for the first time that spring, the cry of a curlew. I never rode to hounds again, though Emma continued to do so until the day we moved from Cowling Hall.

There were many happy, unforgettable times during that first phase of our family life in Yorkshire. Despite my initial misgivings, it became a place where I felt able to give my children a traditional and safe upbringing – to make them feel valued and loved – partly because my own childhood had been so bleak and fragmented. Perhaps it sounds old-fashioned now, but I was anxious to give Emma, Erica, Jennie and Johnny an enduring sense of values – of honesty, decency, and a proper regard for other human beings – a moral code to help guide them and equip them for their journeys through life. In time they would come to need these values – more than I could ever have imagined. Because disaster – and then tragedy – soon came to visit us.

5

I had married Bunny as a young and naive innocent, without ever having had a chance to get to know the real man behind the mask. Our life in India had the kind of artificial glamour in which he had flourished. He was always exceptionally good company and a natural socialite: charming, articulate and deceptively sober, even if he was known for being 'pencil-shy' – reluctant to sign the chitty for drinks at the bar.

ONCE WE SETTLED INTO MARRIED LIFE IN YORKSHIRE, HOWEVER, BUNNY'S LESS ATTRACTIVE TRAITS BECAME HARDER TO DISGUISE AND I BEGAN TO KNOW BETTER THE MAN THAT I HAD VOWED TO SPEND THE REST OF MY LIFE WITH.

There had been several early warning signs, I now realise – his obsession with his former girlfriends, wanting to name the children after their cherished memory; his decision to move us into what was really a most unsuitable house simply because of his fond childhood experiences there; his indifferent approach to work – easily overlooked in a colonial setting, but not so easy to ignore in the confines of Britain. There was his spent inheritance, his reluctance to deal with the bills, and his constant reassurances that some wonderful financial event was just about to happen.

Bunny was born out of his time; he should have been the eighteenth-century squire he longed to be. He was a dreamer, dressed in tweeds and engaging in country pursuits, refusing to think about the harsh realities of life. He never really grew up; he was a Peter Pan who lived in Never Never Land where money grew on trees and no one ever thought about tomorrow. His years in Yorkshire must have been a great disappointment to him. Despite being a leading light in the local Conservative Association, an outspoken member of the village and cricket committees and the life and soul of the blood-sports set, he had hoped for a far grander lifestyle back in England. As the country set began to tire of him, he could see his hitherto unquestioned popularity slipping away from him, and he feared what it might reveal.

In a desperate attempt at bravado, he continued to assume an aloof air, an arrogance almost, to the point of believing himself to be above everyone, even the law. He took pleasure from trying to 'beat the system' and assumed that he could evade it at will, though he was rarely to succeed. He was constantly trying to impress people with what were clearly delusions of grandeur – creating wilder and wilder fabrications about what he did and what he had. The courage the drink gave him propelled him, concealing an inner insecurity.

One day in 1973 we had arranged to spend a day grouse shooting on the moors with a friend and neighbour called Charlie Wyvill. I had planned everything in advance, so that Tompee would take care of the children in my absence. When the shoot was over, I returned home alone to relieve her for a few hours, before she came back to babysit for me, as I joined the shooting party for supper at a local pub. Meanwhile Bunny had retired to another hostelry further up in the Yorkshire Dales with the beaters and the gamekeeper, Freddie. I arrived at the rendez-vous for supper, but Bunny failed to appear.

The meal was almost over when a telephone call came from Freddie to tell me that Bunny – whom he insisted on calling 'Mr Julian' – had been arrested. In a state of inebriation, he had crashed his Land Rover into the stone parapet of Ulshaw Bridge between pubs. Though unhurt, he remained slumped, intoxicated, over the steering wheel. A passing priest roused him from his stupor, whereupon Bunny unleashed a tirade of abuse at him. Not surprisingly, the priest beat a hasty retreat and telephoned the police. When the police car approached the scene, siren wailing, blue light flashing, Bunny came back to his senses. Jumping out of the Land Rover, he slithered down the river-bank, wading knee-deep into the freezing water, clad in his brand new (and very expensive) tweed jacket and trousers, to hide under the little humpback bridge. The police car pulled up, the officers examined the Land Rover and looked about for any sign of the driver.

Bunny, hiding under the bridge, still befuddled, having made one stupid mistake, went on to make a second. As the police were about to give up their fruitless search, he emerged a moment too soon, only to be immediately spotted by the policemen, and arrested for driving whilst under the influence of drink. Exasperated at the news and fearful of what this might mean for his job, I went with Charlie to find him and to recover his guns from the Land Rover. Returning to Charlie's house for coffee, we discovered Bunny in the bath, trying to sober up, while two policemen stood by, ready to interview him. Having got the information they required, they told Bunny they would see him in court the following week. Just as they were about to leave, he called out ebulliently:

'Meet you for a brandy beforehand?'

Needless to say, Bunny was charged with drink-driving and a court date was fixed. When our local postman delivered the summons, which came in the form of a registered letter, he initially forgot to ask me to sign for it. As he turned away, I called him back, not realising what the letter contained. When Bunny found out, he was furious with me, because, he said, if I had failed to sign for it he would have been able to deny all knowledge of it. I was shocked at his dishonesty, something which was completely alien to my nature. But dishonesty and deception continued to play a major part in the breakdown of our marriage.

Not long after the court case, at the end of which Bunny was fined heavily and lost his licence for a year, I received a telephone call. It was Peter Russell, Bunny's cousin and, I thought, employer. He didn't mince his words: he accused Bunny of being bone idle, a scrounger and a liar. He expressed his deep disappointment and anger, because he had only given him the job in the first place as a great favour. Peter told me he hadn't seen or spoken to Bunny in ages and had long ago given up on him, allocating his area to someone else. He wished me and the children good luck before hanging up.

Putting down the receiver, I tried to take in what Peter had told me; that Bunny hadn't worked for him in over a year, although he had been pretending to me all along that he had. I knew he worked on a commission basis, and met clients at all hours of the day or night, and I had simply believed him when he told me that he was off to meet so-and-so, or have dinner with someone. Now I realised that I had been the victim of an elaborate con. He wasn't working or earning, and yet we still had a roof over our heads and food in the refrigerator – God only knew how.

When I confronted Bunny about the situation, he admitted everything immediately and dismissed my concerns.

'Oh, I wasn't sacked exactly; it just didn't work out. I thought I mentioned it,' he told me, before packing up the Land Rover for yet another shoot. Losing his job was like water off a duck's back. He sought escape in fishing and shooting, the one thing he was exceptionally skilled at. He simply did not have the strength to countenance his familial responsibilities.

Armed with this new knowledge, everything began to fall into place – the letters from the bank, the unopened bills; the strange telephone calls from people wondering where he was. To this day, I have no idea what Bunny did with all his money. I know that he made several foolhardy financial decisions, only to lose more cash. I later discovered that he was involved in litigation over some of his debts in Leeds, and that he had gained a reputation as a bit of a nuisance locally, 'pinching' untaxed red diesel from a local farm, borrowing machinery and tools and failing to return them, and taking more than his fair share of the 'bag' when it came to pheasant shoots.

Gradually, inevitably, funds became desperately short and I began to realise that we were no longer going to be able to maintain our way of life. As the bills piled up, unpaid, every day became a battle for me. The more I tried to tackle our problems with him, the more defensive and hostile he became. He would always try to deflate the argument by saying: 'I don't see what's wrong. Don't we live well enough?' waving his arms around magnanimously to indicate the comfortable house in which we lived – and for which he had not apparently paid the rent in several months.

As the situation worsened, I began to lose any respect I had for him. There was little room for love and so we lost that too. I kept a brave face throughout our deteriorating relationship, in order to hide my distress from the children. I said very little to my family, and nothing at all to our friends. At first I was hopeful that we could somehow overcome our troubles, that one of Bunny's friends would indeed come up with a magical job as Bunny kept promising. But lie after lie was heaped one upon the other and Bunny literally forgot where one lie ended and the next began. And there was much worse to come.

One Saturday evening at Cowling, in the late summer of 1973, I was frantically busy as usual, making preparations for the children to go to school the following morning. Bunny was out somewhere, leaving me to clean the children's shoes, iron their uniforms and make sure they had all finished their homework. I had made the sandwiches for his cricket match earlier that afternoon and not seen him since.

Emma had been so engrossed in the kitchen garden all day, planting up her autumn vegetables, her fingers black with mud, her hair straggly and wind-blown, that she had failed to find time to do her homework. Now in a frantic panic, she couldn't find the *Janet and John* Ladybird reading book she needed, and I was searching all over the house to try to find it – the drawing room, the nursery, the kitchen, her bedroom. In desperation I flicked through a pile of papers lying on a large oak chest, which stood in the hall. As I did so, I came across six letters addressed to Bunny – sent to a *poste restante* address – all in the same handwriting, neatly held together with a single rubber band. I stopped dead in my tracks.

My throat knotted as I studied the envelopes. Somewhere deep inside I think I knew what they contained. Fighting to control my emotions and with a sinking heart, I stuffed them back under the pile of papers and decided to investigate later. It was eight o'clock and there was still so much to do, not least to read the children a bedtime story. I remember it was *Thumbelina* that night, the story of a tiny little girl saved from a sunless marriage to a mole by an exotic swallow who flew her to Africa. It was one of Emma's favourite stories.

Fairy tales so often end with, 'They got married and lived happily ever after,' and those were the words that echoed in my head the day I married Bunny. But I knew, that night, that that particular fairy tale had been shattered.

Once the fairy tales were over and the children fast asleep and oblivious to the turmoil raging in their mother's heart, there were no more excuses not to face the truth. I braced myself to read the letters. Pouring myself a large drink, I sat down heavily and slowly opened the bundle, my hands trembling as I did so.

'My dearest, darling Bunny . . .' they began, and I read on in a state of utter shock and disbelief. Not only were they love letters, but they were written by a woman I knew. Local to our village, a few years older than me, married with children, she was someone I had previously considered a friend. I felt as though I had a chicken bone stuck in my throat. And then the waves of misery started to wash over me. During the long days and nights that followed, I was numb with shock; sick to the stomach at the treachery, the clandestine nature of the affair and the thought that it had been going on right under my very nose. I couldn't eat for three days – and I agonised over what I should do. I hadn't been able to read the letters fully, I couldn't bring myself to take in all the sordid details of my husband's sexual relationship with this woman, and yet I desperately wanted to know more. Was the feeling mutual? Had Bunny returned this woman's obvious affection? Or was she chasing him, in the misguided belief that he had something to offer? There were no references to letters from him, after all.

I decided, for the while, to say nothing to Bunny, in the vain hope that our daily life could go on with some semblance of normality. I needed to find out more, and I resolved to try to intercept the next few letters to see what the woman's plan was. It was incredibly hard to pretend that nothing was wrong, especially on the rare occasions when Bunny was home. We still slept in the same bed, after all, even if we had drifted apart sexually. It was a battle for me to keep up a brave face, for the sake of the children, and I didn't always succeed. With the girls away at school during the day, I would often find myself collapsing into floods of tears. Johnny, who was still too young for school, would sometimes find me in this state.

'Why are you crying, Mummy?' he would ask, his eyes wide with alarm.

'Oh, I've hurt myself, I bumped my knee,' I'd lie, wiping my eyes, and Johnny would bend down and tenderly kiss it better.

I felt I had no one to turn to. I was guilty and ashamed; I blamed myself for not being a good enough wife to Bunny, for being constantly tired, for not responding to his advances. Searching for the adulation and love that was his life's oxygen and which he had not found in me, he had turned elsewhere and embarked on an affair. I knew I was at least partly to blame. Later, as my feelings of desperation failed to subside, I confided in my doctor, but his attitude was typically male chauvinist. He listened to my tale of woe and refused to prescribe me any medication. He told me to accept the situation in which I found myself. I will never forget what he added as a parting shot:

'In Africa a man would have many wives.'

I remember thinking what a strange remark it was, especially when, much later, it turned out to be so prophetic.

With Bunny continuing to stick his head firmly in the sand, our debts were mounting at a frightening rate. Concerned about what rights I had, if any, I finally plucked up the courage to make an appointment to see a solicitor in Leeds. I arrived there nervously and falteringly explained my circumstances in full. He listened silently to my story, and then pointed out the stark facts. Having two separate homes would inevitably double our costs, he said. Why didn't I stay with things the way they were and see what happened? He had so little constructive advice to offer that I came away wishing I hadn't bothered to go and see him. I had hoped for more support.

Desperately unhappy as the weeks and months rolled by, I finally turned to my sister Sue for advice. Concerned as to how I could afford to live anywhere else, she also advised that I should stay with Bunny at least until the children had grown up. But that was years away and I was utterly confused about what to do, but I was learning that my decisions in life had to be mine alone. Meanwhile the affair went on, and the debts, the terrible debts, haunted me day and night.

Things went from bad to worse in the course of the following eighteen months. I intercepted a letter from Bunny's lover and discovered that she fully expected him to get a divorce and marry her. She clearly assumed she would have a life with Bunny and wanted to be the mistress of Cowling Hall. It was also clear from the wording that she mistakenly believed he had money. Furious, I picked up the telephone and dialled her number to tell her a few home truths. Trembling with anger and nerves, I told her that if she was after Bunny for the wealth he pretended to have, then she was more stupid than I thought. I don't think she believed a word I said. Contacting her husband a few days later, I discovered that he had known about the affair all along, and was as saddened as I was by it. But we both agreed that there was nothing much we could do.

Bunny came home unexpectedly that night and challenged me. He now knew that I knew, he had found out that I had called her and had intercepted her letter. He was furious. There was no contrition. He literally chased me around the house to get the letter back, until I locked myself tearfully in the lavatory. I didn't know what to do, I considered flushing it down the toilet, or even eating it, but realised how ridiculous that would be. Unlocking the door, I calmly handed it back to Bunny and pushed past him, informing him that from now on he would be sleeping in the guest bedroom.

The bills kept piling up. I had no income of my own and any small savings I'd had dwindled to nothing. What food I bought came entirely from our Family Allowance, collected eagerly by me each week from the local post office. I began to wonder about getting a full-time job to help ends meet, but with four children aged between four and eleven at that time, it would have been impossible, so I took on some part-time secretarial work for a local farmer instead.

Our bank manager started bombarding us with letters and phone calls. After fobbing him off for so long, I discovered that Bunny had been stringing him along too, claiming that he was waiting for substantial funds from India. It was a complete cock-and-bull story and one day I snapped and stormed into the bank to tell the manager so.

'These so-called funds from India are a figment of Bunny's imagination,' I informed him, before bursting into tears.

The manager reached into his pocket and handed me a clean white handkerchief. He was mortified for my sake and for his, and was kind enough not to berate me over my husband's debts. From that day on, if I ever caught sight of him approaching in our small village, I would dart across to the opposite side of the road and duck behind parked cars to avoid having to face him. The children thought I was going mad.

I knew that Bunny had no savings and no legitimate source of income, but, inexplicably, he continued to come home with goods for me and the children, many of them luxuries which we could ill afford, and which we could certainly have lived without. I couldn't think where the money was coming from. And then, one day, a dreadful realisation dawned: Bunny was Treasurer of the local Conservative Association.

By the time I began to suspect the true seriousness of our situation, I was at my wits' end. There was no point confronting him about anything any more. I suspected that he had backed himself into a corner and 'borrowed' money from the Tory coffers with every intention of paying it back, one day, before anyone found out. They did eventually discover the truth – several hundred pounds were missing and legal proceedings were started against Bunny. He was quietly asked to leave the Association, but by then he was living a Walter Mitty existence, where fact and fantasy had become inextricably linked. I don't think he ever really understood how much he hurt me, or other people; and he continued to behave like a plausible Irish rogue, avoiding the police and those who were on his trail, leaving me mentally and emotionally drained, and covering for him.

He spent more and more time away from the house. I was filled with fury and despair; I began to hate the man he had become. Time and again I thought: 'How can you do this to us? How can you claim to love your children, and yet fail to provide for them?' I had come to accept that he no longer loved me, so I decided to offer him a truce: he would go away for twelve months, after which he could decide whether he wanted to stay or leave. I was secretly terrified that he was trying to force me to leave him, to abandon our home and children so that his mistress might move in. I stupidly believed that if I stayed on at Cowling Hall without him the children would have their own home as security and we would manage somehow. Meanwhile everything seemed to be cursed.

Bunny had a pedigree Springer Spaniel bitch called Sash who fell pregnant during these dreadfully worrying few months, when we had no money to pay for anything. Going into labour, she got into difficulty and I had to take her as an emergency case to the vet. After a long and difficult labour, she eventually gave birth to fifteen puppies. Having admitted to the vet I had no money to pay him, he very kindly waived the fee. I then realised that I simply could not cope with fifteen puppies at this, the most awful time of my life, and I tearfully asked him to dispose of them.

Choosing one to keep, I came home with Sash and her solitary puppy, feeling like a mass murderess and as low as I had ever been.

Bunny greeted me cheerfully at home with the news that he had agreed to give a retired racehorse a home. He pointed to the beast snorting in the paddock. In utter disbelief, I blew my top, insisting that he return it immediately. Chastened, he did so, but such events only added daily to my pain and mortification, as our friends inevitably got to know of our troubles. By the time the bailiffs first came to the house, and then appeared on the doorstep every day – and I do mean, without exaggeration, every single day – I think I was verging on semi-madness. They were always polite, almost unctuous, because they knew us as members of their local community, but they persisted in asking for Bunny and serving various summonses on him for goods and money. One of the outstanding debts was, I remember, for £20 damage to Ulshaw Bridge into which he had crashed his car whilst drunk.

Somehow, somewhere, my sense of self-preservation came to the fore. Ashamed and humiliated to be doing anything so clandestine, I secretly gathered together all my jewellery, what little silver we had, and my gun, and asked friends to store them for us; I even hid some things in a secret place in a local barn so the bailiffs would not get their hands on them. But I couldn't rescue everything. We had a very old grandfather clock, dating from the eighteenth century, with an exquisite oak casing, which stood in the hall at Cowling. It was unusual as, deliberately, it had only one hand on the clock face. When I could stall no more, when time had literally run out, the bailiffs came and took it away, carefully detaching the pendulum and manoeuvring it outside. They told me that it would fetch in the region of £100 which would be used to clear one of our debts, though now I realise that it would have been worth far, far more than that. I remember the children gathered in the hall, standing silent, thumbs in mouths, perplexed that this fixture from their home was being removed by a group of strangers.

> *Stop all the clocks, cut off the telephone,*
> *Prevent the dog from barking with a juicy bone.*

from 'Funeral Blues' by W. H. Auden

To my very great shame the bailiffs' actions and the subsequent sale of the clock 'to pay off debts' were reported in the local newspaper. The secret was well and truly out and there was nothing I could do to stop our family name being dragged further through the mire. The telephone had already been cut off, and one day in the blazing summer of 1975, a man called to disconnect the electricity supply. Johnny, aged five, was cooking Yorkshire puddings in the oven at the time, a passion for him at that age, and an economical way to fill the children's stomachs for me. When I answered the door, and the meter man told me rather sheepishly why he had come, I begged him:

'Would you please just allow me half an hour more, so that I can finish cooking our meal?'

He graciously went away and sat in the shade of a tree down the lane for thirty minutes, before dutifully returning and cutting off the supply. From then on, I cooked all our meals on a little Primus gas stove, and we had to make do with no hot water or electric light. The last straw came one morning when an envelope was delivered by hand: it contained the final notice of a court eviction order. To my amazement Bunny didn't bat an eyelid; he was not at all alarmed and carried on with his own pursuits as if nothing had happened. He refused to attend court so I had to go alone. I had no choice but to go and plead for the future of my children.

His attitude finally destroyed any hopes I'd harboured that my marriage could be saved. I knew now that it was over forever, and in a sense I was relieved. If we were evicted then someone had made the decision for us, Bunny and I would be separated at last, and maybe I could start to pick up the pieces of my life again, and those of my children. But first I had to get over the legal hurdles. I had never been inside a courtroom before, or in trouble with the law in any way whatsoever, and I was terrified at the prospect. In the weeks before the hearing, I had many a sleepless night; and when I did sleep I suffered from dreadful nightmares. Barely able to cope, I begged my doctor for some sleeping pills. He very reluctantly agreed to give me some, on the condition that I went to see a counsellor. I hated having to accept that I now needed professional help, but I had no choice but to agree if I wanted those pills.

On the day I was due to appear in court, I made sure the children were either at school or with friends. I drove myself alone to Northallerton county court, ten miles from where we lived, too embarrassed to ask anyone to accompany me and praying that no one would recognise me when I got there. The judge listened to my appeal to him to allow us a few more months to try and raise some cash, made careful note of the case details and asked several questions of the solicitors representing the landlords about the many failed efforts to pin Bunny down. Finally, he pronounced sentence. He had no choice, he said, but to refuse my plea and grant the eviction order. We were given four weeks in which to leave Cowling Hall.

With only a few weeks to pack up a decade of life with all its trappings. Trepidation gripped my heart and I honestly thought that I was going to faint. Frozen to the spot, staring straight across the crowded courtroom at the bewigged judge, trying to accept his judgement with dignity, I heard his words echoing round and round in my head as I tried to take in what this would actually mean. I was homeless. The children were homeless. The dreadful realisation made my jaw drop to my chest, and tears welled in my eyes.

'Will that give you sufficient time?' the judge asked, more gently.

I must have looked a forlorn and sorry sight.

'Yes,' I replied; I could find no other words.

'And where is your husband today?' he asked, his forehead creased into a frown, a frostier tone in his voice.

I faltered. There was total silence in the courtroom, while everyone waited for my response. Eventually I managed to string a few phrases together.

'Well . . . I'm not quite sure, your honour,' I began, honestly. 'I . . . I think he may be fishing . . . fishing for salmon . . . I think on the River Tweed.'

The words sounded so unreal in that place. I had just been told that my home was being taken away, for the simple reason that my husband had failed, for ten months, to pay a peppercorn rent of £6 a week, and instead of being in court, he was fishing for salmon on one of the country's most expensive stretches of river, as if nothing had happened. There was no more he could do to hurt me. Or so I thought.

Emma, photographed in Paris in 1981 (*Chris Booth*)

My parents while they
were living in Assam

Fishing with my ayah
on the Brahmaputra
river in Assam

With my younger sister
Sue while staying in
Worthing in 1951

My wedding on 10 November 1962 in Doom Dooma, Assam, flanked by household servants

With my husband Bunny and dogs, Spark and Kim, on a fishing trip

Cooch Behar palace, the home of the Maharaja of Maharanee, where we enjoyed some truly sumptuous evenings

Emma insisted on having a ride on this boat; her love-affair with hats had started young

She also had an early liking for beads and shows them off here to great effect

Back in England, she became a true Pony Club girl and was besotted with horses

A family group during our early days at Cowling Hall; *left to right*: Jennie, Bunny, Johnny, Emma, me, Erica

Cowling Hall, our home in Yorkshire

Emma at the controls of a single-engine aircraft in which she flew to Australia with Bill Hall (*W.D. Hall*)

Emma and Bill ready to leave on the next stage of their flight (*Clive Hyde*)

Emma with Willie Knocker on safari in the Kerio Valley, Kenya

Emma in one of her wonderfully bright outfits surrounded by colleagues from Street Kids International

A local matting industry in Leer reinstated by Emma after interruption by the civil war

A Nuer luak (homestead) in Leer, Southern Sudan (*Peter Moszynski*)

Children displaced by the civil war, such as those Emma was able to help through her education programmes (*Peter Moszynski*)

Children playing a game of bau (*Peter Moszynski*)

I walked away from the courtroom utterly humiliated but, in a strange way, resolute. I now knew, beyond question, that I would soon be parting company from Bunny after thirteen years of marriage. I would have to find ways of surviving for myself and Emma, Erica, Jennie and Johnny. And for them, I had to be strong. When Bunny eventually came home that night, the worse for wear, long after the children had gone to bed, I was waiting in the kitchen, and took a deep breath as he walked in.

'We need to talk, Bunny. This is desperately important,' I started. 'I'm terrified about the future, and about what is going to happen to me and the children.' There was silence. He put down his fishing rod and tackle and peeled off his quilted fishing jacket. I continued carefully: 'I went to the court hearing today. The eviction order was confirmed. We have four weeks to get out of this house. *Four weeks*, Bunny, did you hear? What on earth are we going to do?'

His eyes glazed over as they always did when I talked about money and he headed straight for the drinks cupboard.

'Just a moment – I want to fix myself a drink,' he said. 'Do you want one?'

'No, I don't. I don't want to drink, I want to talk,' I replied, trying to quell the rising anger in my voice.

Standing by the refrigerator, he carefully poured himself a large whisky, opened the refrigerator and dropped two ice cubes into the glass. Turning, he looked me in the eye for the first time in months. I suddenly noticed how much he had aged, how deadened his eyes were. He had always been much older than me, but now he really looked it. His once-relaxed expression, the one he wore when he was regaling dinner party guests with his madcap tales in Assam, had gone. Standing before me was a middle-aged man for whom reality was too painful to face. I almost felt sorry for him in that moment. Unable to hold my gaze, his eyes dropped to the floor, as an expression of shame and guilt flickered across his features.

'Listen to me,' I told him, my voice catching. 'I've ceased to care about *her*. But I can't stop caring about our children. Our home is going to be taken away from us. What are we going to do?'

Bunny sipped his whisky. 'We'll, we'll manage,' he started. 'Things'll be all right in the end . . .'

I had heard that line so many times before, but this time it wouldn't wash.

'But *how*, Bunny?' I implored. 'How can they be all right, unless we do something positive? Don't you want to protect our children? You don't appear to have grasped the fact that we are about to be thrown out onto the street!'

Bunny sipped his whisky once more. 'We'll manage . . . things will be all right in the end,' he said pensively, his mind visibly struggling to ignore the truth. Brightening suddenly, he gave me a wry smile and did what Bunny always did best – change the subject. 'Incidentally,' he said, his eyes hopeful that I would not persist with the conversation any further. 'Did I tell you, I hooked a huge salmon today, a really big one, but it got away . . .'

This was not a time for incidentals. Stopping mid-sentence, Bunny suddenly found that he was standing face to face with me, and the expression he saw in my eyes was not one he had ever seen before. I am a good tennis player, I have an excellent backhand, I was fourteen years younger than him and coiled up like a tightened spring. The swing of my arm sent his glass of whisky flying through the air, creating a golden arc across the room. Then I was gone. I was gone forever.

My world fell apart for a while after that. For several days, I felt completely unable to carry on, to keep pretending, keep fighting. I could not see what I had done to deserve having this pain inflicted upon me. I had been brought up – though not terribly happily – as a child who believed in fairy tales and happy endings. I believe that, if you were Christian of spirit and the stars were auspicious, you would meet a kind and caring man, that you would marry him, have his children, and that you would be cared for as long as you lived. I tried not to let my innate Catholic guilt make me believe that I had somehow done something to deserve this fate. I had been a good wife and mother, but I had been treated to nothing but lies, lies, lies.

Now my stars had gone out. I had four children and I was being abandoned forever, left to cope alone with money worries, eviction from my home and emotional betrayal. What I didn't realise then was that I was also stepping out of the prison of my own past. I was also learning a lesson: that apparently you can have all you want or need in life, and then it can be taken away from you. The children had been pretty well protected from events until now. But, as I rummaged in the attic and the cellar, clearing out belongings and filling huge wooden crates, there was no longer any point hiding the truth. Our house of cards was on the verge of collapsing.

Emma, at eleven, missed nothing with her watchful eyes and sharp mind. She, too, was learning the same lesson and her childhood ended there. From then on, she became my companion and confidante, an essential prop for me, though I sensed that it began to drive a wedge between the friendship of the two older sisters – Erica realised that Emma and I were, of necessity, growing closer and closer. Circumstances had forced us into making crucial, life-affecting decisions together, conspiratorially, and Yo resented being left out.

My sister Sue was a rock. She hurried north from London to help me pack up at Cowling. When she arrived and saw the look on my face, her first words were:

'I had no idea things were as bad as this.'

She led me into the house and made me tell her everything. With her help, I began to get a grip on life and threw myself into organising the move.

From that day on, I was forced to rely largely on the kindness of friends, relatives and neighbours as I lurched through life, trying to gather all the shattered pieces. Wanda's mother, Erica, who was devoted to Bunny, but who had also taken a shine to me and the children, had very kindly negotiated on our behalf accommodation in a cottage next to the stables in Aysgarth School – the school Bunny had attended as a child. As a single parent with no income and four children, I was not a particularly attractive proposition as a tenant, but the governors of the school seemed to overlook that. I knew the cottage was going to feel claustrophobic after a house with six bedrooms – we would have to make do with one living room, a tiny kitchen and two rooms upstairs – but I had no choice. The school also offered me a job as a junior matron, though one with purely administrative duties, which turned out to be darning socks. It was not exactly what I had had in mind for a future career, but I accepted it gratefully, knowing that the wages would at least enable us to pay some rent.

Now there was just the Hall to pack up and we would be off.

Having filled the house with ten years of family living, I scarcely knew where to begin to dismantle our life. At the same time I was desperate to maintain some normality for the sake of the children. It was by now the middle of the summer holidays, so the children were not at school. I didn't want them always to remember that summer as the one when we lost our home. Jack, a local gamekeeper who was a family friend, kindly surprised us with a black-and-white working Cocker Spaniel puppy whom we called Toto, in remembrance of Emma and Erica's *ayah* in Assam. The little dog provided a welcome distraction while we were packing things up, as he tore about the place ripping up heaps of newspapers and unravelling balls of string, somehow making us laugh in the middle of such turmoil.

The chickens, the donkey and two ponies all had to be found new homes, and I did my best to explain to the children that they were only going away for a while and that they could still visit them. I found Johnny crying his heart out in Nellie's stall, unable to understand, and Jennie clutched a favourite pet chicken, Henny-Penny, to her with a determined look in her eye. A few days later, while Sue distracted the children, the animals were quietly taken away.

I stored some of the larger furniture in a neighbour's barn, but sold many possessions to raise much-needed funds. Bunny's belongings were bundled up into a couple of suitcases in his absence and left for him in his bedroom. I had hardly seen him since the whisky incident. Before long the removal vans arrived and started to load up our life in boxes. By the time they had driven away up the long drive towards Aysgarth, we were left with an empty, echoing house. As I closed the huge front door behind us and turned the key in the lock on that blistering August day in 1975, I made my way towards my little Renault 4, unable to see very clearly for the tears. Driving away from Cowling Hall for the last time, never to return again, the children's bewildered faces peering back at it from the rear window, I wondered if Bunny had even remembered the date.

He eventually returned to the Hall later that night and packed up his few remaining belongings. By then working as a farm labourer, getting work when and where he could find it, he accepted the offer from a friend to live rent free in a tiny crofter's cottage high up in the Dales, a place of few comforts and even less hope. When I went to see it after the tragic events which were to follow, it was cold and damp, filled with dirty pots and pans and empty vodka bottles; the remnants of an isolated bachelor existence. It looked little more than a tramp's hovel.

We had fallen from a great height; a far cry from the days of the Jorhat races and the yellow waistcoat, the spacious colonial bungalow and servants waiting upon our every need. But little did we know, we had much further still to fall.

6

We remained in the cottage at Aysgarth School for three months. I had so little money that we had no choice but to live extremely frugally. There was no refrigerator and no heating. The children – more often than not led by Emma – crept into the vast walled kitchen garden of the school most evenings and stole home with armfuls of booty from the veritable glut of vegetables and fruit. Our one major consolation was that the school boilers were in our building, so there was a constant supply of piping hot water for baths, showers and general washing. Sometimes, if only to wash away my feelings of despair, I would have three baths a day, languishing in the steaming water, my tears mingling with the soap bubbles.

THE OTHER CONSOLATION WAS THE WEATHER; THE LONG, HOT SUMMER HELPED US ALL TO ENDURE THE DRAMATIC CHANGE IN OUR CIRCUMSTANCES, ALTHOUGH I KNOW THE CHILDREN FELT QUITE BEREFT WITHOUT THEIR BALLET CLASSES, PONY CLUB AND OTHER LITTLE LUXURIES PREVIOUSLY TAKEN FOR GRANTED. For the time being at least, the children's school life remained constant. Emma and Erica were both at the Convent of the Assumption School in Richmond and their headmistress, learning of our fate, was tremendously sympathetic and supportive. I struggled to meet the school fees, partly by selling some of our belongings, partly with the help of family and friends, and by applying to various educational trusts. I used all my ingenuity to try to keep the children's education intact and managed by a whisker, over a period of time. It was something I clung on to – that if they could stay in the same school among the same friends, then somehow everything would turn out all right. And at least if they had an education, they had a future.

Although Bunny and I were no longer talking, he kept in contact with the children, and came to see them fairly regularly, Emma in particular. She spent one day a week with him and he came to trust and confide in her. She was torn, poor child, between her mother and father – friend and confidante to both, each one relying on her – a huge responsibility for a twelve-year-old girl. The price she had to pay was her innocence. In the course of that year she grew from a child into a young woman, with worries way beyond her years.

By November 1975, we had to leave the cottage, it was simply too small. There were complicated legal implications; we might have been considered sitting tenants if we stayed any longer, the school explained. Once again Sue came to help me pack up for a second time. Our next home was Burtree Cottage in the village of Little Crakehall, some two miles away, where Jennie and Johnny attended the local primary school. A former farm labourer's dwelling, now untenanted, it was let to holiday-makers during the summer months, but the owners agreed to let us move in over the winter, for a nominal rent.

Slightly more spacious and with a greater degree of privacy, the cottage suited us very well, although I knew that we would have to vacate when spring came. Unable to think much beyond that, I knew now that at least we had five months to settle in and establish new routines. My father joined us for Christmas with Wendy and Bill Burton in Cambridgeshire, and we did our level best to overcome our sadness at spending our first Christmas as a broken family and with none of the festive traditions of Cowling Hall.

Once Bunny and I were officially separated, there seemed little point in staying married, so I continued with the process of suing him for divorce on the grounds of his adultery, naming his mistress as the co-respondent. I was granted legal aid to pay for the proceedings and had to attend the final hearing in Harrogate, scuttling in shyly, only to find to my great embarrassment that there were barristers at the court with whom I had regularly dined. The decree nisi came through on

20 January 1976. The marriage was over and I felt nothing but a sort of cold numbness.

Bunny continued to live an itinerant life, moving from place to place in our area, staying with anyone who would give him food, comfort and a roof over his head. The woman with whom he had first had an affair dropped him like a hot potato when she realised that he had no money. I remember standing in the kitchen garden at Aysgarth School after we had been evicted, receiving a message from her, via an intermediary, that I could 'have him back'. Launching into a ferocious pruning of a fruit bush, I told the messenger acidly:

'Well, I think it's a little late for that.'

Stuck away in his tiny cottage, or slinking from place to place so as not to attract unwanted attention, reality finally caught up with Bunny. Peter Pan had to grow up. Realising that he had lost his wife, his children, his home, his job, his mistress and any money he had ever had, he took to drink and sank into a deep despair. The police were still after him, there were numerous creditors, and litigation pending in various courts. His few friends in the county, people who chose to overlook his many foibles, remained loyal and were extremely kind to him, and it was through them that I heard any news.

After a while, rumours began to circulate in the neighbourhood that Bunny was threatening to commit suicide. One of the master's wives at the school was the first to tell me, and others followed. I laughed the rumours off, dismissing them completely as little more than self-pity and dramatisation on Bunny's part. I maintained that he was far too selfish to carry it out. Still my troubles with him were far from being at an end. He had eventually been charged with embezzlement over the funds he had taken from the local Conservative Association and was of course unable to repay. During his court appearance, he pleaded for leniency, claiming that he had been forced to turn to embezzlement, in order to finance 'his wife's extravagant way of life'. The local newspapers duly reported every word, and my public vilification was complete. I was so disgusted and embarrassed, I seriously wondered how I would ever be able to show my face in the small and highly respectable community in which we lived.

Sickened and appalled, as soon as I heard I marched down to the village telephone box – we had no telephone of our own – to call the police. In a cold fury I demanded to know what I could do to take legal action against the newspapers, to deny all they had said about me and state the truth. I was told by some hapless station sergeant that the court proceedings were covered by reporting privilege and there would be no easy or immediate means of redress. On learning this, I stumbled to the home of some neighbours, and cried my heart out with shame and misery in their farmyard. Strangely, I never blamed Bunny for what had happened. I knew that he was a broken man and guessed, correctly, that he had been encouraged by his solicitor to provide some explanation for his actions. After that, Bunny and I no longer communicated – I had had enough of the past, and I wanted to protect my future. But that future was about to produce a terrible event.

It was February 1976, and the bleak grey days dragged by, bringing early nights, drizzle and gales. Life felt damp and cold, as the mists from the Dales drifted in, clinging to our hair and clothes. Everyone walked with their heads down against the wind and the waterlogged ground sought out holes in our wellington boots and left muddy footprints in the hall. To give the girls something to look forward to, I arranged for Emma and Erica to spend a few days in the historic city of York with friends during the forthcoming half-term school holiday. I drove them to Northallerton station in a hopeful mood. They were looking forward to their trip and we all giggled on the platform as Toto cowered between our legs every time a train whistled past. Their train arrived and I helped them into their seats before waving them goodbye.

Setting off for home, I decided to stop off at Bedale to attend to some matters. I joined a queue of damp people in the post office, each one dripping tiny puddles at their feet, and noticed that Freddie the gamekeeper was also there. He doffed his cap and said good morning, averting his eyes. I was in a hurry and I didn't linger to strike up a conversation with him. Freddie was probably extremely grateful that I hadn't: he knew something which I didn't – though that knowledge was only minutes away, for me. When I reached Burtree Cottage, I noticed a Volvo saloon parked outside. I recognised the car and the two people standing by it, Wanda and Marion, a mutual friend, both buttoned up to the neck against the weather. Even before I switched off the engine, I knew something was wrong.

The previous evening there had been a strange and dark episode that had left me feeling uneasy. The children were home from school, the eldest doing their homework. The coal fire was lit and we were locked in and settled down for a long winter's evening. There was an unexpected knock at the door. I opened it to find two uniformed policemen standing in the doorway, serious expressions on their faces. I asked them in, grateful that my two youngest were in bed.

The officers unbuttoned their coats and told me they had come to question me about Bunny's whereabouts. I flinched slightly at the mention of his name, worried what he had done now. But, no, it was nothing to do with money or embezzlement. Unusually, it was something even more disturbing. His former girlfriend, the one whose letters I had found, had telephoned the police because the oil pipes leading from her domestic fuel tank had been deliberately severed with a knife, leaking the contents all over the drive and onto the main road. Apparently Bunny had been ringing her constantly throughout the day, but she had hung up on him every time. The police naturally assumed him to be responsible.

'Do you think Mr McCune could have done something like this?' one of the officers asked me, doubtfully. They were local lads, they knew Bunny as a bit of a rogue, but vandalism really wasn't his style.

'It isn't in his nature to have done such a thing,' I replied, honestly, but a strange tingling sensation crept up from within me. 'But if he *is* responsible, then he must be in a desperate state.'

Trying to get him off the hook, I told them that, in any event, I believed Bunny had gone away for the weekend. I knew that he had been invited to go with friends to a race meeting in the south of England, because he had asked Emma to join him. She'd declined his invitation because she wanted to go to York.

They thanked me for my time and disappeared into the cold and foggy night, leaving me to wrestle with my conscience. I felt a chill creep into my heart. There was something very sinister about their visit. I felt as if it were some sort of omen. I wondered whether I should go out into the bitterly cold night to search for Bunny, to warn him that the police were after him. But if I found him, he would probably be drunk and then what would I do with him? Would I take him to friends, or to hospital? I couldn't make up my mind.

As always with Bunny, in the end I took the path of least resistance; effectively giving up on my husband for the last time. I tucked Emma and Erica in to bed, stoked up the fire, locked the doors and watched a late-night thriller on television, trying to quell disturbing thoughts.

> Yet each man kills the thing he loves,
> By each let this be heard,
> Some do it with a bitter look,
> Some with a flattering word,
> The coward does it with a kiss,
> The brave man with a sword!

from 'The Ballad of Reading Gaol' by Oscar Wilde

Now as I turned off the engine, got out of the car and approached my two friends, Marion and Wanda, standing at the front door of the cottage, I sensed that something was terribly wrong. The events of the previous night flashed through my mind – haunting me – as they would for evermore.

They were both white-faced. Without speaking, I unlocked the door and they followed me into the cottage. Once inside, I turned to face them.

'What's the matter?' I said, with mounting panic, fearing that something had happened to one of the children. 'What is it? Please tell me straight away.'

'Maggie, you'd better sit down,' Marion said, reaching out to manoeuvre me into an armchair. 'There's some awful . . . some dreadful news about Bunny.' She took a deep breath. 'He was found dead this morning . . . I'm afraid it seems that he committed suicide.'

I froze. And I had to force myself to believe it was the truth. Then somehow, like an animal threatened by grave danger, I instinctively wanted to run away. Escaping Marion's clutches, I flew up the stairs and flung myself onto the bed, my face buried in the eiderdown, shaking with the convulsions of uncontrollable grief.

'Oh, no,' I howled in disbelief. 'Why, why, why? What a terrible waste of a life. He was so self-assured, so good at so many things. He had so much more talent than me. *Why, why, why?*'

There was nothing anybody could do to console me. The months and years of pent-up emotions, of persuading myself that I was better off without him, vaporised. He was my husband and he was dead, leaving me a widow at thirty-four. He had effected the final abandonment of his four children. It was more than I could bear.

> *I am the great sun, but you do not see me,*
> *I am your husband, but you turn away.*
> *I am the captive, but you do not free me,*
> *I am the captain you will not obey.*

from 'I am the Great Sun' by Charles Causley

Over the next ghastly few hours, I learned the sad story of Bunny's final few hours. Like pieces of a jigsaw puzzle, eyewitness accounts of his last movements were slotted into place to create a whole picture. He had been seen in several pubs in Bedale the previous evening, behaving strangely and not in his usual sociable way. He had also delivered his two beloved Springer Spaniels to Freddie, the gamekeeper, asking him to look after them for a while. Putting his final affairs in order late that night at his bleak cottage, he had driven his tatty old van – now his only form of transport – into a muddy field on Manor Farm near the village of Masham, on land owned by Marion and her husband Richard. The farmer who worked this land went out at dawn the next day, to check on his livestock. He walked by the vehicle parked on the edge of a field, and noticed that there was a man inside, apparently asleep. When he returned from his rounds an hour later, the vehicle was still there, with the man still inside. Thinking this unusual, he decided to report it.

Richard returned with him to investigate, and it was only then that they noticed the hose pipe, leading from the exhaust to the inside of the van. In the strengthening light of that cold February morning, Richard wrenched open the door and, to his great shock, recognised Bunny. He was about to see if there was anything he could do, but one look at his face, one touch of the cold car bonnet, made him realise that his friend was in the sleep that would last forever. On the passenger seat were six hand-written letters in white envelopes – four of which were addressed to women Bunny had known and loved, and two to men. One was for me.

The next few days were a complete blur as I was led around like a lost child. Marion packed some necessities for me to stay with her overnight and, with Toto, ferried me back to her house. We needed a plan of action, I was told, as I sipped mug after mug of warm, sweet tea and tried to stop myself from trembling. My friends were marvellous and set everything in motion for dealing with the funeral arrangements. But first, there were the children.

Marion phoned Crakehall Primary School to tell the staff and then drove to collect Jennie and Johnny while I telephoned our friends in York to break the news. We had decided not to spoil Emma's and Erica's holiday and allow them an extra carefree day.

'Please keep them away from any local television news pro-grammes, or newspapers,' I asked my friends hoarsely. 'I don't want them to learn of their father's death before I have had the chance to tell them myself.'

Hearing Marion's car in the drive as I replaced the receiver, I braced myself to face Jennie and Johnny and tell them that their Daddy was dead. Marion ushered them into the drawing-room, and – at her suggestion – we all sat down casually on the carpet to play a board game; with appropriate irony, the game was called 'Sorry'. The children were a little perplexed at their enforced truancy from school and began to ask questions. A few minutes later, Marion gave me a telling look, and slipped out of the room, quietly closing the door behind her. Jennie was only six years old, and Johnny was five.

I began to tell them what had happened, as gently and sensitively as I could, sparing them the true details, but letting them know that they would never see their Daddy again. I told them that he would be happy and safe in heaven. They looked at me and then at each other and began to cry. I could no longer hold back my own tears as I rocked them both gently in my arms. They were so young, they scarcely understood the meaning of what I was saying. It is only in maturity that we find ourselves carrying, for the rest of our lives, the true weight of grief and sadness.

My father came down from Dumfriesshire to join us that night. He had always got on well with Bunny, from those early shooting days in Assam, and he was genuinely sorry to hear the news. It was wonderful to have him there, both for my sake and for the children, even though Emma and Yo remained temporarily oblivious to the situation. The following day, the formalities were set in train. I was interviewed by the local police, who were gentle in their treatment of me. They told me more about the six suicide notes, letting me know to whom they were addressed. One was handed to me, but I couldn't face opening it yet. I stuffed it into a pocket to read in private and stumbled from the room. The days blurred into each other.

It seemed an age before I had to drive to Northallerton station to collect Emma and Erica to go through the ordeal of telling two children, once again, that they had lost their father. They were so much older; they would understand much better, they would hear tales at school, read stories in the papers. I felt I had no choice but to tell them the simple truth, and I wanted the truth to come from me alone and no one else. By this time I was in a state of shock. I cannot honestly remember exactly what I said, when or where, but I do remember both girls' crestfallen faces, the tears coursing down their cheeks. Emma sobbed:

'But Mummy, I didn't get a chance to say goodbye.'

Neither do I have any clear recollection now of when it was, or where I was, when I read the two-page letter Bunny wrote to me. I will never disclose its contents to anyone. But I remember thinking after I had read it that it was probably the first time that Bunny had been totally frank and honest with me, which made it all the harder to bear. Most of my married life I felt I never really knew the man inside Bunny. I could never have a really meaningful conversation with him. He was, and had chosen to remain, an enigma. He had too many shadows and tracks to cover, going back to long before we met. He could be honest only in death, it seemed, not in life. Now that almost a quarter of a century has passed, my bitterness towards him has faded from my heart.

He had a great many good qualities, but was destroyed by his own weaknesses which lured him into a maze, at the centre of which he could find no other way out.

I was fortunate to have friends who protected me as much as they could from the rawest aspects of the tragedy. I didn't want to go to the mortuary to identify the body, so Richard went in my place, to spare me the ordeal. Nor did I attend the inquest, which passed a verdict of suicide. It was odd, but once I knew of Bunny's death, I kept wondering whether his latest girlfriend had heard about it and how she was coping. Although I was now divorced from him, I took it upon myself to assume responsibility for all the arrangements. Bunny died on a Monday and I arranged a private cremation on the following Friday, placing a small announcement in the local newspaper.

When that Friday came, I remember driving through a misty morning into Bedale. It was *Wuthering Heights* weather – thick fog, damp roads and an aching chill in the air. I sought sanctuary in the local florist shop, whose windows were all steamed up. The women were hard at work making up elaborate wreaths, which I suddenly realised were for Bunny's funeral. I was desperately short of cash but, with the few pennies I had, I bought five daffodils, and a few sprigs of green privet. Shy, bewildered – as if caught in some strange dream – I left the shop clutching my humble offering in one hand.

My local vicar, Frank Ledgard, a close friend who had been responsible for receiving me into the Church of England, had arranged to drive me and my father to the crematorium. Meanwhile Frank's wife, Cicely, looked after Emma and Erica at their rectory. Our plan was to spend the weekend after the funeral with friends in Sheffield, and the children's guardians, close family friends, set off to take Jennie and Johnny ahead.

The service itself was totally private and most people respected my wishes to keep away. At the crematorium, it all seemed so clinical, so sombre, so completely distant from the man himself, the witty charmer who had swept me off my feet on *shikar*. I couldn't afford an expensive affair; I had to apply for a council funeral grant to pay the bills. His simple pine coffin was laid out on the little conveyor belt before me – my tiny posy incongruous amid the other floral tributes – and I stood, clasping my hands so tightly together that the whites of my knuckles showed through, holding myself in as the curtains slowly opened and he was committed to the flames.

> He was my North, my South, my East and West,
> My working week and my Sunday rest,
> My noon, my midnight, my talk, my song;
> I thought that love would last forever, I was wrong.

from 'Funeral Blues' by W. H. Auden

Outside, a few people had gathered quietly, to pay their respects. I emerged from the funeral parlour, lost in thought, floating along in a sort of daze, pushed gently forwards towards the car that would ferry me home. I felt a light tap on my shoulder. Turning, I saw a tall, gaunt woman, a stranger.

'I don't want to intrude,' she told me gently, 'but I really wanted to meet you.'

She spoke warmly of Bunny and told me that she had befriended him and had looked after him during his final, dark days. She spoke of him with genuine affection, and of course she was distressed by what had happened. Our conversation was brief, my look at her face transient, but I have never forgotten it, even though I was never to see her again. Some years later, I was told that she, too, had committed suicide.

Frank drove my father and me back to the rectory at Bedale. It was a twenty-mile journey which passed largely in silence, each of us lost in our own thoughts. Emma, Yo and Cicely were waiting, pale and anxious. I think we spoke very little. It was an event which had to be consigned to the past. We drove to Sheffield as planned and returned home after a long weekend away, to carry on with our lives.

I have a deep regret, which still troubles me to this day, that I should have involved the children in their father's funeral to a greater degree. My maternal instinct was to protect them from the pain. But with hindsight, I think perhaps if we had lived through this more as a family, it might have helped them come to terms with the first tragedy of their lives, even though they were so young.

Bunny's death was a tremendous loss for all of us, not just for me. It marked the end of a road along which we could never return. It was a world ending, without even a whisper. I know that Emma agonised over her decision not to go to the races with him and felt that she might have been in some way to blame. It was too close, too painful for her ever to discuss with me, but years later, an old boyfriend of Emma's, her first love, told me how she had poured her heart out to him about the terrible chain of events that affected her so deeply.

Once we were back at Burtree Cottage, I needed to tie up all the loose ends, and there was further discourse with the police in the wake of Bunny's life and death. Tentatively, shyly almost, those who had remained friends with Bunny approached me about the possibility of a memorial service for him. Shocked and saddened by recent events, they wanted an opportunity to say goodbye to him in a more appropriate way. Still shattered, I gave my blessing and Charlie Wyvill and a few others arranged a service in a tiny Norman church in the middle of a field on Charlie's estate. This time Emma and Yo accompanied me, though Jennie and Johnny remained behind. We said prayers and sang hymns. A local parishioner played an ancient organ, whilst her plump son pedalled and pumped the bellows which made it work.

The stresses and strains finally took their toll on me, both mentally and physically. Within a few days of the service, I was completely felled by a chronic bout of influenza. I retired to my bed, away from the world, away from reality, for the next two weeks to hide, drifting in and out of the life surrounding me, waking sometimes and hearing Bunny's voice echoing in my head. My feverish dreams took me back to India and to the places we had been. The sunlight glinting on the water of the Brahmaputra River, the Palace of Cooch Behar, the times when we were together.

Our time at Burtree Cottage was coming to an end. As April approached, in 1976, the owners informed me that they had already booked their first holiday let for the Easter break. It was impossible for us to stay. With no more bolt-holes open to me, I had no choice but to apply for a council house, and travelled to Thirsk to be interviewed by a surly and unsympathetic employee of the county council social services department. It was all I could do to convince him that I had no option but to move.

'Why do you need a council house when you are living in a perfectly good property, with three bedrooms and two bathrooms?' he asked.

I think he thought I should just stay on at the cottage indefinitely and await an eviction order, regardless of any promises I had made to the landlords.

'There is such a thing as loyalty, you know,' I told him curtly. 'These people have been very kind to me, and have become friends. I have no choice morally but to leave as I promised.'

He raised his eyebrows unsympathetically and did everything he could to block my request. After several visits to his sunless smoke-filled offices, I was at breaking point. My fellow claimants were veterans of the system – shabbily dressed, some with filthy children clambering all over the chairs and their parents, as they waited patiently.

But I found it unbelievably demoralising, stripping me of all my dignity, independence and privacy. I was so shocked that I had to declare all our savings, every single penny, right down to the children's post office savings accounts made up of monies given to them for their birthdays and Christmases over the years. It was the most humiliating experience I had ever been through and still the man I had to deal with remained unmoved.

In the end, I think he gave in only because he saw the desperation in my eyes. I had threatened to rent an old caravan to live in and drill holes in the roof for rain to pour through onto me and the children.

'Would that score me enough points to qualify?' I asked, bitterly.

Giving in finally, he offered me a rather nasty house on a notorious local council estate in Bedale where, for our accents alone, I feared that we would be set upon. I was prepared to accept a home at any cost, but a close friend with contacts in high places thankfully intervened on my behalf, and after that false start, we were eventually allocated a house in the more gentle environment of Thornton Watlass, three miles from Cowling Hall and in the farming community where we were known. We moved there in April 1976.

In many ways this modern semi-detached, pebble-dashed house was perfect for our needs. We had sufficient space and there was an extremely well-kept garden full of cauliflowers; Emma was thrilled. It had three bedrooms, a bathroom, a solid fuel fire, kitchen and tiny sitting room. The neighbours were nice and our friends continued to be kind and supportive, inviting us for Sunday lunches and outings to their baronial halls. But, by this time, I was in such a state of abject dejection that I loathed the house from the minute we moved in. It felt a terrible blow, to be relying on the state. I made little effort to make the house homely, deciding that we would make do with the bare necessities – curtains, beds, our trusty twin-tub washing machine and a few pots and pans.

At every possible opportunity, I made sure that we escaped to Scotland to stay with Gramps – in his lovely little cottage with a burn at the end of the garden. But our return to the council house after holidays and weekends spent in Dumfriesshire only served to lower my spirits still further. I was haunted by the fear that we might be evicted at any moment, and would be homeless. Somehow, and to this day I can't remember how, I managed to keep Emma and Erica in their convent school at Richmond, whilst Jennie and Johnny remained at Crakehall Primary School. I relied on the kindness of friends and fellow parents to give the children lifts to and from school to help alleviate the costs. I tried to get hold of money any way I could and even took a part-time job, two days a week, as a petrol pump attendant in Crakehall, earning the princely sum of fifty pence per hour in a vain effort to ease myself out of the state system.

I remember coming home one winter's night to find that Toto, our dog, had chewed up a pound note I had left out for the coalman for a much-needed sack of coal. Bursting into tears, I hunted high and low for the little fragments of paper, until I had pieced enough together to make up the part with the serial number on it. Sheepishly, I sent it away to the bank to claim a new pound note.

Each night when I returned to what I considered to be our dismal surroundings to plan and cook some frugal meal such as cauliflower cheese, quiches or bacon risotto, my heart sank. I felt battered by my experiences. I had suffered enough pity and social ostracism to last a lifetime; I had used up most of my energy and powers of initiative trying to ensure that my children would still feel loved, fed, clothed and provided with a good education, and I had literally come to the end of my tether. I was dejected and self-pitying. When friends or relatives visited, I would run away or hide – anything but have to face them. I was my own worst enemy because the ones who did still visit us were true friends, those who didn't mind being seen on a lowly council estate. But, by then, I was totally downcast, sinking deeper and deeper into a state of abject misery.

The turning point came one hot and sticky evening during the summer of 1976. I came in from work one night and, ignoring the children, crept upstairs and flung myself, exhausted, upon my bed, shutting myself away from the world. My hair was dishevelled, my clothes crumpled, and I started crying. After a while the bedroom door slowly opened and Emma entered, twelve years old, tall and self-confident, her dark hair glossy and her eyes bright. She quietly pushed the door closed behind her and stood looking at me with a steady gaze. There was a flash of something in her eyes. Fear, maybe. Or anger.

'Mum, why are you letting yourself go?' she asked quietly. I could hear something I did not recognise in her tone. I lay limply on the bed, unable to answer at first.

'Well . . . I'm not really. I don't know what you mean,' I replied, raising myself onto my elbows and wiping my eyes.

She refused to falter. 'Look at yourself, Mum,' she said, her voice firm. 'You are letting yourself go.' I suddenly recognised her tone; it was the same one I had adopted myself so often before when trying to deal with Bunny.

Finding it hard to hold her gaze, I opened my mouth to speak, to give her some reasonable excuse for my behaviour, but the words just tumbled out in an emotional cascade.

'Emma, I've been unhappy,' I began. 'I *am* unhappy.' I threw my head back on my pillow, turned away from her and sobbed. 'What is the point of it all? I hate my life and I hate this house.'

She stood firm, her body language rigid and taut. 'But that isn't a good enough reason to let yourself go,' she chided, her voice quavering slightly as she resisted the urge to run over and comfort me. Softer now, she insisted: 'You have *got* to pull yourself together.'

Sniffing and sitting up, my eyes red-rimmed, I looked up at her sorrowfully. 'I . . . I know I should,' I stammered. 'But sometimes it's hard . . .'

Emma shook her head slowly. 'No, it's not,' she contended. 'Not if you really want to . . . And you *must*.'

I looked up at her in surprise. Her uncompromising stare somehow managed to be both critical and compassionate at the same time. For a moment, I wondered who she was, this assertive creature before me.

'Mum, go and wash your hair,' she said firmly, seeing that the worst was over. She reached for a towel and handed it to me. 'Have a bath and dress in some of your good clothes, and come downstairs and join the rest of us.' There was a pleading look in her eyes. She had run out of ammunition and she hoped it had been enough.

Slowly, I rose to my feet, took a deep breath and smiled. The unfamiliar muscle movement tugged tightly at the corners of my mouth. 'Okay. I will,' I said with a sigh, moving obediently towards the bathroom. Relieved, Emma nodded her approval, turned on her heels, and was gone, leaving me remembering a time when I had confronted my own mother. This time I realised that my own child was no longer a child; that she had slipped through my fingers and was gone. This was my moment, and that of my daughter. There was no going back.

What I wanted more than anything was to buy a place of my own, but I couldn't imagine how this could be possible. It was obviously the cheaper option for us to stay in the council house, allowing me more freedom to buy a few luxuries for the children, or take holidays. But I felt instinctively that until we were free of the social services, and standing on our own ten feet, we would not be able to shake off the past and all its ghosts, which still haunted me.

I decided to hold a family conference and invited all my children to sit down with me around the table in the gaudily painted kitchen, to discuss our future. Emma was by now thirteen, Erica eleven, Jennie seven and Johnny six.

'I think I can safely say that we have reached the bottom of the barrel,' I said, studying the cracked linoleum and the little black stove. 'The good news is that there is only one way out – up. But I have to make some very difficult decisions and I need your help. Hands up who wants to leave this house and try to find somewhere else to live, somewhere of our very own.' The four little faces round the table each lit up at the suggestion. Four pairs of hands shot up into the air and waved around gleefully. They had made their first executive decision.

I had already taken a look at a very run-down property, Alverton House, a 200-year-old, grey stone semi-detached cottage, which was up for sale in the village of Little Crakehall. It was very cheap for what it was and I had seriously considered whether it might be worth purchasing, and doing up, although I realised that it would have been impossible for us to live there while the renovation work was in progress. On a whim, I put in an offer, considerably lower than the asking price, and was not surprised to discover that someone else had offered more.

'Oh, well,' I thought. 'It was probably a silly idea anyway.'

One evening not long afterwards, I was out walking Toto when a car pulled up alongside me. It was Mr and Mrs Hudson, the original owners of Alverton House. They told me that the sale had fallen through, and wanted to know if I was still interested. I very badly wanted to have our own home, but it seemed such a pipedream, given that I had so little money. Faced now with the possibility that I might be given a second chance, however, I decided to keep my options open and pleaded with them for a little time to think about their offer.

Walking home that night, the butterflies in my stomach were doing triple somersaults. How on earth was I going to raise the cash? What was I thinking of? I had all but decided to telephone the next day and tell them I was sorry, that I had made a mistake in my calculations, when my sister Sue called.

'I did something really stupid today,' I told her, laughing. 'I nearly bought a house.' I told her what had happened, making light of my foolishness, but she wasn't laughing.

'Tell me everything,' she said and insisted on the smallest details about Alverton House. I told her what it looked like and how much it cost. I said I had already ascertained that I would be eligible for a council grant for much of the work but that it would be an enormous project. Listening carefully, she said suddenly:

'Why don't I give you some of the money that Mummy left to me? It should have been yours anyway.'

I was speechless. It was such a generous offer that it took my breath away. Still an impecunious nurse with a small baby at home, I was sure she needed all the money she could get. Not only had she come to my rescue in such a kind and unexpected way, but she was using Mummy's money to do so. She gave me no choice but to accept.

The kindness continued. Aunt Margot, my fairy godmother, and her husband George offered to help with the bill for renovating the property, over and above the council grant. A surveyor told me the house was basically sound, a builder eventually agreed to take it on (after two who said they wouldn't touch it with a bargepole) and the bank agreed to fund part of the project if I could stump up the rest of the cash. Thus it was with the help of my wonderful family and friends, and with my heart in my mouth, that I was able to renegotiate it for the sum of £4000. Alverton House was to become a home. Our home. The first I had owned in thirty-five years. I could hardly believe it.

The renovations were extensive and would take more than a year, but I knew it would be worth the wait. I had something to look forward to at last, a light at the end of what had sometimes seemed like a never-ending tunnel. Regaining some personal confidence, I started to think about going into teaching. I had enjoyed being with children ever since Emma was born, I had loved running the little playgroup in Assam, and although I had no real experience, I knew that I would be good at it.

Nervously, I applied for a teacher training course at St John's College in Ripon, after confirming that I would be eligible for a full grant. But when I received a letter of acceptance, I panicked and realised that it would not be a good time to become a student, even if there was a long-term goal. Quite apart from adding to the financial burden, I knew that, in my delicate emotional state, I could not accept failure if I didn't make it through the course. Setting aside my ambitions, I accepted a job as secretary to the headmaster of one of the large state primary schools at Catterick Garrison. It was only nine miles away and the hours and holidays would be much more compatible with having four young children. I began working there in September 1976, a job I was to stay in for six years, and which provided us with much more financial security.

There were several major hurdles still to overcome and I did not always cope as well as I would have liked. I knew that we would have to stay on at the council house until Alverton was ready, but I didn't realise how dispiriting that would be, especially when – in the spring of 1977 – 'cowboy' electricians, employed by the council, came in to rewire the house and left it in a terrible mess – floor coverings ripped up, dust and plaster everywhere.

I ran to the village telephone box in floods of tears to call the council and complain, but they just didn't want to know. I had never felt so close to mental breakdown as I did that day. Walking back to the house, hardly able to face the clear-up job that lay ahead, I resolved to whisk the children to Scotland for a few days and build up some mental reserves first. Gramps welcomed us as usual, and his calm reassurances that everything would be all right bolstered me enormously. When we returned to the council house, we found a note pushed through the letterbox from a friend who had called and seen the mess through the window. It read:

'You simply can't stay here, you must come and stay with us.'

Once again, through the kindness and sympathy of friends, we managed to get through.

By the summer of 1977, more than a year after Bunny's death, hope was dawning: the work was almost complete at Alverton, and we were able to move there in August – our fifth move in two years. At last we had a rock on which to rebuild our future. It was the year of the Queen's Jubilee and our little village green was the venue for fancy dress competitions, picnics, sports events, dances and huge bonfires. There were organised celebrations everywhere, and we had our own private party.

With a new sense of purpose in my life, I set about decorating the house, enlisting friends, relatives and children. Emma – a great lover of natural wood – helped me to strip the ceiling beams of years of lime and plaster; a real labour of love. Yo, a meticulous, methodical little person, helped me lay a patio in the back garden. Friends dropped by to help us paint and hang wallpaper. All of this we managed to achieve before the winter set in. We had our own house at last, a place really to celebrate Christmas. It was to be the start of ten tranquil years.

7

My greatest challenge during the decade which followed was to acclimatise myself to being a single parent. It was hard enough scrimping and saving just to make ends meet, but with four boisterous children to steer through life as well, there was little time left for anything but to survive. Despite the hardships, however, we quickly settled into a comfortable routine at Alverton House – it was warm and dry, there was room enough for all and, most importantly, it was ours.

TO SAVE MONEY, EMMA AND YO HAD STOPPED BOARDING AT THEIR CONVENT SCHOOL, WHICH MEANT THAT I HAD TO COMPLETE A DAILY TWENTY-FIVE-MILE ROUND TRIP TO AND FROM SCHOOL. Jennie and Johnny were still at the local primary school, and had to learn independence early – letting themselves in after school with a key, making something to eat and doing their homework until I came in. All the children increased in self-sufficiency in those first few years at Alverton, learning how to enjoy themselves with simple pleasures such as roller-skating, cycling and playing hopscotch. Johnny made his own little wooden go-cart and somehow persuaded me to tow them on it behind my Renault 4 – amid shrieks of laughter.

In the golden summer months, secret dens were made out of grasses, the children frolicked with Toto in the cornfields and hedgerows, we played Pooh-sticks in the beck running through the village, and fished it with a worm. There was the village fête and the smell of freshly cut grass; the first flush of roses and the flowers and vegetables to tend to in the garden. Dragging herself away from the plants she loved, Emma was loaned a horse to ride, and threw herself wholeheartedly back into the one activity she had most missed.

Our main summer holidays were spent with my father at his delightful cottage in Duncow, Dumfriesshire. Here the children were free to roam and play in the pine woods or the burn; fish and camp, picnic by the sea or walk across the wide mud flats of the Solway estuary. We'd collect mussels and wild flowers along the shore; build camp fires to keep warm and cook sausages for lunch. These holidays inevitably held sad memories of our times there with Bunny in happier years, but I felt it was important for them that life was seen to go on; that their grandfather could still take an active role as the only adult male in their lives, and that they could remember their father with fondness.

Back at Alverton in the evenings and during the winter months, the children played endless games of cards and Monopoly, games which often ran on for days – until one of them ended up owning so much property or owing so much that only an argument would conclude matters. There were, of course, the inevitable squabbles of family life as the children began to establish their individuality, and I tried to maintain order without curtailing their vitality.

Emma, particularly, had a free spirit, and I loved the vigour with which she pursued her hobbies. She pressed wild flowers and mounted them in scrapbooks (reminding me of my own childhood). She grew plants from seed in the garden, scattering them haphazardly over the soil with the result that they grew in a random tangle of growth, more picturesque than any formal plan. Whenever a new cucumber, marrow or courgette was ready, we were made to sit down together, with due ceremony, to eat it. The other children protested loudly when she decorated their plates of food with bright red and orange nasturtium flowers she had also grown, but she insisted they were edible and would brook no complaints.

She collected shells with fervour whenever we were at the seaside and carefully chipped fossils from the rocks with a hammer and chisel. If anyone we knew intended to travel to some remote part of the world, she would beg them to find the prettiest specimens for her collection.

She was gregarious, rarely seeking solitude and filling our home with her friends. Our house was snug and welcoming, with a relaxed atmosphere often different from the austerity of their large North Yorkshire homes. I would arrive home to find a horde of gangly teenagers crammed into the sitting-room, drinking lemonade and chatting. And I regretted the day I finally had a telephone installed, because thereafter it rang constantly, most of the calls from suitors for Emma and Yo.

Pretty soon, boys began to flock to the house. Emma's husky voice and her height made her appear much older than her years, and she and Erica blossomed with the attention. They enjoyed playing the field and not affiliating themselves to one boy or another. They would stay up late in the sitting-room, playing games, laughing and talking, and I would have to retire with cotton wool in my ears in an effort to get some sleep before work the next day.

The only respite I got was when they wanted to watch a particular television programme. Then they would all troop off somewhere else to see it in colour, rather than try and focus on my old black and white set. Apart from its antiquity, it had the infuriating habit of shutting down in the middle of some gripping film or whodunit, when the meter money ran out. We would be left suspended in mid-air before a mad flurry of movement ensued, torches flashing from room to room in search of a fifty pence piece to resume the electricity supply before we missed the ending.

Throughout her life, Emma delighted in going to parties. She never showed any of the normal spells of shyness which affect most people's childhood and had plagued mine. Despite our reduced circumstances, the children remained friendly with a lot of the wealthier children in the area and as they reached their teenage years, they were invited to some rather lavish parties. In our social circle, there was a penchant for making them as grand as possible. Even after she had left Yorkshire, Emma made every effort to return for such events which she considered would one day become a dying art.

When Emma came home I was often reminded of her simple childhood pleasures. The memories would surge back . . . frost-laden ice-skating parties in winter, when the flooded fields on freezing days were transformed into pleasure grounds. Our breath puffed out in great clouds of steam and sometimes we would play ice hockey at night, under a cold winter sky speckled with brilliant stars.

Emma, the adult, relished playing hostess, which she did with consummate ease, and would invite friends to dinner. Enlisting Jennie as kitchen skivvy and waitress, and Johnny as bartender, she and Yo would dress up to the nines and hold court. I had strict instructions to sneak to the cinema or elsewhere with the younger children once the main course had been served. No successful dinner party has its host's mother or younger siblings hanging around just as things are getting interesting.

One of Emma's most striking characteristics was her amazing dress sense, born partly out of need. From her youth, playing with her *ayah*'s beads in Assam, she had an eye for the exotic and, because we didn't have the money to buy her expensive silks or ball gowns, she became adept at making do with what we had, or with what she could find. She never tired of putting outfits together, mixing fabrics and patterns, jewellery and hats with tremendous style. One party dress was fashioned out of black dustbin liners, worn with my longest evening gloves and pearls, and another striking outfit – half-white, half-black – was made out of cheap remnants. She had a sure eye and was forever rummaging through jumble sales or charity stalls, coming home triumphantly with broken beads and old silk scarves, or any other interesting scraps bought with her pocket money. She would then work on them, turning them into something individual, stylish and unusual, in which she invariably looked elegant. It was a trademark that would endure for the rest of her life.

As far as her schoolwork was concerned, a determination set in and she worked studiously for her achievements. She did well at school, getting eight 'O' levels in 1981, before sitting down with me to discuss what she should do next. Art was still her best subject, and she wanted to take Art and History 'A' level. The problem was, where? Much as I loved having her around, I knew that it would do her good to get away for a while, to experience another part of the country, see new horizons, and meet new friends. When my sister Sue kindly agreed to have Emma to lodge with her, and Martin and their children, in Surrey after Godalming Sixth Form College accepted her application, the stage was set. She was seventeen and she was leaving home.

It was a terrible wrench at first, not having her with me. In the previous few years – possibly the most difficult of my life – she had become my rock, my co-conspirator and, perhaps most importantly, my best friend. But I still held very strong views on education and I knew that the facilities offered in Surrey would give her more scope. Plus, I wanted her to escape Yorkshire for a while. Whilst I had done my very best to anaesthetise the pain of the previous years, the district would always remain a place of great sorrow where everyone knew her past, remembered Bunny's death and maybe, just maybe, treated her differently because of it.

However hard the decision had been to send her away, within weeks I knew I had been right. Living in the south suited her down to the ground. As if to set the pattern for her life, she began to surround herself with interesting and individualistic people at college. With them, her personality began to cohere: she was never afraid to speak her mind on the issues about which she felt strongly, and yet she had the ability to remain friends with those whose ideas she refuted. From quite a young age, her opinions were well formed and worth hearing; people loved talking with her. Her uncle Martin, especially, had a strong influence on her – the first father figure in her life for some time – and encouraged her to provoke discussion and thought, even if they often differed in the end. She could be charming and disarming even when she disagreed with an adult's view.

It was at Surrey that she embarked on a carefree, adventurous stage of her life. She still liked to shock with her zany clothes, and would perform mad stunts, such as she did one Rag Day when she and three fellow students dressed up as cowboys and boarded a train at Milford. Charging up and down the carriages, holding people up with air pistols, they demanded money for the college coffers. There were no ill intentions, just youthful zest and high spirits, but one elderly lady passenger was genuinely confused and reported the incident at the station. The police made contact the following morning and issued Emma and her friends with an official caution.

Casting her net further afield, Emma set off on her first foreign holiday as an adult – spending a summer in Italy on a EuroRail pass with three girlfriends from college. She was always completely unabashed about baring her body and shed her clothes at every beach opportunity, sunbathing topless or naked, relishing the freedom her naturist spirit hadn't enjoyed since her childhood in Assam. They slept on beaches and in youth hostels and, for a few cherished days, in a beautiful chateau belonging to a handsome young Italian they met called Luigi. Emma loved Italy, and thought of the trip fondly for many years afterwards, keeping letters and photographs, snapshots of a time when she felt she hadn't a care in the world. In her floating dresses and bohemian beads, Emma began a period of intense wanderlust, something I think she probably inherited from Bunny.

Within a few months of returning, she was planning her next trip. The following summer, she hitchhiked to Greece via Yugoslavia with a friend, Henry Leveson-Gower, persuading smitten long-distance lorry drivers to allow her to sleep in their little bunk beds in the cabs – a courtesy which hardly needed to be afforded to her, as she had always had the ability to sleep just about anywhere, and at any time. Poor Henry was left to converse with the drivers as best he could in whichever foreign language was appropriate while Emma slumbered on.

Knowing that I had made the right decision by sending Emma to Surrey, I arranged for Erica to follow her to Godalming Sixth Form College a year later, leaving Jennie boarding at the local convent school and Johnny boarding at Aysgarth. Alverton House seemed incredibly quiet and empty after Erica had left. I found myself missing the constant stream of visitors and telephone calls, and although I occasionally went out with friends or, very occasionally, on a date, it was an essentially lonely time for me, as I prepared myself for life after the children. How different from what I had imagined when I first married Bunny. No seven children, no comfortable home in the colonies, little money. It all seemed so far away, that golden time when I lived on the sun-kissed tea garden in Assam.

With my heart in my hands, in 1982, I decided to leave my job at the Catterick Garrison. My plan was to move to London for a while, to live and work there. I would be closer to Emma and Erica and it would be a chance for the other children to get to know London when they came to visit me in the school holidays. Staying with any friend or acquaintance in the capital who would put me up, sometimes sleeping on a mattress on the floor, I signed on at a night school for a secretarial refresher course in an effort to graduate from a manual typewriter to an electric one, and searched high and low for a temporary job during the day to help pay my way.

Jobs at that time in London were extremely difficult to come by. I found myself tramping the pavements in vain, clutching copies of my CV, arriving unannounced at the front doors of dozens of companies to see if there were any vacancies, only to be rejected on the grounds that I still had two dependent children. One afternoon in Piccadilly, after a particularly bad day of rejections and rudeness, I stopped for a moment in my tracks, indifferent to the expressions of strangers rushing past, and closed my eyes to scream inwardly at Bunny: 'How could you have done this to me?'

As the traffic roared by, I remembered back to another day in London years before, when I had thought about throwing myself under a bus. But my persistence and determination did eventually pay off and I was offered a temporary job with Hatchard's bookshop in Piccadilly, helping in their natural history department for the three month run-up to Christmas. I enjoyed my time there and the people I met were interesting.

On Christmas Eve, I booked my train ticket to travel back to Yorkshire, where I discovered the children home from their various schools awaiting my arrival. The house – which had been empty for several weeks – was decked with holly and a tree, and a full turkey dinner was prepared, ready to cook. They were very proud of my endeavours in London, they said, but had missed having me at home for weekends and wanted me to know how much. It was a wonderful gesture and I truly felt as if I had come home.

In the new year of 1983, I started to look for a job back in Yorkshire, painfully aware of my limited prospects in London. The search took six weeks, and was almost as disheartening. Growing increasingly desperate, I was prepared to take anything anywhere, so long as it paid. I even chased a job in a meat factory, but was turned down. Friends, however, alerted me to an interesting post working with a company called Tennants Fine Art auctioneers in the market town of Leyburn. With their recommendation and my tenacity, I managed to secure the job in which I was to stay for three-and-a-half very happy years, in what proved to be my most interesting position. All thoughts of moving south were once again put on hold.

After passing both her 'A' levels with good grades, Emma then had to decide where to go next. Newcastle University offered her a place to study art, and so did Oxford Polytechnic. I was glad and relieved when she chose Oxford. I knew it would provide her with more opportunity, living and studying in the world-famous university city. Once again, I was right. It was during her three years at Oxford that Emma's personality flourished, and her intrepid nature allowed her to embark on the very first of a series of quite remarkable experiences. The umbilical cord had been well and truly severed.

She found a house to share initially with Anna Baldock, Jo Mostyn, and one other friend. To help them settle in, Jo's mother and I drove south in our respective small cars, packed to the roof, transporting our daughters' goods and chattels for their big new step in life. Jennie and Johnny came along and we all converged one damp Saturday afternoon in September 1984. The house, though spacious, felt bleak, bare and empty. On arrival, we were desperate for a hot cup of tea, but there was no electricity and we were too late to have it connected, so we adjourned to a local pub for a high-spirited evening.

Spilling out of the pub, full, warm and happy, we bumped into – quite literally – a group of young men who erupted into a violent fight. It flared up in a matter of seconds, with no apparent warning. Hefty fists flew past my nose as I grabbed the girls and pulled them away. The brawling men rolled into the car park, and my poor little Renault 4 – with Toto barking furiously inside – suffered permanent dents to its bodywork. The ugly scene died down as quickly as it had flared up, and the young men dispersed into the night, leaving us a little shaken and me quite fearful for Emma's safety in the world she had yet to discover.

We crept back to the house and each found some space on the floor to sleep, rising early the next morning to put all hands to the pump. Between us, we hung pictures and curtains (rejects from Cowling Hall), unpacked boxes, cleaned the kitchen and settled down to a large brunch, before heading home. As I left, I gave Emma a hug and pressed a £20 note into her hand – all that I could afford. Fortunately, her grant soon kicked in, and with the £20 a month I continued to send her, and by supplementing her income working as a waitress in the evenings, she just about scraped by, although her letters home always ended with the words: 'Please send clothes etc'.

Emma threw herself into her course work with her usual energy; all her projects were interesting and varied, often portraying deprived people in society, including one in which she photographed a tramp, a nun and a business executive as three contrasting subjects to illustrate 'a day in a life'. On one of her rare weekend visits to Yorkshire, we sat around the kitchen table, her moody black and white photographs spread out in front of me as she explained her ideas. The liberated atmosphere of Oxford fuelled her imagination and allowed her taste for the unusual free rein. She would be seen riding her bicycle through the city's streets wearing something more usually seen at an evening cocktail party than on a drab weekday morning. Onlookers likened her appearance, in her colourful flowing dresses and gowns, billowing scarves and floppy hats, to someone from a Noel Coward play, but admitted that she had both the courage and the poise to carry it off.

For several months, she wore a long purple velvet coat, a hand-me-down from a family friend. With her stature, high cheekbones and dark hair, she gave the appearance of great beauty and elegance, and she relished the attention she received. Friends said that in Oxford there were times when Emma could never really decide if she was European or ethnic – she seemed torn between the two, having been born in India, and raised by colonials in the English countryside.

It was her striking and somewhat bohemian appearance which first caught the eye of Sally Dudmesh, herself a pretty blond anthropology student, who met Emma while the two of them stood studying a college notice board. Instantly attracted to each other, Sally and Emma quickly became and remained best friends. Sally said afterwards that it was like meeting her own sister. Born and raised in Africa but with a British passport, Sally was to be one of the first and perhaps most important catalysts in Emma's life, the reason she took an interest in Africa and the Third World. It was Sally who introduced Emma to another person who was to become an important thread: Willie Knocker – a blond-haired, slightly thick-set white Kenyan, who was a student himself and natural history enthusiast, who was Sally's boyfriend at the time. Ex-Army, Emma found him bossy, sharp-tongued and opinionated, but she always enjoyed the challenge of picking a fight with him. He, in turn, dubbed her 'Lady Cruella de Ville' for her rapier tongue. From then on, their friendship was sealed.

Joining the group, Annabel, the beautiful and intellectual eldest daughter of our local vicar and old family friend Frank Ledgard, moved to Oxford for her first postgraduate job. When Annabel found a house to share with her own contemporaries, Emma followed. I was a little unenthusiastic when I heard – I thought Emma was abandoning her student life too prematurely to live with older people without the same goals in life and with more money than her. Each of them was a high-flyer in his or her own way. They created a miniature Bloomsbury Set of artists, sculptors, scientists and landscape gardeners. But, as ever, Emma adapted and the house they shared, The Old Post Office at Littlemore, a charming cottage with a spacious but unkempt garden, was to become her main home for the next three years.

She upgraded to a moped from a bicycle and bought some bantam chickens, hoping that the sale of their eggs would help towards the housekeeping, a plan which worked until someone left the garden gate open and they all disappeared. She planted vegetables and sweet peas in the garden and wrote to me fulsomely of how the formerly scrappy lawn – with her tender loving care – had grown a beautiful pale blue carpet of wild speedwell. Years later, a meadow of speedwell happened upon by chance reduced me to tears and a longing that she could have been there to see it.

Always able to relate to older people, Emma became good friends with her landlords, Teddy and Jeffie Hall, and – in due course – with their sons Bill and Martin. Twenty-six years old, a dashing young graduate of Exeter University, Bill was working for his family firm, which specialised in scientific engineering and computing. Flying was his passion, he had obtained his pilot's licence at the age of nineteen and, three years before he met Emma, had bought his first single-engine aircraft, a Robin *Aiglon*, a light four-seater.

The first time I met Bill was rather unexpectedly one Sunday that winter. Johnny and Jennie were giggling conspiratorially all morning, in on some big secret, when the telephone rang. It was Emma.

'Hi Mum, I'm in Bedale,' she said, 'I've come for lunch.'

I was pleased and surprised – even more so when I discovered that Bill had flown her with Annabel from Oxford for lunch. We had a lovely spontaneous family gathering, before I drove Bill and the two girls back to a tiny grass airstrip near Thirsk. He seemed very nice, although the complete opposite to my untidy, disorganised daughter in his sports jacket and corduroy trousers – 'stiff upper lip' as Emma described him, and she was right. Driving home after dropping them off, I wondered absent-mindedly if it was a case of opposites attracting.

Bill had a penchant for long-distance solo travel and had already been to Kathmandu and to America via Iceland and Greenland, but his big dream was, one day, to fly to Darwin, Australia, where his great-grandfather had made the family fortune. It was a 15,000 mile journey which would take 120 days, and Bill knew he couldn't possibly do it alone.

'I'm game if you are,' Emma told him, volunteering to be his companion and guide. Bill could hardly resist this bubbly young woman who would, if nothing else, be great fun to have along for the ride. Emma then had the small problem of winning me over to the idea and, much more of a challenge, persuading her tutors that she could afford to take three months off from her studies and still complete her degree. She came home one weekend that winter with a new light in her eyes. I mistook it for love at first, or at least for the love of a man. Bill's name was on her lips every second sentence. But, after a while, as the full story began to unfold, I realised that the sparkle in her eyes was not for anything physical. It was for adventure.

My initial reaction was one of horror. Not so much about the obvious dangers involved in travelling across half the globe in a single-engine aircraft with someone she barely knew. No, my horror was that she could even consider taking time off from her studies at such a crucial time in her career.

'But you can't go, Emma,' I insisted, stirring the gravy for the roast chicken with renewed vigour. 'You couldn't possibly afford such an interruption in your course. Be sensible.'

The look she gave me was humbling. I felt like a boring old killjoy, and my forehead furrowed as echoes from my own past – my mother's disapproval of everything I did – came back to haunt me.

Emma sensed my indecision and seized her chance. 'But, Mummy, *please*,' she urged. 'It's the chance of a lifetime. It would be like a magic carpet, carrying me to places I have only ever dreamed about.'

By the time I looked up she knew she had won the argument. Waving my wooden spoon at her, I nodded my head slowly.

'Okay, Emma, but on one condition . . .' I began.

She threw her arms around my neck and hugged me to her. Pushing her away, I looked straight into her clear green eyes and spoke firmly.

'You can go, if – and I mean if – your tutors say you can spare the time off.' Nodding and smiling, I could see she was already planning her packing. She knew that with a little gentle persuasion, her tutors would be even more of a pushover than I was.

Sure enough, in a moment of pure inspiration, Emma conceived an idea that convinced the college to allow her the time off. She claimed that her bird's eye view would give her a wealth of ideas for visual art. She could take a camera and photograph the ever-changing colours and textures of landscapes as they flew over seas and deserts, jungles and mountains, using the slides when she got home to base all her future projects on. With her characteristic incisiveness, it did not take long for her to persuade them. Having negotiated a six-month extension to her degree, Emma and Bill began to plan their trip in earnest. Emma threw herself wholeheartedly into generating publicity, contacting newspapers and radio stations around the world and arranging to give them blow-by-blow accounts of their journey. It was a most valuable experience, and one on which she was to draw years later. She had never shied from publicity, she had loved the camera from childhood and knew how to manipulate it to her best advantage.

Bill concentrated on organising fuel stops and raising the money needed to finance their hotel stays. I had every confidence in him. He was a serious and capable young man who had negotiated his own time off work and had very carefully planned his route. As he and Emma pored over maps and charts, plotting each step of the way, their excitement – and mine – grew.

'There are two important stipulations,' Bill told Emma, warily. 'I don't think it would be a good idea for you to wear any of your hippy clothes on this journey. It's sure to cause problems the further east we go. Every time we land, they'll think we've got a cargo of drugs on board.'

To his surprise and to mine, Emma nodded her agreement. He was the captain after all. Finding his courage, Bill set out the rest of his terms. 'And the second thing is that you won't be able to wear any of your weird jewellery. All those metal bangles will make the navigational equipment go completely haywire.' Emma pouted, her hand flying defensively to her wrist. That was like asking her to travel naked. Reluctantly, however, she agreed, bequeathing them to a delighted Jennie.

The terms agreed and their bags packed, it was all systems go. So on Saturday 11 January 1985, at High Wycombe Park airfield, Buckingham-shire, not far from Oxford, Jennie, Johnny and I assembled with Bill's family to see the two young travellers off in their tiny plane, bound for the other side of the world. I was as nervous as a kitten by the time I reached the snow-covered airfield, but when I saw the plane – nick-named 'Birt' – emerge from the hangar and realised it was scarcely larger than my little Renault, and far more flimsy, I felt a pang of fear in my chest. The magnitude of their endeavour hardly seemed feasible, but Emma was so excited that, as always, I was swept along by her exuberance.

Bill remained calm as the final checks were made, but he was concerned that they should get off on time and keep to their schedule as Emma fiddled and fussed, packing all their essential belongings into the cramped cabin space, leaving no room for comfort. The little plane bulged with maps of the world, survival kits, a life raft and jackets, rulers, calculators, the odd bar of chocolate and an extra fuel tank. Fortunately we had – at Bill's father's suggestion – swapped Emma's enormous old suitcase for a tiny portmanteau, capable of carrying only fifteen kilos of her personal effects.

Bill started up the engines and, after a few emotional farewells, they took off as we waved from the ground and watched them disappear into the heavy, snow-laden clouds. I waited silently on the runway, listening to the noise of their little engine fading into the distance. For a brief moment, I wanted to change my mind, to call my daughter back, to tell her I was wrong. The previous evening I had looked up the word 'adventure' in the Oxford English Dictionary and found, to my consternation, that it meant: 'Chance of danger or loss; risk, jeopardy; a hazardous enterprise or performance.' I was heartened only by a hasty look at Chambers Dictionary, which defined adventure as: 'A remarkable incident; an enterprise or commercial speculation; an exciting experience; the spirit of enterprise.'

Emma and Bill encountered problems almost as soon as they set off. The weather was bitterly cold over Europe and ice storms threatened seriously to delay them. Bill decided, in mid-air, to change their flight path and try to skirt the land mass of France. Trying to make his new route understood by the French air traffic controllers, he came across the first serious language barrier. Poor weather and communications continued to dog them. On the leg from Athens to Crete, Emma had to shine a torch out of the little windows, to make sure that great sheets of ice were not forming on the wings, a hazard that can weigh the plane down and be fatal in sub-zero temperatures. To compound the danger, their little plane was buffeted by strong crosswinds and a Greek air traffic controller's strike meant that they had to land at Corfu without any assistance at all from ground control. Emma told me later that on this part of the journey she had felt tangible fear.

The *Aiglon* could fly at 130 miles per hour at an altitude of 10,000 feet for approximately six to eight hours at a stretch before having to be refuelled, so they had to touch down in many foreign lands. After France, their route took them to Italy, Greece, Egypt, Saudi Arabia, Bahrain, Pakistan and India. They planned to stop for three weeks in India as tourists, before flying on to Burma, Thailand, Singapore and Malaysia, meeting Annabel in Bali on '29 March at two o'clock', halfway through her nine-month tour of the Far East. I marvelled at their confidence in hoping to keep their date.

Then they would fly on to Australia, stopping at Darwin, Tennant Creek, Alice Springs, Ayers Rock, Broken Hill, Melbourne, Sydney and finally Rockhampton near Mount Morgan in Queensland, to visit the gold mine which had been owned by Bill's great-grandfather in the late nineteenth century. Then they would head home. It was an epic journey in such a small and potentially fragile aircraft, travelling so many miles and through such a variety of climatic conditions. So much of their time was spent flying over the sea, or over inhospitable terrain in which they would have been unable to survive had they been forced to land, that it was a miracle that they encountered as few problems as they did.

Bill's chief concern after France was the compass on which they were so dependent. An air bubble appeared in it, altering its accuracy dramatically and giving them variations of up to 15° on the reading. Leaning towards Emma and shouting at her over the engine noise, Bill instructed her to study the maps fastidiously and point out beacons and landmarks – roads, railways, rivers – to guide them in lieu of the compass. It was travel in the best adventurer's tradition. Bill had a wing-leveller, a type of automatic pilot, which allowed him brief periods to study the maps himself, but it was Emma who bore the chief responsibility of navigator and co-pilot.

Reaching the deserts of the Middle East, their little plane was suddenly forced upwards by violent heat thermals that threatened to destabilise them, possibly pushing them into the path of the Jumbo jets criss-crossing the skies overhead. There were blinding dust storms, the fear of which made them wary of travelling on windy days. Travelling further eastwards they braved driving monsoon rains which deluged their aircraft and made it impossible to see out, while the cacophonous din of thunder and lightning crashed and flashed all around them. Over Karachi in Pakistan, the engine's ignition system suddenly failed, causing the couple several heart-stopping moments. Bill – with his pocket screwdriver and engineering expertise – was fortunately able to fix the problem just before they plummeted to earth, pulling out the dashboard in mid-air and using sticky tape to hold together some faulty wiring, temporarily. On other occasions, the alternators broke down more than once and a faulty heating pipe had to be plugged hastily with Plasticine.

Not all their difficulties were airborne ones. It had been Emma's task to organise the visas for entry into all the countries in which they were scheduled to land – including Saudi Arabia which is notoriously bureaucratic – but she sweet-talked them into handing the visas over without much ado. To arouse as few suspicions as possible with the officials with whom they would have to deal – especially in the Middle East where an unmarried couple were not allowed to travel together unless working – Bill wore his captain's regalia, and Emma borrowed something akin to an air hostess's uniform, complete with two undeserved gold stripes. But, in the confined chaos of the tiny plane, she soon lost one of her stripes, inevitably drawing attention to her fictitious status, and causing them more than once to be delayed and closely questioned by burly officials. They then had to prove that they were not smuggling drugs or harbouring any secret political motives. It was sometimes very difficult to convince hard-faced immigration officials that they were simply two intrepid travellers.

Bill had specifically asked Emma to break with a long-held tradition of hers and wear a bra – he could just imagine the raised eyebrows at some of their destinations where an ankle is enough to get the local blood boiling, let alone an unshackled nipple. Emma dutifully wore one as they took off, but discarded it within hours, claiming it was too uncomfortable to wear. Bill sighed, grateful that at least her white uniform blouse had two front pockets.

At Delhi they had another sticky moment when they discovered that theoretically it was impossible for them to return to their plane because they had no airline ticket or commercial crew pass. Bluffing it out, and briskly waving their international driving licences above their heads, they got through the security barriers unhindered. In Jeddah, however, the officials weren't so easy to dupe. Emma was frogmarched off and locked alone in a room until Bill had refuelled, because unaccompanied women were forbidden to move around freely.

The landing fees varied dramatically – from US $300 for just two hours in Jeddah (the same as a Jumbo jet) to US $2 per night in Rangoon. They were grateful for their extra fuel tank when they reached the Far East. Several of the more remote airports did not supply Avgas, the light aircraft fuel, and they had to siphon and hand-pump the fuel they had from the tank to the wings, a laborious business. They stopped each night and stayed in local hotels before setting off again at dawn. Claiming to be aircrew, they negotiated fifty per cent off the room rates at luxury hotels like Raffles in Singapore, and I was thrilled when Emma also managed to stay at the Tollygunge Club in Calcutta, a place where I had spent many happy hours, twenty-four years before.

Once they reached countries notorious for bad food, their chief concern, mid-air, was going to the lavatory, and they were careful not to eat anything which might upset their stomachs. They had urinals with them for emergencies, but amazingly, they managed to train their bladders and bowels to coincide with fuelling stops. In India, Emma and Bill visited Patiala, a small principality in the foothills of the Himalayas. Emma, born in sight of that vast mountain range, spent her twenty-first birthday in the shadows of the very same snow peaks where I had spent my own twenty-first. She was also in a place not far from Dehra Dun, where my parents had married. I thought of her all day, glowing with pride that she was doing something so liberating on such a momentous date.

In a letter home from Patiala, where they were staying with a friend of Bill's, called Uvi, a former maharaja, Emma wrote:

'We managed to get ourselves visas (only through Uvi). We must have been the only Westerners in the area and everyone stared at us as though we had just stepped off Mars. We spent three days up in the Himalayas near Simla, which is the old summer capital of Delhi. I celebrated my twenty-first birthday in those glorious mountains, and where better? The sunsets were incredible and the whole area quite breathtaking. Sadly, Uvi had a magnificent summer palace called Chial a little further up the mountains but the government confiscated the property, like so many others, and it is now a sad, run-down hotel. It is heartbreaking to see all these government-run old properties like the Old Fort at Patiala. They are all slowly decaying as the government, after demanding all the property, now has not the means or the will to maintain them.'

Emma and Bill made an unscheduled detour to Kathmandu to overcome a two-week maximum limit on their landing on Indian soil, and because Emma wanted to go. Bill was delighted to share this wonderful and beautiful remote place on the roof of the world with Emma, someone whom he now considered a very dear and close friend, but nothing more. Flying out of Kathmandu through a valley flanked by mountains, they were stunned by a carpet of opulent red rhododendrons, a most magnificent sight as 'Birt' had just enough power to lift them up over the mountain range and on over Varanasi.

Flying in to Dum Dum Airport in Calcutta, they were met by the local press, whom Emma had alerted in advance. When her photograph appeared in the local daily newspaper, Dr Rhakal Chowdhury – sipping coffee over breakfast – nearly choked. Snatching a telephone to call a former medical colleague now living in Britain, he asked:

'But is this *our* Emma?'

He was the doctor who had assisted Bill and Wendy Burton at the birth of Emma, twenty-one years earlier, in the tiny tea garden hospital in Assam.

Bill and Emma made it to Bali, and met up with Annabel as planned, on the very day and at the very hour they had said they would. They had a glorious time together. During the trip they had mostly stayed at safe and recognised hotels, sharing a room for cheapness, but, when they reached Bali, Emma was determined to seek out places well off the beaten track. Bill capitulated and admitted later that he often had a better adventure when Emma picked the accommodation, including the place in Bali which he loved so much he eventually took his own bride there on honeymoon three years later.

I heard from Emma sporadically during her journey, depending upon the local postal service, but I cherished all of her postcards and newsy airmail letters. Her journey was followed by the local newspapers, both in Yorkshire and Oxford, and she kept all her promises to them to remain in touch. During one interview with Radio Oxford, she calmly said that if they needed to make a forced landing in the sea, she would scramble onto a rock and sketch the waves until help arrived. Typical. Half-way through her trip, however, and the day after my forty-third birthday, the telephone rang at my home around nine o'clock in the evening and I picked it up to hear her husky voice.

'Hi, Mum,' she called down the phone cheerfully, 'I just wanted to share my magic carpet with you. We are in Australia, it is just after sunrise and Bill and I have climbed Ayers Rock.' There was a pause, and a contented sigh. 'And Mummy, it's the vastness of this place that takes your breath away.'

Tears welled in my eyes. It was marvellous to hear her voice and I was honoured that she had chosen to share one of the greatest moments in her life with me.

Though Bill and Emma were very different – he an academic and scientist, she so artistic and flamboyant – they made excellent travelling companions, and their unforgettable adventure was completed successfully. Crossing the English Channel early one misty morning, they saw the white cliffs of Dover looming out of the murk.

'Well, we made it,' Bill grinned, a lifetime's dream fulfilled, a journey ended.

Emma couldn't speak. The moment was too significant. But for her, it marked the beginning of a journey, not the end.

> *I was a traveller, the guest of a week;*
> *Yet when they pointed the white cliffs of Dover,*
> *Startled I found there were tears on my cheek.*

from 'The White Cliffs' by Alice Duer Miller

They landed back in England on 1 May, having flown a total of 30,000 miles. Emma had spent Bill's 'safety money' on an assortment of foreign garments and jewellery for herself, but her one extravagant purchase of the whole trip had been a beautiful length of turquoise-blue raw silk, a gift for me to make up into something really special. I was touched.

She was positively buzzing in the weeks after her return and couldn't wait to see her aerial photographs from the dozens of films she had sent home by post. I had never been able to make head nor tail of the slides and transparencies, but she threw herself amongst them on the floor and wasted no time in selecting the best. She spoke with awe of the astonishing variety of images which she had seen unrolling on the surface of the earth below her – the patterns made by man and the weirdly abstract or formless regions. True to her word, and to her tutor's delight, within two weeks she had arranged an exhibition of her pictures taken from her often steamy little cockpit. It was to be entitled 'The Earth From Above', and was to be shown at the Poster Gallery in Oxford in the following October. Her trip had been a triumph.

She was thrilled by the responses she received when people heard about her journey and delighted when people asked if they could buy some of her prints. Word got out and before long she was invited to write up her experiences in a two-page article in *Harpers & Queen*, entitled 'Aussie Odyssey'. It was her first proper contact with the world of magazines and she was intoxicated by it. She loved the sense of power writing gave her, she flirted with the fame, and I felt instinctively that she would almost certainly store the experience away somewhere, to be used later to her own advantage. The article was published along with twelve of her photographs, depicting, among other things, the fields of France, the Arabian desert near Luxor, roads in Jeddah, parched paddy-fields in India, terraced Himalayan lowlands in Nepal, a jungle clearing in Malaysia and a salt lake in Australia. In her final paragraphs, she wrote:

> *'The contrasts of smells, foods, cultures and religions all held their fascinations, but for me the most interesting aspect of the trip was having the opportunity to view the earth's surface from a bird's eye perspective. Flying at low altitudes enabled us to see the landscapes below with clarity most of the time. There were the odd days, particularly in Europe, when the plane was cocooned in a veil of cloud, or we rose above the cloud level and entered into that silent, surreal world of cotton-wool lumps . . . but, most of the time, geometrical fieldscapes, arid deserts, soggy swamps, wriggling rivers and snow-capped mountains all passed beneath us. Roads were like rivers as they snaked across the surface of the earth.'*

The article was very well received and I wondered if this was where her future lay. She had always been so good with words and now, it seemed, she had had her first taste of fame. With her extraordinary looks and flamboyant clothes, I could well imagine her working somewhere for a chic London magazine, designing lay-outs and supervising photo shoots. It was a career path which I knew would suit her very well. I wondered if this was where she would end up making her mark, because as someone once said, love her or hate her, Emma always knew how to make her mark.

Whatever the future held for my eldest daughter, I was pleased to see that the media attention hadn't gone completely to her head. She was never so starstruck that she refused my request to come to Yorkshire later that year and give a talk in the local village hall to raise money for charity. With the hall packed and everyone eager to share her experiences, Emma – using an ancient projector I borrowed from a neighbour – talked us through every step of her journey with a panache worthy of a veteran public speaker. It was an event which dazzled the people of Crakehall and was a talking point for months afterwards. Thereafter they dubbed her 'a latter-day Amy Johnson', after the pioneering British airwoman who flew solo from England to Australia in 1930, only to be drowned after being forced to ditch her plane during the Second World War. It was a title I know Emma secretly relished.

8

Returning to Oxford after her great adventure was hard for Emma. Although it continued to provide intellectual and emotional stimuli, all of which she soaked up, her new-found sense that the life she craved lay beyond the scope of ordinary experience made her painfully aware of Oxford's limitations. I sensed her restlessness, and knew she was finding her college work sheer drudgery. Losing the impetus to finish her thesis on the artist Leon Underwood, despite all her reassurances to me and to her tutors, she had to ask for an extra year to complete it. She needed constant encouragement from Annabel, my urging, and the tremendous patience of her tutor, and all the while she daydreamed about her trip and how much it had meant to her, nostalgic for its excitement.

HER CONCENTRATION LEVELS WERE NOT HELPED BY THE FACT THAT SALLY DUDMESH AND WILLIE KNOCKER HAD LEFT FOR KENYA, A LONG-PLANNED HOLIDAY FOR THEM BOTH, AND EMMA WANTED NOTHING MORE THAN TO GO WITH THEM, EVEN THOUGH SHE KNEW THAT, FOR THE MOMENT, IT WAS OUT OF THE QUESTION. In one letter home, she wrote: 'My situation is awful in a sense, seeing possibilities, but with too many responsibilities to just get up and go.' She was learning one of life's salutary lessons.

Africa was her latest passion. The dark continent appealed to her sense of the exotic. She was mingling with several people in Oxford who spent much of their time talking about Africa, listening to African music and discussing the political situation there. The colonial lifestyle they and Willie and Sally spoke of in Kenya reminded her of her childhood in Assam – a warm climate, beautiful wildlife and scenery, servants and sleepy days. By contrast, England suddenly seemed small and staid, Oxford stifling and boring. Yorkshire was no longer somewhere she identified with, and Surrey was too suburban. She wanted to fly to foreign lands to explore and experience as much as she could. By the spring of 1985, the lure was becoming too great. She announced that she could wait no longer and was planning to take a grand summer tour with Willie and Sally, from Zanzibar to Cameroon, in July.

Saving hard for the air fare and struggling to finish her thesis, she did whatever she could to supplement her grant, posing nude for still-life drawings, and working part-time as a cleaner and waitress in a local hotel. In the summer of 1985, she got a job at an Indonesian restaurant called Munchy Munchys, working for Tony and Ethel Ow, who employed her thinking that her looks and voice would attract the customers. They were right. But it was not all plain sailing, having my daughter as a member of their staff. She wore huge wooden bangles from the wrist to the elbow and when they asked her to remove them for health and hygiene reasons, she refused. On her very first day, when she reached to pick up an empty glass from a table, her bangles slid down her arm and sent the glass crashing to the floor. Only then did she comply with their request.

Later, as she relaxed into the job, she would regularly arrive for work covered in paint, having been helping friends redecorate their flat in London, to earn a few extra pennies. Ethel and Tony had daily rows with her about her appearance and her attitude. On at least one occasion she was sent home, protesting loudly, to clean herself up before she could start serving tables. But she soon settled and the restaurant provided her with discipline and a chance to experience life in the real world. More importantly, from a mother's point of view, it gave her one good, hot meal a day for the year that she was there.

Munchy Munchys was one of those unlicensed venues where many young students met, lingering over the bottles of wine they brought in themselves, to discuss issues which mattered to them. Unpretentious and reasonably priced, it was also patronised by the dons, the rich and the rare, and a few passing celebrities. But it was through the younger clientele that Emma extended her contacts with African students, articulate young men whose families had sent them to Oxford to receive an English education. Brought up in a prejudice-free family, where individuals were treated as such, regardless of their colour, she found herself sexually attracted to black men, joking that white men always reminded her of earthworms.

The Sudanese were by far her favourites: tall, gentle people with whom she felt an instant affinity, and not only because their height matched her own. She became fascinated by what they told her of their country – its culture and politics – particularly those regions affected by war, famine and disease. Trying to discover more about the place to which all her heart strings were pulling her, Sudan gripped her imagination by being one of the most remote, inaccessible and undeveloped areas of the world. She resolved to find out more.

The name Sudan, literally translated, means 'Land of the blacks'. It covers an area of approximately one million square miles, about ten times the size of the United Kingdom. Sixty per cent of the population are Muslims, fifteen per cent Christians and the remainder devotees of older religions. More than one hundred different languages are spoken by nearly six hundred separate tribes or ethnic groupings, and two-thirds of the population are nomadic pastoralists, herding livestock or eking a living out of the harsh environment. Arid deserts cover the north, savannah grasslands the central regions, and equatorial woodland and swamp extend over the south.

War had raged in Sudan since 1955, the year before the end of Anglo-Egyptian rule. In 1983, the Sudan People's Liberation Army and Movement (SPLA/M) was formed under the leadership of Dr John Garang, a member of the Dinka tribe, backed by the Mengistu regime in neighbouring Ethiopia. Gradually, the SPLA took control of large areas of the south and the battles with the forces of the Muslim north raged on. Three decades of war had devastated this lush and fertile land. A combination of displacement and poor rainfall in 1984 and 1985 claimed 300,000 lives from famine or drought-related diseases on the Horn of Africa, and prompted the United Nations to launch Operation Lifeline Sudan. Images of starving children, their mouths and eyes covered in flies, were beamed across the world. Sudan was truly on the aid map, but like Ethiopia, Somalia and so many other Third World countries, the plight of its people was virtually forgotten as soon as the television crews packed up their cameras and moved on.

Because of the war, the infrastructure of Sudanese village life had all but gone. Warmongering was now the only trade. Children who should have been in school spent their lives carrying Kalashnikovs and marching for miles through fetid swamps. Young fingers that could have been planting and harvesting crops, or fishing the Nile, held hand-grenades and stripped weapons. Millions of women, children and the elderly were forced to become refugees in the process, abandoning their crops and homes in the mass flight from the fighting.

In the politically explosive climate of mid-1980s Oxford, Emma was surrounded by young men and women who were campaigning passionately for the release of Nelson Mandela, the ending of apartheid in South Africa, or the cause of the Nicaraguan Sandinistas. In typical Emma style, she rejected the trendier political bandwagons and chose instead to champion the one place that hardly anyone in the world had heard about. It was a choice that was to change her life forever, as she was drawn deeper and deeper into its web. Her transition from a keen and interested art student to a largely political animal concerned solely with those less fortunate than herself was not an overnight process. It took several months of all-night debates, long hours of reading and weeks of meticulous inquiry on her part as she armed herself with all the facts. But it was an experience that affected her radically. Abandoning those friends who did not share her passion, she became increasingly moody and temperamental as she courted the danger and excitement of Sudanese politics.

She began to lead a rather secretive life, staying out all night and not explaining to her flatmates where she had been or with whom. In the words of one of her friends at the time Emma was 'constantly pushing out the boundaries, moving on and experimenting with life'. She took a black boyfriend called Jude, and then another, called Louis. Her home and personal life seemed to be filled with clutter – art projects, political pamphlets, history books and endless empty coffee cups. She finally gained her degree in early 1986, by which time she was completely obsessed with the problems of Sudan and was doing volunteer shifts at the Refugee Studies Centre in Oxford. Abandoning all thoughts of a career in art or her trip to Africa, she moved to London in mid-July to live with Sally at her flat in Barons Court, west London, and started work as an assistant at the Sudanese Cultural Centre in Rutland Gate, Kensington, helping new students to find accommodation and to settle into London life.

Emma always said the word 'cultural' was rather misplaced when it came to the services the centre offered students. It was a tall, thin, elegant building outside, but inside all was chaos and decay. The caretaker was a man called Mr Robinson, who had worked for the centre – an arm of the Sudanese Embassy – for sixteen years. He had gout and was unable to climb the stairs to see to the necessary repairs of the old and crumbling building. The roof leaked, electrical wires hung from the ceiling, and the toilets refused to flush. There was a library downstairs but the filing system was so incomprehensible that it was impossible to trace a single book.

It was in London, nonetheless, that Emma learned a great deal more about Sudan. Her job was to handle student administration grants and she soon knew which side she was on. Most of the students and diplomats were Arabs from the north, and the few southern Sudanese students all suffered terrible prejudice at their hands. Emma complained that they were treated as third-class citizens, one step lower than a Muslim woman. Indignant on their behalf, and through the influence of those around her, she soon entered a dangerous arena, decrying the new famine in the south and protesting in any way she could. Radical politics weren't my only worry for her. To my horror she marched across London to Marble Arch in a militant anti-apartheid rally – although she did confess afterwards that she would never do it again, because of the blisters. She visited the Notting Hill Carnival, had another relationship with a charming Nigerian called Eddie, and informed us all that she was planning on going to Africa at the earliest opportunity. I was bewildered and bemused by her activities. Failing to see the warning signs, and ignorant of the subjects which fired her passion, I think I secretly hoped it was a phase she would grow out of.

Energised by her new ability to shock, she arrived in Yorkshire for a grand twenty-first birthday ball, a fancy-dress party in one of the baronial halls, with Eddie on her arm. She delighted for years afterwards in telling the story of how the hostess, a titled lady, had approached him halfway through the night and congratulated him warmly on his clever use of black paint. Seizing every opportunity to become involved with the matters close to her heart – which were encompassing much of the Third World – Emma became concerned with Band Aid, the high profile pop and rock charity project which raised millions of pounds for deprived African children, temporarily abandoning her job to try and help raise public awareness and divert much-needed funds to Sudan. She was on a steep learning curve and, surrounded by people who knew a great deal more than her, she often felt out of her depth. Realising that what she needed to do was to drop everything and go to Africa for herself, she contacted the United Nations and the Voluntary Services Overseas (VSO) about the possibilities of working in Sudan for a period. She was on a mission. Writing to me from London that summer, she said:

> 'I plan to go to Africa in a year. I am hoping that the United Nations Refugee organisation will sponsor me. My knowledge of Africa is so minimal, I am ploughing my way through fat books about the refugee situation. See you soon, Emma.'

Her plan actually came to fruition sooner than she hoped. By spring 1986 she had secured herself a trip to Khartoum, her first visit to Sudan. She flew off without giving me a chance to say goodbye, but wrote to me often from the bustling capital, with its streets laid out by the British in the pattern of the Union Jack. Khartoum, she said, had a very Arabic feel to it; a world of deserts and tent encampments, ancient civilisations and age-old customs. People thronged the streets; men dressed in dazzling white turbans and hooded cloaks – *jellabiyas* – and the women were swathed in brightly coloured lengths of cloth. The breeze was constantly warm, scented with spices and aromatic herbs. She was in her element.

Writing to me from Showak, where she was initially the guest of an assistant manager for a refugee project, with her own room and a beautiful garden all to herself, she said:

'You will be very concerned to hear that I am being treated like a queen. The Sudanese hospitality is overwhelming, kindness that we do not know about in England. As a guest, I am not allowed to cook, wash, iron, make my bed or even go anywhere unaccompanied. The latter is a blessing in Khartoum, as there are no street names, the houses are not numbered and nobody knows where anything is. You begin to appreciate the knowledge of London's taxi drivers.'

A month later, she wrote to me from the city of Falasha and said that she had decided to extend her stay in Khartoum, having got herself a three-month job teaching English literature and art in a school run by Italian nuns, under the auspices of the VSO. After that, she hoped to get a further extension so that she could learn Arabic and gain some teaching experience. I was surprised, because after her initial delight with Sudan, her first few letters home had spoken of her difficulties in settling into the life – dealing with the heat, the flies, the mosquitoes, the lack of alcohol and the strict segregation between men and women – especially when most of her friends were men, and her favourite vices were drinking, smoking and playing cards – activities that only men could enjoy by law.

There were, however, some advantages to life in Khartoum. She was, by then, staying in a cultural centre guest house around a large courtyard, and often had the place to herself. She wrote:

'It is a very conducive lifestyle. One can lie on a bed and sleep at any time and not be called lazy. One can be late and not be called unreliable, eat as much as you want and not be called greedy, be as large as you want and not be called fat. The women are generally enormous. Even I am considered a thin chicken here, which is a change.'

She travelled to the oasis town of Kassala, a reception centre for refugees from Eritrea, where she came across a nomadic tribe whose women are kept hidden from view and can only emerge wearing a full head-dress. Emma was fascinated by their lifestyle and hoped to be allowed to take some photographs of their eyes for a later exhibition. Her job involved teaching forty pupils English, using the books *Jane Eyre* and *Cry, the Beloved Country*, from 7.30 am to 12.30 pm, four days a week, with the afternoons free to paint, read or sleep. She caused great amusement among the local children by collecting scrap metal from the streets to use in sculpture classes for her pupils. They joked that she was running a 'Keep Sudan Tidy' campaign. In her spare time, she swam in the Nile every day to keep fit and stay cool, and lived on a staple diet of beans, bread and a light pancake called kisra. Her biggest concern was the mosquitoes which, she said, were eating her alive.

By March, she was desperate to come home. The pay was not good, the living conditions were getting her down and the other, male, guests had started to treat her like the female servant. She also had other concerns. She wrote:

'I have spent the last week trying to extract the Eritrean houseboy at the guest house from prison. The Sudanese government is clamping down on urban refugees and they are now being regularly picked up. If they carry no identity card, which is usually the case, they are imprisoned. The fine is £Sud200 (approximately £1 sterling) which is too much for a refugee to afford. The consequence of this operation is that the jails are crammed with refugees who are held indefinitely. You can imagine the state of these prisons. There is no food, washing facilities etc. Thus many die of disease and starvation. UNHCR, the United Nations body which is meant to protect refugees, ignores this whole issue, saying that there are no refugees in Khartoum. As there are few work opportunities in the camps themselves, it is no wonder people drift towards the towns in search of better opportunities. My day at the prison as a mere visitor was certainly unpleasant – flogging and beating are common punishments. Even pregnant women are humiliated in this way. The judge stank of alcohol at ten o'clock in the morning and was obviously doing quite nicely, thank you, on the incoming fines.'

She hoped to come back to England and start up a VSO-sponsored newsletter for Sudanese refugees. She asked me to book her a ticket out.

'The heat is quite oppressive and I am continually soaked in sweat. My face remains a glossy-red tomato colour. The electricity is inconsistent,

often we survive for days without water, electricity or fans, and this is just the start – as the water levels of the Nile drop, the power machines become redundant . . . The heat is killing me, I now sleep outside and fight off the mosquitoes, the lesser of two evils. When the wind howls, it whips up a substantial dust storm; the sun is obscured and the air is impregnated with dust. Then we are trapped and have to sweat it out inside the house. The flies crawl around your face, but it is pointless to wave them away. They, like the mosquitoes, are persistent creatures. It is strange the flashbacks that I get when away from England. Vivid childhood scenes return. Even my dreams are quite fantastic, recalling faces and places that consciously I had quite forgotten. I feel like writing it all down. I am sure Freud would have a field day.'

By the spring of 1986, my own restlessness had once again got the better of me and it was with some sadness that I decided to try and let Alverton House and move south in search of pastures new. Although I had made so many good and lifelong friends in Yorkshire, my two eldest daughters were established in the south – Erica working as a legal secretary and living in London, and Emma using the capital as a base from which to save for trips to Africa; Johnny was at a boarding school in Derbyshire and heading for the world of television, and Jennie was on a catering course in the south of England, and about to work her way round the world as a cook, with a tiny rucksack and an independence of mind that terrified me.

The time was ripe to start to create a new life for myself and to move on. Alverton had been a good and stalwart friend. Its thick dry stone walls made of huge boulders had sheltered us. As I locked the front door behind me, I felt quite fearful at stepping out into the world once more, without its comforting sanctuary. I was driven to Darlington station, where Sue, a good friend, was waiting to travel to King's Cross with me. She and her husband, Robert, lived in a company flat in central London during the week and returned to their Yorkshire home at weekends. They kindly offered me the use of their flat for two weeks while they were away on holiday, and had armed me with a list of companies to chase for possible job interviews. Sensing my trepidation at leaving Yorkshire for good, Sue bought me a large gin and tonic with the words:

'Drink up, I think you deserve this.'

I was soon feeling very much better.

Using their flat as my base and public transport to get around, I began the process of knocking on doors. Although I sensed an initial reluctance by some of the temping agencies to take on a forty-four-year-old widowed mother of four who had limited London experience, I did eventually get a placing with an agency whose recruitment staff had sufficient confidence in me.

'Maggie, just keep your head down and work hard,' they advised, and I did exactly as I was told. For the next fifteen months, I was gainfully employed without a single break in the arts and publishing world – initially moving between flats belonging to friends, until I could eventually afford to rent my own small flat in Battersea, south west London.

I was enormously grateful for the start the temporary agency gave me, but after being in full-time employment for so long, I wearied of the strain of temporary work – never knowing where I would work next from one week to another, unable to forge friendships with people who realised I would only be with them for a short spell. Being single and living alone in London is isolating and expensive and I had been accustomed to being surrounded by friends and family.

Emma was by then briefly back in London from Khartoum, and working again for the Sudanese Cultural Centre, while planning her next trip to Africa. She kept in touch with me fairly regularly by telephone and we met for supper frequently, although she had her own life and friends. She never stopped worrying about me, however, at times lecturing me about personal safety.

'You should always take a taxi late at night, Mum,' she would say. 'If you get mugged, you won't get much sympathy.'

It was Sue and Martin, not me, who first discovered that she had a new boyfriend. My sister and brother-in-law, who had been so kind to her during her student days, hadn't seen her for two years and when she rang, unexpectedly, to invite herself to their home in Surrey for the weekend, they were delighted. Sue, especially, had formed a close bond of friendship with her eldest niece and was looking forward to having her to herself for a couple of days to catch up on all the news. They asked Emma to come early so that they could see her before they had to go out to dinner on the Friday night. But, instead, she telephoned to tell them she'd be late and they ended up having to leave the dinner party to collect her from the station. Much to their surprise and annoyance, she was not alone. The man she was with was introduced to them as Belay, an Ethiopian refugee working with Band Aid.

Sharing his wife's disappointment with Emma, Martin gave her the third degree about her behaviour before he and Sue retired to bed. When they woke up in the morning, Belay had gone. So, too, had the special bond between them and Emma. Although they remained friends, they never recaptured the same depth of friendship after that incident. Sue and Martin had crossed that line from being equals to being somehow parental, at a time when Emma was obviously feeling overly sensitive about her status. Hearing of the row, I reassured Sue that Emma only had herself to blame. She had a habit of wanting to shock, of foisting issues and situations on people, like the time she ruined a dinner party of mine by speaking in brutally graphic terms of the terrors of female castration in Sudan. She was testing us, and had obviously abandoned her western inhibitions. But she often forgot – or didn't care – that others hadn't.

Emma soon became deeply involved with Belay, moving into his east London council flat as his lover. Friends who visited her there instantly noted a change in her appearance. She looked drawn, gaunt, had stopped wearing her elegant clothes and seemed tired. She was very much more serious about the political issues which aroused her passions, and told people that she had finally found a purpose to her life. She brought Belay to meet me and I liked him. He was quiet and gentle in a powerful sort of way, although I was never quite sure who was using who in their relationship – was Emma using him as an opening for relief work in Africa, or was he using her to help him get a foothold in England? It was difficult to tell.

I discovered much later, and not from Emma, that she had accidentally fallen pregnant by Belay, only to miscarry his child, something she had tried to brush aside. But she became quite ill afterwards and went to stay with her godmother, Wendy Burton, and her husband Bill in Cambridgeshire to convalesce. Her relationship with Belay, however, was doomed to fail and thereafter went through a difficult patch. By this stage, Emma was twenty-two years old, and experimenting with everything that life had to offer. Frustrated at her inability to get a second teaching tour in Khartoum, she became upset and confused, and – for a while – slightly lost her way. She somehow got mixed up with a crowd of people who were taking drugs and drinking too much, and she started to follow suit. Kalid, a kind friend and another of her lovers, whom she met on her first flight to Khartoum, could see where she was heading and decided to rescue her.

He promptly removed Emma from the London scene and took her to see an old friend of his, Liz Hodgkin, and her mother, Dorothy, who lived in a house called Crab Mill near Ilmington in the Cotswolds. He asked them to take care of her for six months and forbade them to let her return to London. Dorothy Hodgkin, a Nobel prize-winning molecular biologist, had well-established connections with Sudan. The Hodgkins had an 'open house' for many Sudanese when Emma became their guest. Liz was in the final months of her own PhD and Emma quickly endeared herself to everyone by assuming the role of housekeeper and chief cook, boiling up huge quantities of mince flavoured with cumin seeds and carrots, for any visitors who might descend, freeing Liz to concentrate on her studies.

Through their kindness and hospitality, Emma was gently brought back from the brink. She lost no time in rehabilitating herself to a life in the country, working with the land again, digging up potatoes, planting vegetables and picking spinach and blackberries. Liz always said Emma was a natural hunter-gatherer and was never happier than in the fresh air and countryside. Her confidence restored and her experimentation days over, Emma returned to London. Liz followed to take up a job with the London School of Oriental and African Studies (SOAS). Emma joined political groups campaigning for peace in southern Sudan and, with Liz and others, set up a four-page newsletter called 'Sudan Update' which attempted to disseminate information coming from the front lines, and whose sympathies ran counter to the official government in Khartoum. At one point 'Sudan Update' was considered no longer necessary, but

Emma insisted that they must continue to publish. 'Sudan Update' survives to this day.

In December 1986, Emma returned to Khartoum to take up another teaching position, a job which was to last until March 1987. Any plans I had for spending that Christmas with my family at Alverton House were dashed. Emma was in Sudan, Erica was on a kibbutz in Israel, Jennie in Northern Ireland and Johnny was on holiday in South Africa. I returned to Yorkshire from London alone, and spent the day with friends toasting my children – scattered to the four winds and each one in a trouble spot. At least there were no family arguments.

When Emma returned from Sudan she began applying for post-graduate courses, and in June 1987 was offered a place at SOAS to study for an MA in African politics, paying her way by continuing to work at the Sudanese Cultural Centre as a student liaison officer. She was focusing her interests with renewed determination and I was glad to have her home. I was still on the quest for a permanent job in London, and I was delighted when I managed to secure myself a full-time position with a property developer in Chelsea. I grew in confidence and felt better able to make important decisions about my future. One sunny summer morning as I walked over Albert Bridge to work, stopping to look at the River Thames and its swirling currents, I made up my mind to move out of London for good, sell Alverton House and buy a property in Surrey, commuting in every day. One of the keys to my decision was the fact that I simply wasn't ready to hang up my gardening tools yet. Gardening had always been an infatuation for me and I didn't even have a window-box in Battersea. I realised that I wouldn't be happy until I was back on my knees with a trowel, digging and planting the soil.

The attraction of Surrey was twofold; I could afford something slightly bigger than I could in London, and it would bring me closer to my sister Sue. She, by this time, was the mother of three children, Peter, Michael and Annabel (known as Freddie), aged between seven and eleven, and was well ensconced in her lovely pantiled house. What a different life they had led, I often thought; all three children born and raised under the same roof all these years; their parents together, while us McCunes seemed to have led a nomadic existence, moving from house to house, flitting from county to county, country to country.

Sue had been a rock to me in recent years and I had grown inordinately fond of her. I had seen more and more of her and come to rely on her in many ways, something I could never have envisaged on that bleak day when I met her again in the Parkers' parlour in Worthing all those years before. Now here I was, seeking her out and looking forward to us becoming even closer as neighbours. Staying with her and Martin for a week to test out the commuting, I was surprised to find it often took me the same amount of time to get into London on a fast train as it had line-hopping across town. That settled it. I began my search, and within a few weeks, I found the house I still call home – Little Farthings, a small semi-detached, red-brick, turn-of-the-century property near Godalming with a narrow but quite lovely cottage garden. I couldn't wait to start burying my hands in the earth. I was thrilled and excited; this was the first house I had ever chosen just for me, not because the company owned it, or Bunny wanted it, or for the sake of the children. It was mine and mine alone.

The children were still scattered. Johnny was finishing at boarding school in Derbyshire, Jennie and Yo were both in Israel, unaware of what I was up to in England. Emma was, I knew, probably off to Africa at any minute and would be lost to me for a while. At my request, she did spare the time to come and view the house with me, giving it her seal of approval, and – when I eventually moved in during December 1987 – it was she who helped me to decorate and unpack our previously stored belongings from Yorkshire.

For eighteen months our precious belongings had remained in store, and so much in our lives had changed during that time. I was a very different person now and, so I realised, were my children. As I unpacked the flotsam and jetsam of our Alverton life, discovering the children's favourite pebbles, shells or marbles collected during the years they grew up in Yorkshire, Emma's wild flower scrapbook, and her equestrian rosettes, I wondered if I had been quite mad, paying storage and removal charges for such trifles. But then again, were they trifles, these precious little fragments of a past life? Or were they all parts of the jigsaw, the puzzle that was about to unfold in a way I could never have envisaged.

After spending my first Christmas, and new year, at Little Farthings with Emma and Belay, and the rest of my family, we resumed our separate lives. I didn't see very much of my eldest daughter during 1988, a year which turned out to be quite difficult for me. Friends who knew what I had been through in the previous twelve years had always said that one day, something would snap. And snap it did. My back went getting out of the bath one evening and for six weeks I was a complete invalid, able only to sleep on the floor at my sister Sue's house, nursed night and day. The children were all shocked to see their mother ill for the first time in their lives. Emma, vulnerable and insecure with Belay, burst into tears at the news, one of the few times I have known her cry.

My employers at the Chelsea property developers were initially sympathetic, but just a few weeks after returning to work, I went down with a virus, erethema nodosum, which affected my legs leaving me limp and feverish, and had to take another six weeks off work. Not surprisingly, they decided to dispense with my services, giving me a month's notice. It had been my first full-time job since arriving in London and I had blown it. My confidence was shattered.

Emma spent most of that year based in London, trying to make her relationship with Belay work, and studying at SOAS. She was still working part-time at the Cultural Centre and planning a field trip to Africa to continue her research into refugee and cultural politics. After recovering from my various ailments, I temped in Surrey for six weeks – a miserable and depressing experience – before finally securing myself a job in November 1988 at the London Stock Exchange, working for a Surrey-based company.

I loved my new job, and surprised myself by how much I enjoyed the City life. I hoped to be able to stay. But after only one week, I overheard two colleagues talking.

'Well, she seems very nice, but we can't keep her with such limited computer skills,' they said.

I realised it was me they were talking about and I was alarmed. I didn't want to lose my job, so from that moment on, I embarked on a tough challenge – to teach myself the tricks of the trade. Whenever anyone had a minute spare to teach me a new command on the computer, I wrote it down and committed it to memory. With overtime and a bit of extra homework, I was proficient enough in computer skills to be offered a permanent job within a few weeks. I had taken on the challenge and won.

Fired up with enthusiasm and growing in confidence daily, I applied for and was accepted for another job a year later, at Bear Stearns International, an American investment bank. It was the start of a career that was to last four-and-a-half years, moving me from the City to the prestigious new Canary Wharf development in London's Docklands, as secretary in the corporate finance division. At last, I felt I had arrived.

It was in March 1989 that Emma finally fulfilled her ambition to travel to Kenya to see Sally Dudmesh and Willie Knocker. Sally was by then working as a jeweller, and living in Africa permanently. Willie was a naturalist, and a consultant aid worker. They were delighted to see their old friend and surprised at how passionate she had become about Sudan. She became more and more magnetised by the country and its politics, particularly by the war in the south – the longest war of this century – and by the fate of the region's native Nuer and Dinka tribes.

Emma was at a crossroads in her life by then and had an inner restlessness; she was trying to find herself and to resonate with something. The plight of the Sudanese somehow held enormous appeal; she was excited by the possibility that, by doing something so completely different from all that she had ever known, she could truly become whole. Her interest was further fired up by the changing political landscape of Sudan. In June 1989, the three years of relative calm, afforded by the country's first democratically elected government, was shattered by a military coup led by Brigadier el-Bashir and his National Islamic Front. On seizing power, the new government banned political parties and systematically destroyed the organised opposition, retaking by force many of the areas in the south previously held by the SPLA.

Transfixed by the politics of it all, seduced by the people and the landscape of Africa, Emma returned home to London just long enough to split with Belay finally, and to persuade her SOAS tutors that her studies would benefit enormously if she spent the summer months in the country she had come to love. Using the same charm she had used in persuading her Oxford tutors that the Australian trip would enhance her potential, she won the day and, by August 1989, she was back on a plane to Kenyatta International Airport. What neither she nor I quite appreciated was that, this time, it would be for good.

Launching herself completely into the African way of life, Emma persuaded Willie Knocker to take her on safari almost as soon as she arrived. She wrote to me from there; her letters were fulsome in their praise.

'We spent a night at Pika Pika Dam, listening to the lions roaring through the game reserve where we spied a large herd of elephants crossing the plains – perhaps a hundred or more – a most spectacular sight. The Kerio River runs gently by our campsite, situated at the mouth of a large lugga, a dry river bed. A dancing acacia tree stands between where I sit and the cool, crocodile-infested river.

Beyond, the landscape rolls away into vast semi-desert, completely uninhabited. Thorny trees, bushes and flowers attempt to thrive in these dry lands, blasted by the sun during the day, drained of water during the dry season. Birds hop and call, bright blue superb starlings. The 'Go-away bird' (the Grey Loerie) – is normally considered an enemy of the hunter because its long drawn out call startles his prey – was completely silent, undisturbed by our presence. Five eland came nervously down to the river to quench their thirst. We wash in the rocky shallows to avoid the crocs – we spied one yesterday, his eye and nostril just tipping above the surface. Half a goat, dried, roasted, stewed or boiled, sufficed as our food supplies.

Willie and I may perhaps have the possibility of working with UNICEF in southern Sudan – US $3,000 a month each – it may be worth postponing my MA and earning some pennies. Anyway we shall see – will keep you informed. Now planning a week's trek into the Masai country. Lots of love, Emma.'

A month later, she had obviously decided what she was going to do. In a letter dated 5 September 1989, she said:

'I have almost been offered a job with UNICEF to rehabilitate schools in southern Sudan. If the job is confirmed, then I will postpone my MA *for one year and remain in Kenya. The reasons being: (a) It will be a fascinating job and a wonderful break. It seems these kinds of jobs are to be found if you are in the right place at the right time. Once in the network it seems easier to get other jobs. (b) Working for the UN is extremely lucrative. For the first time in my life I may be earning decent wages. What do you think? (c) You will all be able to come and stay!'*

Her mind was clearly made up and she was simply letting me know what she had decided and why. I could hardly disagree with any of her points and, as her letter was covered with endearing doodles of palm trees, sail-boats, zigzag patterned snakes and crocodiles, I could see that she was in a place that truly inspired her creativity and sense of fun. How could I refuse?

The UNICEF job she referred to was to be another major catalyst in her life. She had been offered a position with Street Kids International (SKI), a charity set up by a Canadian lawyer, Peter Dalglish, in northern Sudan, under the umbrella of UNICEF, and which he wanted to extend to the war-torn south. Peter was, and is, an idealist who visualised humanitarian ideals to create social and political change. He gave up his law practice to devote himself to aid programmes after witnessing the famine in Ethiopia, and he particularly wanted to save the young Sudanese boys who were being press-ganged into joining a child army, fighting for a cause they hardly understood. If he could break the cycle of despair that led these hungry, poverty-stricken children towards a life in military uniform, then he hoped to help effect peace.

Peter decided to expand the scope of his enterprise to southern Sudan and asked a friend and colleague, Alastair Scott-Villiers, if he could recommend anyone. Alastair had briefly met Emma at Oxford, and he and his wife Patta were now veteran aid workers with Operation Lifeline Sudan. Over a lunch of chicken curry at the Fairview Hotel in Nairobi, Peter and Emma were introduced and hit it off straight away. Peter wrote later:

'She was tall, elegant and strikingly beautiful. In some ways she was an unlikely choice to take up the responsibilities as the co-ordinator of our proposed schooling programme in southern Sudan . . . but over the

course of the lunch I realised that Emma was exactly the right person for the assignment. She had already travelled extensively in Sudan, and had taught herself passable Arabic. She was resourceful, committed and ferociously independent . . . I knew that with her natural charm Emma would do a fine job of extracting whatever supplies we needed from the most recalcitrant UN official.'

Emma felt passionately about education, something she had inherited from me. She saw it as a vehicle that would improve one's own position in life, and also the position of whole communities. But after three decades of war, the region's educational system had been shattered – the schools had been bombed, the teachers had fled, there were no papers, no pencils and no textbooks. If a village was lucky enough to have a teacher, or someone who was prepared to impart their own reading and writing skills, the children were taught in the shade of a tree, drawing letters with their fingers in the sand. With her spontaneity and vision, Emma shared Peter's dream of using education as a vehicle to address the wider problems of the underprivileged in southern Sudan. She used to insist that she was not feeding hungry mouths, but hungry minds.

Peter warned her that it would be a logistical nightmare. Not only would she be working in the middle of a war zone with all the attendant dangers of being bombed by government forces, or captured and killed by rival factions, but she would be operating in a land where the rainy season prevented travel for much of the year between April and October and where communications were virtually non-existent and resources in short supply. Never one to refuse a challenge, Emma accepted the job and within weeks had persuaded UNICEF and Band Aid to part with more money – to help fund SKI's first office in the town of Kapoeta in southern Sudan, just over the border from Kenya, and to buy her a US $30,000 Toyota landcruiser, complete with winch and tapedeck.

By November 1989, after setting up the necessary funding and staff, she was en route to war-torn southern Sudan to begin work. She wrote in her diary that she felt as if she was on the 'cusp of the earth', flying into the cradle of mankind.

'This was the tip of a huge region. Landlocked, bordered by nine other African countries, it is dissected by the central artery of the Nile, which weaves its way through the Sudd, an enormous swamp of reeds and papyrus, on its journey to the Mediterranean Sea. The vast plains of water are a whole world in themselves – alive with fish, herons, pelicans, reptiles, elephants, antelope, white-eared cob. The richness of life is staggering. As we flew, I began to find the landscape so infinitely flat that it was unnerving, almost frightening. I grew up in the Yorkshire Dales, but this raw openness made me feel exposed.'

Arriving in Kapoeta, captured from the government eighteen months earlier, Emma was met by a little sea of schoolchildren, following her curiously, as she made her way to her new home, a UN building, past a battered SPLA sign which read: 'United We Stand Divided We Fall'. The local school had no doors or windows and the roof was caved in. Later, she wrote to Erica.

'News from this end is new and bewildering. Kapoeta still bears the marks of battle. The house in which I reside is peppered with bullet holes. However, some sense of normality is slowly returning – a small market, a hospital and a school. There is no currency available so commodities are exchanged – soap and salt being in hot demand. The wind blows every morning, throwing up dust, the heat is hot and dry but by nightfall all is quiet and the sky exposes a panorama of twinkling stars. Gun shots can often be heard – perhaps a dog, or a drunken soldier? The military camp is set back from the town. Every morning I am woken by the troops singing, beautifully, I may say, as they exercise around the block.

Her work took her to many parts of the Upper Nile, visiting schools and being introduced as 'The Tall Woman from Small Britain'. Doodles of a tall thin woman in a miniskirt began appearing on the walls of the school huts wherever Emma was expected. The children would always stand up respectfully from their positions on the floor when she entered their humble classrooms, singing in unison their song of greeting: 'Our visitor, our visitor, we are very glad to see you.' Accompanied constantly by at least three armed guards – necessary for her own protection but also to make sure that she didn't see anything she wasn't meant to see of SPLA activities – Emma would take note of what each village or town needed in terms of school materials, give them what she could, and return to Kapoeta, often several hours' drive away.

The risks to her life were immense. Sporadic fighting between government and SPLA forces caused death and destruction all around her. And the war wasn't her only danger. In her very first week, being driven back from a village called Chukudum, nestling at the foot of the Imatong Mountains, laden with fresh potatoes given as gifts by the school children, she was involved in a car accident which could have been fatal. The UN Resident Project Officer, a sarong-wearing Burmese called Maung, was driving. Emma wrote:

'I asked Maung to take the wheel because I was tired. It was a decision I was bitterly to regret. I had forgotten that Maung had worked as a bureaucrat in Rangoon. The moment he took the wheel, we raced off at top speed, skidding round corners, hurtling blind over narrow bridges, only inches wider than the car. "Maung!" I shouted. "You don't need to drive so fast!"

"Ah, but I'm a good driver!" he yelled, stepping on the gas. Instead of negotiating a sharp bend we came to, Maung ploughed on straight ahead, he was wrenching at the steering wheel, and the car skidded out of control. It flew up a steep bank and overturned. None of us moved. When the potatoes had settled, with dull little thuds, there was complete silence for a few seconds. Then a desperate scramble to get out. I realised that I was shocked, but unhurt, and could wriggle out through the open window. I was amazed to see all the others crawl out unharmed. The only injury – poetic justice – was sustained by Maung.

"Oh, help me, I am injured!" he wailed, mopping a tiny little cut on his forehead.

"Don't be ridiculous. You are perfectly all right," I told him crossly. "You could have killed us. Why were you driving like a lunatic? You are absolutely NOT a good driver." '

On another trip home along a winding bush road, Emma caught sight of something strange in the distance. Straining her eyes to see, she could hardly believe what loomed ahead of her – a MiG jet, parked in the middle of nowhere, perfectly intact. Her driver explained that the pilot had run out of fuel after a bombing raid a few months earlier and had managed to land his aircraft with only minor damage to the under-carriage. He was unhurt and had walked forty kilometres to Bor, before SPLA soldiers caught up with him. Emma squinted into the sun and saw that the Libyan Crescent had been crudely over-painted with the flag of Sudan. The MiG's only occupants now were bees, a huge swarm of them, flying in their thousands in and out of the open cockpit window to reach their honeycomb.

There were natural wonders too. The Sudanese obsession with their cattle fascinated Emma – the beasts form an integral part of their lives, they are their currency, the subject of barter and worship, of theft and grievances, of holy rites and sacrifice. She never forgot her first trip to a cattle camp, a place on high ground where children are fattened on milk and taught the ways of the pastoralists. The boys learn how to make ropes, tend to the cattle, and to fish and hunt. The girls are taught how to milk the cows, to sour the milk and to make household items from their skins. She wrote:

> 'The group of curious onlookers swelled. It is always like that in southern Sudan; wherever you are someone always appears from nowhere to greet you. The elderly leant on their sticks or fishing spears, thick ivory armbands encircled their ashened arms, and they puffed at pipes held in the corners of their toothless mouths. Some had pieces of cloth tied in a knot at the shoulders, others were naked, smeared with ash. The children giggled and laughed, practising the little English they had learnt in school: "What is your name? How are you? Good morning," when it was late in the afternoon.
>
> The young men arrived later, their hair dyed orange from cattle urine, with strings of colourful beads around their waists. Brass ankle and arm bracelets made from empty shells polished with sand com-pleted their splendid attire. One arrived with a catfish hanging on the end of his spear. We were unable to persuade him to part with his catch.'

Once, during her spell at the Sudanese Cultural Centre in London, Emma had taken a Sudanese student, in Britain for the first time, to the Cotswolds for the day to see something of the English countryside. She asked him what he would like to see: a village, a church, a pub?

'Are there any cows here?' he asked.

She took him to a farm and showed him some black and white Friesians living in a byre with their own dung encrusted on their hides. The student was appalled.

'Is this how you treat your cows?' he said.

In Sudan, the people clean their cows every day and polish their horns. The dung is carefully collected for the sweet-smelling fires, and the cattle revered. Although they slaughter them regularly in rituals, they do so only with the utmost respect, and they grieve for them as if they were people. The only thing the young Sudanese was impressed by was the voluptuousness of the cows' udders.

Emma divided her time between the bush and Nairobi – a vibrant city where she had many friends and spent her time going to dinners and parties, and planning safaris and trips to the coast. A great passion was to play badminton, which they often did under the stars, sometimes to music wafting from the house – Patta playing the piano and another friend playing the bassoon – a scene from a quieter, gentler time. A scene which could only happen, in the modern day, in a country like Africa.

The rest of her time was spent in the desolate reaches of southern Sudan, where she was in her element and the contrast couldn't have been more vivid. None of us had been surprised when Emma decided to try and maintain some sort of order in the lives of the people whose infrastructures had been completely destroyed by years of war and neglect. She won people over with her boundless energy and enthusiasm and they, in turn, won her over with their beauty and cheerfulness, all in the face of prolonged adversity.

Disappearing off into the middle of the civil war with little more than a rucksack and a miniskirt, she was a lifeline to thousands of desperately poor people, starving and emaciated children with little food or water who lived amongst dirt, disease and dust. The discrepancies between her two lives hardly seemed to bother her; she loved each facet of her existence with equal measure, and stepped in and out of her two worlds effortlessly; although those who knew her said she was always most at home in the bush.

By sheer hard work and ingenuity, and with a budget of just US$10,000 a year, she re-established one hundred community-based primary schools, purchasing chalk, chalkboards, paper, pencils and text-books in Kenya, transporting them by road and air to remote communities throughout Eastern Equatoria. If she couldn't find what she wanted immediately, she went out of her way to track it down – she wanted the children to read and write in their own languages rather than in English, so she searched high and low for the old reading books published in the 1950s and 1960s by the missionaries. Eventually, she found the original plates for a Dinka book for children called *Marial and the Cow*, and arranged for hundreds of copies to be printed for the first time in more than twenty years.

Nothing fazed her. Regularly running the gauntlet of bombs in a corridor of land she crossed and re-crossed in order to carry out her tasks, she regarded the war as little more than an irritation. When the Sudanese airforce bombed three of the new schools, run by Sudanese volunteers, and killed over twenty children, Emma didn't falter and immediately arranged for the construction of underground shelters. With SKI, Emma really had found her path in Africa. Peter Dalglish wrote:

'*Emma was the most extraordinary relief worker I had ever met. Although she came from a family of means, she was immune to the crass material needs that have paralysed so many of her generation. She wore whatever she could get her hands on, slept on the dirt floors of huts, and ate whatever food was being served in the village. Emma was bitten by scorpions and rats, and survived bouts of malaria and amoebic dysentery. She never complained about the lack of the most basic amenities, such as electricity or running water. Her only luxury was her solar-powered laptop computer on which she used to write me detailed reports from the field . . . With her new wheels Emma would disappear into the field for months at a time. I would hear nothing from her and then an eloquently written report would emerge from the* fax machine at the SKI headquarters in Toronto. Her reports combined personal anecdotes about the children she had come to know and love, alongside statistics about the number of pencils and notebooks she had distributed.'

More than once on her trips to remote villages she got caught in the vast expanses of bush during bombing raids carried out by government aircraft, but she appeared to many to be fearless; she never hesitated to go into the most dangerous areas, and if others wouldn't accompany her, she would go alone. During one trip deep into the bush on her first visit to a town called Leer – a place which would later hold so much significance – she was with some elderly village chiefs and a southern Sudanese education co-ordinator called James Chany Reer, when their pick-up truck sustained a puncture. Waiting for a runner to return with help, they heard the drone of an engine far away. Emma wrote in her diary:

'James suddenly sat bolt upright, cocking his head. He listened for a few seconds.

"My God," he said quietly, looking me in the eyes. "That's a Sudan government Antonov plane."

Most southern Sudanese can distinguish the type of plane from its engine noise; it was a skill I quickly learnt myself.

"James, that plane's going to bomb us," I said. I just felt it somehow instinctively. "We'd better hide the car." I knew that planes followed the roads and a white vehicle would stand out a mile.

"No, no, no," he said. "It won't come, no need to worry. Trust in God."

But I wasn't reassured. I jumped into the truck and hid it under a tree as best I could. It was obvious that the plane was searching for Leer. But low cloud was preventing visual contact. The plane went on circling, the whine of the engine dying away, then coming back ominously.

"We'd better find some cover," I urged, desperately casting around for a suitable place to hide. The chiefs had already run to some safe haven.

"It's all right," James was saying. "You're a hawaga (white person). Nothing is going to happen to you. God will protect you."

I almost laughed, I was so incredulous.

"But James, do you really think that a bomb makes a distinction between a white person and a black person?" I asked. It seemed a bizarre moment to have a metaphysical argument. In any case, in that moment we heard a distant rumble, then another.

"That's only thunder," James asserted.

"No, it's not. They're dropping bombs. And I'm going to find shelter." I looked around in despair. There wasn't even a hollow in the earth. I ran around until I found a little dip at the base of a nime tree. The plane was coming. As it approached the bombs fell in clusters. One, Two, Three. Then a pause. Then again, the explosions getting nearer and nearer. I could feel the earth shake. We were directly under the flight path. Terrible fear possessed me. I rolled myself up into a ball, I shut my eyes tightly and waited. The plane screamed overhead. A few seconds passed.

I opened my eyes and raised my head. The noise of the engines drifted away. As they faded, it was like a kind of sublime music. I tried to get to my feet, but felt too weak. I'd noticed plumes of black smoke had begun to rise over the trees in the middle distance. Pent-up fear burst out of me. I held my head in my hands, shaking uncontrollably.

James came to me. He was more agitated by my tears than the bombs. He didn't know how to deal with a distraught hawaga.

"You mustn't let anyone see you," he implored, wiping away my tears with the tips of his fingers.

Suddenly my anger took over. "I hate the Sudan government," I shouted.

"Yes," said James. "It's so disappointing that they've spoilt your visit to Leer."

The following morning, James came to call on me bearing gifts – a reed fan, roasted maize and fresh milk from his cows – so that I would think better of my stay in Leer. People then gathered outside the school. A cow was ceremonially slaughtered, and we prayed that the bombers would never come again.'

Moving on to the town of Bor, Emma came across widespread destruction and carnage. Five people had been killed in the morning raid by government planes and several had their arms and legs blown off. The German medical team who worked at the local hospital were fleeing as fast as they could, fighting for places on the next outbound flight. Only one nurse had agreed to stay on at the hospital and help with the wounded. A local UN representative and a mechanic were the only people with enough medical knowledge to patch up the maimed and dying, working together in the most basic conditions to carry out amputations and other vital surgery in a makeshift operating theatre. They had to break down the door to the medical store, because the doctor had run away with the key.

Emma helped as best she could, rolling up her sleeves, nursing the less severely injured and tending to the severely shocked. Some of the children she had come to help had been killed, others had fled into the bush, terrified. Those who had volunteered to teach them had been killed. The school was a smoking ruin. Shattered by what she saw, angered by the futility of war, Emma spent the next few days doing what she could. She wrote:

'As late afternoon came, we began to bury the dead. One was a young woman wrapped in a simple cloth. Her face was entirely unmarked; and her expression strangely peaceful. I almost had an urge to shake her gently by the shoulder, to wake her up.'

It was Emma's first direct experience of war, and the sights she saw only hardened her resolve to remain in Sudan and do all she could for its forgotten people.

9

Emma became known as something of a local celebrity in Sudan, limelight she positively basked in. She was certainly the most glamorous aid worker the people of the region had ever come across, with her extraordinary outfits and infectious smile – a complete contrast from so many of the rather dour, colourless and earnest men and women who emerged from the field bogged down emotionally and physically by what they had seen.

HER DETERMINATION TO ACCESS THE REMOTEST AREAS GAVE HER UNIQUE EXPERIENCES IN THE FIELD, AND HER KNOWLEDGE AND UNDERSTANDING OF THE PROBLEMS FACING SOUTHERN SUDAN GREW, SO MUCH SO THAT OTHER AID WORKERS CAME TO RESPECT HER INFORMATION AND HER JUDGEMENT. Always the great negotiator, she persuaded Band Aid to part with cash to fund further projects, and she learned to appeal for financial assistance from other relief charities throughout the world, such as the UN's Operation Lifeline Sudan. Peter Dalglish was right, she could charm the birds out of the trees. It was her underlying love of politics, being in the thick of things, and her continuous flirtation with danger, I think, that drove her on. I always said she would have made a good suffragette. Now here she was, being a suffragette for Africa – even if her MA appeared to be permanently on hold.

The Sudanese people with whom she so closely identified, and whose stature echoed her own, dubbed her the 'white Dinka woman', an honour indeed for a convent girl from Yorkshire. The Dinkas are one of the largest tribes in the south, traditionally known as cattle thieves and, as such, the Nuers' oldest enemy. But the two tribes were closely affiliated in their joint struggle against the Muslim forces in the north at that time, and lived cautiously side by side.

Emma was able to differentiate between the two main tribes quite easily. The Nuer men are identified by their traditional 'manhood markings' caused by raised scar tissue on their faces, just above the eyes. The markings are made on teenage boys aged between fourteen and sixteen as part of an annual initiation ceremony into manhood, at the end of the rainy season. Without anaesthetic, each boy has to endure his face being cut to the bone with a small knife, in six long cuts from ear to ear, which are then packed with hot ashes to raise them above skin level. The scars remain for life and it is said that they can be detected on the skulls of dead men. From the moment of cutting, the boy becomes a warrior and no longer has to undertake any domestic duties. He is given a spear and an ox, and from then on, until he is a father and a husband, his chief interests are dancing and lovemaking.

It was to this ancient people and their tribal customs that Emma brought so much laughter, daily. Driving into their bombed-out dusty villages in her incongruously bright clothes and jewellery, always smiling, always pleased to greet the children who flocked to her like starlings, hands outstretched, calling their cheery hellos – 'Maalε! Maalε! [Welcome! Welcome!] Emm-Maa!' – she would unfurl from her vehicle like a cat and dish out treats to children who had never known any. She was quickly accepted as one of them, a person from the outside who assimilated totally with those on the inside, and yet still had the contacts, foresight and education to know how to get them help and to achieve their goals. For them she represented beauty and hope and, in turn, she had discovered complete job satisfaction; Sudan was the perfect metier for her and her path was set.

Not that she ever allowed her appearance or light-heartedness to delude people into thinking she wasn't serious about her commitment or completely in control. During one long trip back from the bush, she had to sit in the back of a truck with a young armed guard, who stank of alcohol and body odour. She wrote:

'The journey was very uncomfortable. The combination of rancid breath and the discomfort of the back seat made my stomach churn. Something hard was rubbing on my side. I looked down to see a hand grenade sandwiched between our guard and my thigh. Thinking that I was interested rather than alarmed at his grenade, a young soldier took it in his hands and proceeded to juggle. He looked at me and displayed a set of white teeth in a big grin. Clunk. The hand grenade dropped to the floor. Everyone in the back looked down, watching this ball of explosives roll this way and that and bounce in the air as the car roared over another pothole.

"I've had enough!" I said. "Either this man gets out, or his hand grenade gets out – or preferably both – at the next check point!" I had made my ultimatum and at the next junction, the back door was flung open and the body guard parted with his grenade.'

On a personal level too, things were going well. Sally and Willie had decided to go their separate ways and Emma had stepped into Sally's shoes – with her blessing. Emma had admired Willie from afar for many years and had come to respect his advice. Now, as they embarked on a love affair that was to last for some considerable time, it was Emma who did the running initially, who pursued and cajoled. There was even talk of wedding bells. Emma wrote to Yo that autumn and said:

'Willie is still in southern Sudan, earning a lot of money doing exactly what he likes best – walking in the bush. I hope he comes down at the end of October as I miss him very much. If Willie and I do get married, there will certainly be a beano out here. There seems to be pressure coming from all sides to tie the knot – Willie's family, friends and Willie himself talks about the future in such terms.'

Emma told Yo to tell her young cousin Freddie, Sue's daughter, that she might well be a bridesmaid soon. Freddie was delighted at the prospect and so were we. Willie was great and Emma shared his passion for Africa. His family were absolutely charming. His parents Jeannie and Roddy had retired to the Kenyan coast, where Emma and others often went to relax. His sister Roo and her fiancé Simon had Emma as their lodger when she was first in Nairobi. Willie's brother Richard and his wife Jules were also close to my eldest daughter – she acted as a witness at their wedding. So, in many ways, she had already been accepted into the family.

While Emma carried on with her educational projects, flying to and from Sudan, Willie devoted his time to water-well aid projects in east Africa. Their separate work commitments meant that they were to spend several weeks, if not months, apart at one time or another, but initially, they both believed their relationship was strong enough to handle it. I read Emma's letters bemoaning their long separations and hoped that they were right. She had planned to come home for Christmas that year, and had been looking forward to it, but Willie persuaded her to stay in Africa instead and spend the holiday with his family down at the coast. She had a wonderful time, sunbathing, windsurfing and partying, but was furious with Willie because he didn't arrive until new year's eve and she was left alone with his family.

It wasn't entirely his fault, he could never resist an opportunity for a safari and had spontaneously decided to go to Tanzania with a friend, John Horsey, a UN aid worker, fully expecting to be back in time for Christmas. But en route they came across a river full of floating dead fish, and it was apparent that the local villagers had used dynamite. John had chastised the villagers in no uncertain terms, ticking them off for their environmentally unsound deed. When he and Willie neared their camp, towards nightfall, they saw a pall of smoke rising from that direction. Their camp had been attacked and torched, burning all their supplies and possessions, leaving them to find their own way back to civilisation as best they could, a journey that took several days.

Emma resented Willie's absence, she was homesick for an English Christmas and felt extremely let down. It was to be the catalyst in the eventual break-up of their relationship. They split up soon afterwards, the first of many break-ups in what was to become an on-off relationship. Emma sent word to her young cousin Freddie that she wasn't going to be a bridesmaid in 1990 after all. I read her words with sadness and wondered who might be the next man to capture my daughter's heart.

Emma first met Riek Machar Teny-Dhurgon at the Pan Afric Hotel in Nairobi in January 1990, at a wide-ranging conference to discuss the issues facing Sudan. Riek was a war lord, a rebel commander with the SPLA, the right-hand man to John Garang, and someone who was at least partly responsible for the continuation of the war. One man's freedom fighter is another man's terrorist, Emma remembered reading somewhere as she drove to the conference in the hope of meeting him. Terrorist or not, he was the one person who could help her in her battle to provide education for children in the areas his soldiers controlled.

If she was expecting a bellicose African egotist, she was to be surprised. Riek had an easy charm, spoke good English, and was practised at dealing with westerners. After studying for five years at the University of Khartoum, he had taken his MA at Strathclyde Polytechnic, Glasgow, his PhD at Bradford Poly in Yorkshire, and had gone on to lecture in mechanical engineering. In a country with less than two per cent literacy, this inspired respect. A Nuer chief and tribal war lord, whose face was devoid of the traditional manhood markings, his dashing appearance, seven foot height and languid motions attracted Emma from the first, although she tried to remind herself she had other more serious matters on her mind.

After waiting to speak to him in person for what seemed like hours, she finally buttonholed him at the end of the conference. She wanted to discuss, in detail, the many problems she was facing helping children in the regions controlled by his men under the auspices of the Sudan Relief and Rehabilitation Association (SRRA), the relief arm of the SPLA.

'Commander Riek,' she began, bristling, 'do you have any idea how frustrating it is trying to bring education to the children of the Upper Nile region, when all you and your men seem to do is block me at every turn, and the children I am trying to teach keep being marched off into the bush to become child soldiers?'

Riek was astounded by her attitude, and her courage. He knew who she was, he had heard of what SKI was trying to do, but in the middle of a complicated and lengthy war in which his men were killing and being killed, and many of his people were dying, educating the children had not seemed a top priority. His trip to Nairobi was the first time in five years he had taken a break from the swamps and the bush of southern Sudan. Faced now with the formidable vision of a tall white woman with legs like a gazelle, determined to press him on every point she had to make – he was smitten.

Riek has always said that for him it was love at first sight. Emma had beautiful hands, with long, elegant fingers, not dissimilar to his own. She exuded sexual confidence and knew how to use it, flirting with her eyes, and with that permanently smiling mouth. But Emma was far from finished with her tirade against him.

'I want you to know,' she added feistily, 'that I am also holding you personally responsible for my inability to get the teacher training courses set up in Torit and Bor. The SPLA refuses to allow people who could be trained as teachers to leave their own areas. I am also forbidden from travelling to many of the key areas where my work is so important. Unless I have your co-operation, I will have no choice but to take this matter further.'

Riek smiled at her, his grin revealing a large gap between his two front teeth. He asked her quietly, in his lilting voice, if she had ever read a book on the history of the Nuer people by the English anthropologist E. E. Evans-Pritchard.

'You really should,' he added softly. 'It will tell you all you need to know about my tribe.'

Emma was caught off guard. She hadn't read the book, and said so, although she had heard of it. Keen to keep the upper hand, she asked him if he would care to accompany her to the local library the following morning to help her find a copy. Riek agreed. Thereafter, she softened and began to ask more personal questions about his family and background. They found themselves drawn closer and closer together, and before long, Emma realised that the man she had so wanted to meet was even more intriguing than she had expected him to be. For her, too, it proved to be an immediate passion. She liked Riek's confidence and the way he threw his head back and chuckled. His voice was, she said, like velvet. She liked watching him twirl his ebony and ivory cane round and round in his elongated fingers as he spoke, and she loved the blue-black colour of his skin. They made love on that first night, an experience which was to change both their lives forever. Lying in his arms, she felt instinctively that here was the man she had been searching for, even if it seemed that nothing in the long term could come of their relationship.

Within twenty-four hours of their first encounter, Riek had gone, she knew not where. His Nairobi trip was cut short and he travelled to Zaire for a month before returning to southern Sudan where he was despatched by John Garang to command a remote area of the northern Upper Nile front line. Riek and his men were ordered to patrol the bush on foot via Ethiopia and he would be out of contact for seven months. Emma was beside herself with worry during those few months, wondering whether Riek felt the same way about her as she did about him, or whether she alone had felt something special. She tried to make discreet enquiries about him. Was he still alive? Which part of Sudan was he in? Was there any chance of them meeting again? But there was a war on, and high-ranking SPLA officials weren't in the habit of giving a strange white woman a blow-by-blow account of their commander's military movements.

Trying to consign her feelings for Riek to nothing more than a one-night stand, she carried on her on-off relationship with Willie Knocker. But all the while she was secretly dreaming of the tall, dark, handsome stranger she had once met, but who had now vanished from her life without trace. She needn't have worried. With her memory locked in his mind, Riek hadn't forgotten Emma either. Unable to exorcise the image of her, and following the dictates of his heart, he asked whether anyone had seen her on the rare occasions that he was in contact with the SPLA office in Nairobi. The reply was always negative. For those engaged in the serious business of war, the idea of a commander's liaison with a white woman was entirely taboo, as every white person was suspected of being a potential spy. As information of each other's whereabouts eluded them, and in the absence of any further news, Emma and Riek got on with their separate lives.

Having patched up the buildings and arranged the equipment necessary to re-open more schools in the south, Emma realised that her next problem was to address the chronic shortage of staff. To induce people to return to a war zone and teach, or to persuade those there to stay, she needed to reassure them with offers of food, shelter and proper training. Thus it was, in the spring of 1990, that she set off on a six-week tour of Eastern Equatoria to establish two new teacher training centres in the towns of Torit and Bor. She wrote to me after her first week away, sending the letter home via a UN plane.

> *'Torit is a typical African town, largely consisting of thatched mud huts and the odd stone and brick building. We have established a teacher training institute here – formerly the Catholic mission. Rehabilitation is in progress – tree planting, carpentry, painting etc. The destruction of war is depressing. One cannot help but wonder what these places were like when they thronged with teeming activity instead of the derelict buildings, the lootings and the emptiness.*
>
> *The people here are busy cultivating the land for planting – purifying the soil by scattering the remains of chickens and, if wealthy, goats and cows. They fear that people who may have committed some crime have walked across their land. The fathers from the mission told us yesterday that if the rainmakers fail, they are often killed by the women as too are those with the evil eye that scatter the clouds to prevent rain. Apparently, many of the older generation regard white people as descendants of water and therefore with power over the rain. Others call us the red monkeys!'*

Emma continued to busy herself with SKI, flying to and from Nairobi, preparing reports and setting up the infrastructure to promote teacher training and establish schools. Determined that the villagers should become self-supporting in maintaining the schools once they were set up, she devoted much of her energy to investigating ways in which they could grow their own crops to help pay the salaries of the new teachers.

Receiving her first pay cheque from SKI, a significant moment in her life after years of impoverished studenthood, she moved out of Roo and Simon's Nairobi home – where she had lodged for the previous ten months – and set up house with Sally Dudmesh in Koitibus Road, Langata, a leafy suburb of the sprawling city. Sally was always delighted when Emma was back in town; the two girlfriends would spend days catching up on each other's news, making up for lost time.

In July 1990, with money in the bank, Emma could afford to fly home on leave for six weeks, the first time I had seen her in nearly a year. She looked fantastic, tanned, happy and confident. She hired a car for part of the holiday, the first time she had ever been able to afford to, and – using my home as a base camp – travelled up and down the country, visiting friends in Oxford, her Gramps (by then living in Shropshire), and all her old friends in Yorkshire. Coming back via East Anglia she stopped in on Aunt Margot and Uncle George and Wendy and Bill Burton in Cambridgeshire, before touching down with me once more via her friends in London, visiting theatres, galleries and dining out.

There were parties galore; Annabel Ledgard held one for her in London, Sue and Martin held the first annual summer party for her at Springwood, and in between times, she and I caught up on all the news and we reminisced. Her favourite spot was sitting on the bench in my garden, sunning herself and flicking through glossy magazines – a real treat for her – while I pottered among my flower beds, tending to the summer plants. Those were somnolent days, looking up across the hollyhocks and delphiniums, listening and watching as she laughed and chatted, regaling me with the sights and sounds and smells of Africa – all of which seemed so very distant from our quintessentially English setting.

I was still working at Bear Stearns, Erica and Johnny were both in Bristol – him on a business studies course and Erica studying furniture restoration. They shared a house in the wilds of the west country, and it was through Johnny that Erica met her future husband, Hugh, a fellow student. Jennie – who had been missing from our lives for over a year, travelling the globe with a backpack and rarely calling or writing – had recently returned unexpectedly, only to announce that she was planning her next trip. So, for a brief while, all my children were in the same country, and – joy of joys – they all converged on Surrey for Emma's farewell party that August. A glorious day.

Waving her off at the airport the following week. I had none of the usual pangs at seeing her go. Only a few days before she departed, Emma surprised and delighted me by inviting me to Kenya for Christmas, giving me the money for the plane ticket. It would be my first visit to the continent she had fallen in love with. I was thrilled and was already planning my packing.

That Christmas was a significant one in my new, grown-up relationship with Emma. It was her chance to resonate with me, and to share with me some of what she had discovered as the magic of Africa. It was my chance to journey into the unknown, to see where my daughter was living and working, to open my mind to her loves and the life she had chosen in a foreign land.

I was half-expecting Africa to be full of the same sights, sounds and smells as a continent I left long ago. To my surprise, it was so very different, a continent in its own right and full of its own temptations. Exploring with Emma, spending my first Christmas alone with her. I revelled in the new experience. I felt able to breathe again after years of anxiety, financial insecurity and heartache.

Emma collected me at the airport on 8 December and took me to the little house she shared with Sally. On the very first day, she and Willy drove me, Sally and John Horsey up to the Ngong Hills for a walk. At the summit, the landscape was swathed in fog and a strong wind blew my skirt over my head.

'My God,' I thought, 'I've come all this way and it looks no different from the Yorkshire Dales.' But, driving back in the half-light, I saw my first giraffe through the trees, grazing from a tall acacia, its extraordinary outline at one with the African bush. Despite the fog, I was in a very different country.

Emma was still working, so she put me on an internal flight to the most sumptuous hotel I had stayed in for many a year – Hemingways in Watamu on the coast – whose opulence reminded me of life on the SS *Chusan*. The beds were turned down each night, the mosquito nets lowered and I had not experienced that kind of style since leaving India. It was a real treat. I stayed there for nine days, wallowing in the luxury. I made new friends and visited Willie's parents, Jeannie and Roddy, who lived nearby along the beach, and who took me under their wing. We went fishing, 'goggling' (snorkelling), and explored the hinterland.

Returning to Nairobi relaxed and ready for anything, I was swept straight into a wedding party for Roo and Si, who had married earlier that day. It was a bewildering, but most enjoyable affair. The following ten days were spent travelling on safari through Tsavo East, heading back towards the coast, with Emma and friends. By this time we had been joined by Lucy and Simon, the daughter and son-in-law of Wanda from Aysgarth School in North Yorkshire. Sally had organised a huge house party for Christmas day: we stayed in Kilifi at a house which stood on the edge of the Indian Ocean. The day was dreamlike. It began with a feast of tropical fruits for breakfast, followed by many hours of swimming and goggling and, later, many hours of relaxing and chatting under the speckled shade of a huge baobab tree. As the sun went down we prepared ourselves for an evening of celebrations, drinking tequila slammers before settling down to a traditional roast turkey dinner with all its trimmings. The following day Lucy, Simon and I were back on the road, on safari once more. We drove through Tsavo West, northwards, via Nairobi, and on up to Lake Bogoria, having already said our goodbyes to Emma and Sally at the coast.

Flying home on 30 December 1990, I sat back in my airline seat, sipped my gin and tonic and reflected. For me, it had been a rekindling of old memories, my first chance in fourteen years to enjoy the colonial lifestyle once more, and I had loved every second of it. I was content that Emma was surrounded by friends and people who loved her, fulfilled in her work and happy at last, and I felt better able to empathise with her growing passion for Africa. Still single, despite Willie's best endeavours, Emma was, I felt, on the verge of embarking on a new phase in her life with renewed energy. Idly, I wondered whom she might choose to share that journey.

By January 1991, a window of opportunity opened for Riek and Emma to be reunited at last. He had been summoned back from the front line and asked to report to John Garang in the small town of Nasir, close to the border with Ethiopia. Standing on the banks of the River Sobat, a tributary of the White Nile, Nasir had been established in 1912 by the British as their command-post over the local cattle-keepers, and was now a creeper-covered ruin.

The SPLA had established a key military base just south of the old town and Riek was placed in charge of it and several hundred troops. As head of his own new administrative centre, Riek tried again to locate the woman he had never forgotten in the year that had passed. By coincidence, John Ryle, a writer and old acquaintance of Riek's, arrived in Nasir. He was researching a series of articles and there were things he needed to know about the region; but he soon found that he was the one answering the questions.

'Do you know someone called Emma McCune?' Riek asked John within a few hours of his arrival, as they were reminiscing over old times. The answer was yes, John knew Emma from Nairobi and London, and told Riek that as far as he was aware she was currently back in the Kenyan capital. By the time John flew back to Nairobi a few days later, he was carrying in his pocket a short command for Emma from Riek. John promised Riek faithfully that the message would reach its destination. And it did. It read:

NASIR 5th FEB 1991

Ms Emma McCune
STREET KIDS INTERNATIONAL
NAIROBI

1. I would be grateful if you could fly out to Nasir this week to discuss the educational problems pertaining to the Zones under my command. These are Western Upper Nile, Northern Upper Nile and the Sobat Basin.
2. I have been informed by the SRRA Offices in these Zones that you are helping in provision of school materials, etc. I have written to SRRA Nairobi Liaison Officer to issue you the travel permit to Nasir.

COMMANDER RIEK M TENY-DHURGON

Emma leapt into action, begging a lift on a UN plane to fly to Nasir straight away. But when she got there, she discovered to her very great dismay that Riek had gone. He had unexpected business in Gambela, 200 miles away, because of the growing tensions in Ethiopia over whether President Haile Mengistu's regime would survive. Mengistu had traditionally supported the SPLA and if he went and a new, unsympathetic regime came to power, it could have dire consequences for the war.

Bitterly disappointed to have missed him, Emma had no choice but to return to Nairobi and wait for news. As soon as she heard via the radio that he had returned to his base, she attempted three times to get a flight to Nasir, but was further disappointed when fuel shortages and the withdrawal of flight permission into liberated areas conspired against her. There was only one option, to travel overland. It would be a perilous journey, of around 1,500 miles across some of the most inhospitable and dangerous terrain, taking her through the front lines between the rebel and the government forces; across territory controlled by armed and merciless tribes such as the Toposa; and along roads so dangerous, she would have to cut a path through the bush. With such a seemingly insurmountable challenge thrown at her feet, her mind was made up and she packed her bags.

Emma knew it was madness to go, and that she shouldn't go alone, but her heart was ruling her head. She convinced herself that there were legitimate educational reasons for her visit, and that she could also improve her standing by making such a hazardous journey, but in truth, it was her love for adventure and for Riek that drove her on. Her powers of persuasion had never been in doubt and she used them now to convince Willie Knocker that he should drive her there. Their precarious relationship had been in one of its 'on' phases for a little while, and Willie hoped that it might stay that way. The more she pushed him away from her, the more he loved her. He had already asked her to marry him, a proposal she had answered with a 'maybe', and he wondered now, if he went with her on this madcap journey, whether he might just get the answer he was waiting for.

Willie was initially doubtful that they could survive such a journey, but she couched it in such terms that they would be able to rescue aid worker colleagues stranded in Nasir, and that it would be such an epic adventure and the best safari ever, that he couldn't resist. He loved her, after all. Willie loaded up his vehicle with essential supplies – fuel, food and water, and gave a lift to a radio operator who wanted to get to that part of the country. It was February and still the dry season and they set off from Kapoeta near the Kenyan border in Willie's battered Land Rover 'Brutus'. The first stage of their journey to Bor was largely across grassy plains following ancient cattle trails. They drove on through Kongor to Nuerland, travelling through Ayod, Waat and Ulang. En route, they were fortunate enough to see a migrating white-eared cob and tiang, rare forms of antelope. The sky took on the strangest hues of red and pink and filled with palls of smoke from the traditional burning of grass that was going on.

At night, they made love in their bedding rolls, laid out under the stars, to the sounds of hyenas out on the plains. In Waat, they visited the shrine of the Nuer prophet Nyndeng – marked by a circle of small elephant tusks – where they offered packets of salt in return for a safe journey.

From Waat the road virtually disappeared and they had to follow cattle trails flattened by centuries of hooves, north towards Wedenyang, on the south bank of the River Sobat, near Ulang. The last leg of the journey was along a route only recently re-opened after eight years of being out of commission. At one point they became lost, had an argument with their guide, losing faith with him, and ended up hacking down eighteen kilometres of acacia forest to get through.

It was something of a triumph when they arrived, exhausted, at the little army garrison of mud huts at Wedenyang, the first travellers to reach the area overland in nearly a decade. After unloading their vehicle, they waded across the river to meet Riek, standing, legs apart, arms folded, on the far shore in his trademark battle fatigues and red beret. The war lord was more than a little flattered that Emma had answered his call and come so far, although he expressed his surprise at seeing Willie.

'What did you bring *him* for?' were his first words to Emma.

As their eyes met and sparked once more, my daughter was unwittingly entering a new and dangerous world.

The following morning, there was little time for Riek and Emma to be alone. She awoke to find the rebel commander addressing a group of villager chiefs about forthcoming elections and how to organise their schools. Sitting down quietly beside him she looked, Willie said, like a cross between a memsahib and a Sultana of the Nuer, taking part in the discussions and offering what suggestions she could. There were awkward silences as Emma and Riek caught each other's glances and quickly looked away.

Finally, Riek stood up in a single fluid movement and announced to the gathering that he needed to speak to Emma privately. His bodyguards were very suspicious and not at all happy, but he commanded them to remain outside, while he went into his office with her alone. Once inside, they circled each other cautiously, superficially continuing their discussion of social and educational matters, but with other things on their minds. Suddenly, Riek made the first move.

'Why did you travel so far, and on so dangerous a journey?' he asked.

Emma's eyes sparkled as she looked across at him. 'I wanted to see you,' she replied. She hardly dared tell him how many nights he had been in her thoughts in the previous year.

The ice broke and they set aside all pretence at discussing impersonal matters. They sat down next to each other at the table and talked intensely. Sitting side by side, occasionally brushing against his arm, Emma could smell his sweat and feel the heat exuding from his body. He, in turn, looked at her with renewed appreciation, recalling the curve of her back, and the way her long fingers held her pencil or camera so precisely. Emma held Riek's hand, entwining her fingers in his, and told how she had tried to get news of him, or speak to him through the radio via Ethiopia. She asked him why he hadn't replied to her notes or written himself. Riek said he knew nothing of any notes or messages, he could only assume that they had been intercepted and destroyed. Just like Romeo and Juliet, Emma thought.

> *From ancient grudge break to new mutiny,*
> *Where civil blood makes civil hands unclean.*
> *From forth the fatal loins of these two foes*
> *A pair of star-cross'd lovers . . .*

from the Prologue to *Romeo and Juliet* by William Shakespeare

For the next twenty-four hours, Emma and Riek spent most of their time together, locked in intense discussions about the war, international politics and aid, and the logistics of creating educational systems and local economies from nothing. They found an affinity in each other, which went far beyond their obvious physical attraction. There was a shared passion for Sudan, Riek claimed to understand Emma's drive to provide education for the children, he said that he wanted nothing more than peace. Meanwhile, Willie, a keen naturalist, wondered at his girlfriend's absence while he made forays into the bush to study the birds, the habitat, and to fish the Sobat River.

On the evening before Emma and Willie were to make the return journey with three other passengers, Riek had been involved in a series of interminably long discussions with his aides. The sun was setting and, as Emma sat with them, listening, waiting, she wondered if they would be able to spend any more time alone together. Riek must have read her thoughts. Quite abruptly, and with an almost imperceptible wave of his hand, he dismissed his aides and his bodyguards, who swiftly and silently left his hut. Leaning back in his chair, his eyes glinting in the rich orange light that flooded in through the open doorway from the sunset, Riek smiled at Emma, his white teeth flashing at her.

'You know a great deal about politics and this war,' he said, his rich voice music to her ears.

'I'm learning fast,' Emma replied, her own wide smile enticing him to continue.

Riek nodded. 'And in the process, you are learning about my people, the Nuer people.' When he spoke in such a way, Emma was almost able to forget that he was a soldier, a warmonger, and liked to think of him instead as a proud tribal chief.

She smiled again, this time giving him a meaningful look from large green eyes, the pupils soft and dilated. 'I'm always willing to learn more . . .'

'I thought so,' Riek said, rising to his feet. The seven foot warrior took a few paces towards the small window of the hut, and stood with his back to her, staring out across the River Sobat, its waters aflame with the reflection of the sun. He took a deep breath. 'How much do you know about Nuer mythology?' he asked, his accent thick.

Emma shrugged. 'Enough to know that it's worth knowing more.' She had certainly done her homework, she had read the book he had recommended a year before, but there was so much yet to learn, so much she wanted to learn.

Riek paused, his huge hands clasped behind his back, still clutching his ivory cane. 'But do you know of something that is written there?' he asked.

She waited.

'An unmarked left-handed Nuer chief will one day marry a white woman.'

The sun was sinking fast, sending rosy shafts of light into the hut. Slowly Riek turned around until he was facing Emma. Then, very gradually, he raised his left hand, palm towards her and flexed back his long fingers. The silence seemed perpetual, as they gazed at each other. At last Riek raised his eyebrows and half-smiled.

'And so . . . will you?'

Emma betrayed no emotion. She sat stock still for several seconds, holding her breath. Her heart was beating so fast inside her chest, she thought it might burst. Picking up a file of documents, she stood in that effortless single motion of hers, held Riek's gaze for a second, then walked to the little door of the hut. Hesitating on the threshold, she looked back at him, her lips parted, her eyes bright.

'I'll think about it . . .' she said quietly, and walked out into the dusk.

Emma settled into the passenger seat and sat back. Willie glanced across at her through his gold-rimmed spectacles and saw that she had closed her eyes. There was an expression of rapture on her face. He smiled to himself, captivated, now as ever, by her beauty, her serenity. He wished she would give him an answer to his proposal of marriage. They had so much to share and he knew that life with Emma would be different – exciting and dangerous.

They were approaching Kongor, less than a quarter of the way through their return journey from Nasir, and she had hardly said a word. Willie thought that perhaps Emma was tired by the long journey and the gravity of the discussions with Riek, and that she would probably fall asleep, despite the juddering of the Land Rover over the bumpy roads. But he was wrong. She didn't sleep, she remained silent and restless and he wondered what was wrong. That night when they reached Kongor and were preparing to go to sleep in a small tukul, Emma broke her silence, dropping her bombshell on him. Lying in a bed next to hers, he heard a sudden sharp intake of breath as she sat up. Willie glanced across at her: she was staring down at him, her eyes wide open.

'Willie, there's something I have to say.'

He blinked momentarily, then looked back at her. 'Well, what is it?' He was intrigued as to what had made her jump. He had no inkling of what was to follow.

'I don't love you any more.' Her husky voice seemed even deeper and softer in the dim light. It caressed him with its throatiness.

His eyes flicked between her face and the roof of their hut in which a brood of young African barn owls were snoring and chipping their beaks. A joke. Emma's mischievousness. He had played this game with her before and he smiled. 'So, what am I supposed to have done to deserve this?'

'Nothing,' she replied. Her tone was even.

'Well, then I plead not guilty and can't be prosecuted. There's no case to answer,' Willie laughed, turning back to go to sleep. But he felt a strange sense of trepidation that, inexplicably, even though they were in such close proximity, a great gulf was rapidly opening up between them. He was conscious of Emma's gaze still fixed upon him.

'It's not a joke,' she said calmly. 'I mean it.' Somewhere in the far distance, Willie thought he could hear a hyena laugh.

After a second, he swivelled to stare Emma directly in the face. 'Now come on, Emma,' he chided. 'We've got a hell of a long way to go. It's not the time to start playing tricks.'

'It's not a trick,' she insisted, coolly. 'I – don't – love – you – any – more.' This time she really spelt it out for him, making deliberate gaps between her words. Each one was a great gaping ravine down which he was about to fall. Willie stared at her hard, holding his own breath as he did so. There was something in her expression he had never witnessed before. He had seen many things in her eyes – love, anger, lust – but not this. Not this . . .

There was silence. He stared into the middle distance. It was a moment of destiny being rapidly realised, a moment which left his heart as burnt out and dry as the land across which they had just travelled.

Frowning, he looked back at Emma, her expression unchanged.

'But Emma, *why?*' he pleaded. 'What on earth has happened? I thought . . .' His words died away. Looking at him steadily, an enigmatic half-smile came to her lips. He dropped his eyes, unable to hold her gaze.

'Because I have fallen in love with someone else.'

His head spun round to look at her and he was shocked by what he could see. It was true, he could tell. It was in her eyes. She was so smitten she couldn't wait to tell him; couldn't wait until they got home to a more appropriate venue, a more convenient time. Her green eyes were lit up like those of a schoolgirl with a crush.

Willie wished he could shout his response, howl his pain in the night, hear it echoing out of the window and defiantly across the grassy plains, but instead he could only whisper incredulously, '*With someone else?*'

There was a long pause. 'I have fallen in love with Riek.'

Willie swallowed with difficulty. '*Riek?* But that's not possible . . .'

Emma raised her eyebrows. 'Oh yes it is.'

He turned away, taking a deep breath, absorbing this latest blow. Five, ten seconds passed. He cast a sidelong glance at her – at the woman he had adored and believed to be his alone. 'So . . .' he murmured acidly, 'is there . . . no hope for me?'

'No, I'm afraid not. Not now.' That frosty tone, so final. She settled back into her bed, staring up at the ceiling. The silent seconds passed.

And then the anger came. Tidal waves of it. He had been used. Coolly and calculatingly used to drive her to the arms of the man she loved. There was no legitimate educational aspect to the visit, she had beguiled him into accompanying her to Nasir – risking his life and her own – with one thing on her mind, Willie rolled over in his bed and froze her out, his fury poisoning his heart against her, against the woman he had once hoped to have as his bride.

The following morning, they were on the road early, Willie slamming the Land Rover into first gear and pressing his foot down on the accelerator. We have all at some time had to endure excruciating journeys such as these – wordless, with the tension stretched to breaking point – trapped in a confined space with someone we hate for the time being. But from there, in the middle of the African bush, to reach their destination across a heartless terrain that could cause their death at any moment, felt to him as though it might as well be a journey across the universe. Again and again, Willie was on the verge of jamming on the brakes and kicking Emma out of the car in the middle of nowhere, where she may or may not have survived. He had found his nemesis in a desert, and so perhaps should Emma, he argued mentally. But, decent to the core, he drove on, gripping the steering-wheel, his jaw tightly clenched.

There were very real perils to face as they sped along the winding red earth road back to Kenya. Their path was littered from time to time with burnt out SPLA or government trucks, bombed from the air or by ambush. Coming upon a stationary vehicle abandoned ahead, they slowed down and approached with great caution. Driving closer, they could see it was a brand new Land Cruiser belonging to the charity Norwegian Church Aid, and it was a mess. The tyres had been shot out, the windscreen shattered and the vehicle was riddled with bullet holes.

Its occupants, hiding terrified in the bush nearby and severely injured – one with his foot blown off, the other with a bullet in his thigh – flagged Emma and Willie down and told them their terrifying story. The previous day they had been driving to Bor when they ran into members of the Toposa militia laying mines in the road. A fire-fight ensued, the Toposa shot up their car and ran off. Had they not surprised the mine-laying party, then the very road Willie and Emma were travelling along would have been peppered with mines.

It was a salutary thought, but not one that Willie had much time for, as he helped the injured men into his car and set off again silently, heading south and east as fast as he could. All he could think about was getting as far away from Emma as possible; the 'Lady Cruella de Ville' of his Oxford days, who had now been so heartless that even his college nickname for her seemed too tame.

By the time they got to Torit, 130 miles from the Kenyan border, neither of them could stand the atmosphere any more. Willie dropped Emma and the injured men off, and left her there, telling her to get a lift with someone else. As he headed on alone, he reflected bitterly on how his life's hopes had been annihilated by one single word: *Riek*.

10

By April 1991, two months after she and Willie had parted for good, Emma had made up her mind. Determined to get back to Nasir to see Riek, she persuaded SKI that Nasir was the perfect region to continue distributing school materials and setting up new teacher training courses. Where better than right under Commander Machar's nose, she urged, so that the rebel leader could see for himself the value of the programme and support it elsewhere? The argument won and, despite the start of the rainy season, she packed her belongings and hopped a ride on a UN plane.

A RRIVING IN RIEK'S BASE CAMP, CARRYING LITTLE MORE THAN HER TRADEMARK KIKAPU (LARGE AFRICAN BASKET) AND A FEW BOOKS, SHE DISCOVERED TO HER VERY GREAT DISAPPOINTMENT THAT RIEK WAS NOT THERE. He was in Ethiopia once more, on his latest mission to promote the cause of the SPLA. Sending word to him via solar-powered radio that she was waiting for him in Nasir, she received the prompt two-word reply:

'Please wait.'

Emma waited for seven days, alone and confused in a dank, rat-infested house formerly used by visiting expatriates. The electric storms raging overhead were thunderous, the Sobat Basin had flooded with the rains, and she was beginning to lose hope of ever seeing civilisation again. With the heavens pouring forth their deluge, making the muddy ground, known locally as 'black cotton soil', treacherously slippery, she wondered if she would ever get out.

Just at that moment, a Land Rover appeared through the pouring rain, driven by a soldier she recognised as one of Riek's bodyguards.

'Commander Riek requests that you accompany me to his military headquarters at Ketbek,' the driver told her. 'It is ten miles south east of here.'

Emma didn't need a second invitation. Grabbing her kikapu and wrapping a kanga around her hair in a vain attempt to protect it from the rain, she splashed through the muddy puddles and jumped into the vehicle, smiling to herself as they headed out of the town.

The roads were almost impassable; a journey that would have taken fifteen minutes in the dry season took them well over an hour. By the time they arrived at the rain-sodden cluster of little mud huts in the middle of the garrison, Emma was cold, tired and very damp. Ushered towards Riek's tukul, her wet hair plastered to her head, she removed her kanga and wrung it out in the doorway before stepping in. It was dark inside, but as her eyes grew accustomed to the light, she could just make Riek out.

He was lying on his bed, his hands clasped behind his head, his eyes closed. A mosquito net was draped back over him like a theatrical curtain, inviting her forwards. Stepping closer, she glanced at the small black Sony radio on the table next to him, softly transmitting the crackling broadcast of the BBC World Service. As she reached his bedside, and stared down at him lying there motionless, his eyes opened and his face broke into the most enormous grin.

Within a month, by May 1991, Emma was successfully co-ordinating her teacher training project in Nasir, fulfilled and happy in all areas of her life. She was living in Riek's garrison compound, surrounded by armed soldiers and bodyguards, separate from the other relief workers who were based a mile away, and her close liaison with the rebel commander was already causing consternation and friction between herself and other aid workers, not to mention Riek's men, who had no idea what to do with a woman in their midst, let alone a white one.

Emma shrugged off the stares of the troops and tried to get to know them, particularly the bodyguards who followed her lover wherever he went. One, in particular, called Forty-Six after the

Russian-built RP-46 machine gun, was a giant of a man, over seven feet tall, with traditional Nuer markings across his forehead, around his mouth and eyes. Trained by Fidel Castro, he walked with a slight limp from a childhood accident with a gun, and was Riek's most devoted aide.

Few, if any, of Riek's men spoke her language, nor she theirs but, one by one, she learned their names and before long they were like brothers to her. They watched in silent astonishment as she scratched and scraped at the soil around Riek's tukul with her hands and lovingly planted seeds for vegetables and fruit. Watching her so engrossed, watering and tending the tiny seedlings as they grew, the bodyguards began to lay down their Kalashnikovs and kneel alongside her, tilling the baked soil with the sharpened points of their bayonets or hunting knives, and fetching her buckets of water.

Previously only a visitor, Emma now cherished living amongst the people, the camp followers of the garrison, becoming one of them, eating their food, trying to learn their language, helping to prepare their food and bake their bread. They lived on boiled Nile perch and sorghum, a type of sugar cane, and all ate the same food. She danced at their gatherings in the African way, much to their delight, stamping her feet and pulling impish faces at them as she swirled and whirled like a Dervish.

Most aid workers drove around locked in their four-wheel drive vehicles, living together confined to their private compounds, mixing only with their own. Many left, burnt-out, after six months or a year, disillusioned with the magnitude of the problem facing them and what little impact they made, merely scratching at the surface. For Emma it was different; she appeared ready to live as one with the people and commit herself in every way to them. With plenty of responsibilities in the field of education alone, she encouraged the women and children of the camp to come to her with all their complex problems – paving the way for a flood of poorly written letters in pidgin English, asking for necessary items, money or help in finding displaced relatives. In one instance, she personally drove a mother over one hundred miles to a refugee camp to try and find the woman's lost son.

Emma was somehow able to bridge a cultural chasm and to relate to these people as individuals. She had been like that ever since she was a small child in Assam. She had never regarded people of a different colour and culture as a species to study or as a social problem. She regarded them simply as people. And they could tell the difference.

In May 1991, President Mengistu of Ethiopia was overthrown, an event the SPLA and the people of southern Sudan had feared and dreaded. Through Riek's men and radio contact with Nairobi, Emma heard that hundreds of thousands of Sudanese refugees – people who had previously fled to Ethiopia because of the war in their own country – were now returning and about to descend on them in Nasir, the town closest to the border. Whether or not that was the true reason for the influx of displaced people, or whether the entire movement of refugees was orchestrated by certain factions of the SPLA to ensure food and supplies for themselves (a frequent abuse of aid in Third World countries), no one will ever know, but it was clear what the Khartoum government thought. They bombed Nasir unexpectedly, killing thirty-six people and wounding many more, including women and children. Emma was caught in the middle once more, and did all she could to help tend the injured and dying. Using the SPLA solar-powered radio, she put out an urgent call for help to the aid agencies in Nairobi – an act which infuriated the Khartoum government.

Emma had never been afraid of upsetting those in authority, certainly not those in the north, and she cared less now. Her only concern was for the health and safety of the more than 150,000 refugees who descended on the little town, seeking food and water. After Emma's emergency call, Patta and Alastair Scott-Villiers arrived from Nairobi and within days had helped set up a relief camp in a disused army barracks. The refugees continued to arrive in their droves, although many had died on the way, and those who survived were thin and weak. The event triggered world attention as television crews and newspaper journalists flew in from around the globe to cover the latest story from this war-torn area of east Africa. Their arrival, with film crews and cameras, satellite telephones and instant access to the world beyond, fired Emma's imagination. They were there because she had made a call. She realised the impact she could have, and her power over these messengers of doom.

We are they who come faster than fate: we are they who ride early or late:
We storm at your ivory gate: Pale Kings of the Sunset, beware!

from 'War Song of the Saracens' by James Elroy Flecker

It will never be certain whether Emma was fully aware, as in all aid drops to such situations, that some of the much-needed food and supplies were being siphoned off by soldiers, in this instance Riek's own men. In one confrontation with UN aid workers about the problem, Emma and Riek were reported to have served their guests fried bread balls called mandazis, made out of the Unimix high-protein meal sent in for children, on a bright orange plastic plate taken straight from a UNICEF feeding kit. It was a continuous moral dilemma for those providing aid to the Third World – if those looking after the frail and hungry didn't keep their strength up too, then more would die. But at what point did they have to intervene when children were starving and the soldiers caring for them patently weren't?

Patta was far too busy, at first, tending to the sick and starving to have time to talk to Emma or question her friendship with Riek, but after a while – when the worst was over and the relief camp settled into a life of its own – she became perplexed by her friend's behaviour. Emma seemed incapable of understanding why anyone should be hostile to her devoting so much of her time to a rebel military commander in charge of the destinies of thousands. Despite her obvious happiness in her work and personal contentment, Patta began to worry about where it could lead. Then, out of the blue, on the morning of 17 June 1991, she realised that she was too late. Emma appeared in the relief camp, found Patta and tapped her on the shoulder.

'I'm getting married this afternoon,' she announced, her face lit up like a flame. 'Will you come?'

Patta was completely taken aback and spun round to face her friend. 'Married? Who to?' she asked.

Emma grinned. 'Riek, of course,' she replied. There was something in her eyes which told Patta that she knew it was dangerous and might not work, but that she was determined to go ahead.

For Patta, everything suddenly fell into place. The way Emma and Riek were with one another, the intimate familiarity between them. She could see the attraction – both had great charm, stamina, a thirst for power and success, and a great calmness in the face of disaster – but she never thought Emma would go this far. Seeing Emma's eyes shining with happiness, she held back from what she was going to say.

'Of course I'll come,' she replied. Almost as an afterthought, she added: 'Congratulations.'

By midday, Riek and Emma had set out by Land Rover to Ketbek church, a little Presbyterian church in swampy ground on the banks of the River Sobat, accompanied by Patta, an Indian doctor called Bernadette Kumar, and several armed guards. The church was an oval tithe barn with a grass roof built on a mound of mud. There was an air of general excitement as Riek's people heard that something special was about to happen.

Emma's wedding outfit was a white cotton jabi, or netala, an Ethiopian shawl, wrapped around her waist to form a skirt and another one draped across her shoulders. Both were trimmed with a coloured symmetrical pattern on the edges. Riek was in his best khaki combat fatigues with gold epaulettes, heavy black boots and his scarlet beret bearing the gold-embroidered SPLA insignia. He carried his ebony and ivory cane. They hadn't travelled far when the road became impassable due to flooding and their vehicle became stuck in the mud. No amount of pushing and shoving could dislodge it, and for a while they thought that the wedding would have to be postponed. As I write this I can't help remembering how, in another land, a long time ago, events had also conspired against me reaching my own wedding.

Undaunted, Emma suggested that the wedding party abandon the vehicle and set off on foot, a journey of almost two miles, trudging through the black cotton soil. She was determined that the ceremony should go ahead. Riek smiled, shrugged his shoulders and agreed. So off they set, this strange and straggly group, Emma and Riek at the fore, hand-in-hand, grinning from ear to ear, and encouraging the others. On the way to the church members of the bridal party stopped from time to time to gather dried grasses for Emma's posy. Riek, his pistol tucked into his belt.

When they arrived at Ketbek church, Emma was barefoot, her white garments spattered with mud and thorns caught in her shawls, but she remained radiant. Word had preceded them. Chairs and tables had been set out in a small clearing in front of the church. Naked children played in the dust, beating on drums with sticks, and a choir of six women dressed in white home-made surplices thrown over their ordinary clothes, stood singing. Other women were draped in vivid turquoise wraps, tied in huge knots at the shoulder.

The afternoon grew cooler as the sun started to sink, tingeing the air with pink. It was the cow-dust hour when the young boys of the tribe herd their long-horned cattle into the camps and the thick dust raised by their hooves mingles with the sweet-smelling smoke from dozens of small cooking fires, and from those burning dung out on the plains. There was an air of anticipation as villagers and other native tribes-people gathered round, within sight of the church compound, waiting for something to happen as the light turned from golden to a soft, hazy pink.

Riek and Emma took their seats, side by side, in the middle of the clearing, flanked by Kalashnikov-carrying bodyguards and Riek's closest aides, including Dr Lam Akol, his fellow SPLA commander, who acted as a reluctant best man. In front of them was a low table covered in a red cloth. A few feet away was a makeshift altar, a metal-tubing trestle table, draped in a white cloth. Riek indicated, with a nod of his head, that the ceremony should begin.

The master of ceremonies, Riek's adjutant, a gaunt Sudanese man with a tiny goatee-beard on the point of his chin, solemnly appeared in his best robe, undoubtedly passed on through an aid agency – a Western-style pink, quilted dressing-gown, buttoned to the neck and tied at the waist. It was not unlike one I had owned when the children were small. Emma tried very hard not to giggle. The adjutant was amongst those who had wholly disapproved of Emma, who believed it quite wrong for Riek and her to be together, and who did not believe Riek would go through with the marriage. To make him understand that he would, Riek appointed him as the man in charge.

Reading from the Bible, the adjutant chose several long and gloomy passages reminding Riek of the importance of marriage. In an effort to deter Emma, he spoke of woman as being the rib of Adam, and of man's jurisdiction over the second sex. Patta intervened and sought Riek's consent to introduce something more light-hearted into the proceedings, based on love. Permission granted by a highly amused Riek, she read a passage from Corinthians which she had chosen for her own marriage ceremony, as the adjutant leaned over her shoulder suspiciously eyeing the words as she read:

> Love is patient, love is kind and envies no one. Love is never boastful, nor conceited, nor rude; never selfish, not quick to take offence. Love keeps no score of wrongs; does not gloat over other men's sins, but delights in the truth. There is nothing love cannot face; there is no limit to its faith, its hope and endurance . . .
>
> In a word, there are three things that last for ever: faith, hope, and love; but the greatest of them all is love.

from the Bible, I Corinthians 13: 4–7, 13

A second official, James Mut Kueth, a Nuer priest in a traditional black robe with a white dog collar, asked Riek and Emma to stand in front of the altar, and holding their two hands in his, read out the solemn and lengthy marriage vows. Bemused, Emma listened quietly to the words she didn't understand, and squeezed Riek's hand, making him smile shyly. Patta lent Emma a silver dress ring that her husband Alastair had bought her on a recent holiday. Emma bought Riek his ring later. Riek placed Patta's ring on Emma's long finger and the marriage was confirmed.

The ceremony over, the couple kissed, people applauded and the choir sang their lilting tribal songs. Patta took photographs, all of which showed Emma lit from within, luminous in her happiness and love. There was no other celebration, no slaughtering of a cow as Nuer tradition demands – given the present refugee situation, it would have been insensitive. And no honeymoon.

The sun – now a huge red ball of flame in a vast African sky – sank slowly behind the church, and a flock of birds flew off, silhouetted in flight. People gradually dispersed, as they always seem to in the bush, melting into the background, disappearing almost as mysteriously as they had arrived. As a motorboat sent to collect them for the journey back to Nasir waited on the riverbank, the newlyweds strolled hand-in-hand down to the river, the moon illuminating their path. Patta, the only western guest, whose reservations about the marriage had been many and varied, watched the ceremony with tears in her eyes and a lump in her throat. She said afterwards that, somehow, in the midst of a war and a refugee crisis, it had all seemed very beautiful and right.

> *And hand in hand, on the edge of the sand,*
> *They danced by the light of the moon,*
> *The moon,*
> *The moon,*
> *They danced by the light of the moon.*

from 'The Owl and the Pussy-Cat' by Edward Lear

I had no premonition, not the faintest inkling of what was to come, so it was a bolt from the blue. It's true that my suspicions might have been aroused by the fact that, during the summer of 1991 – when we expected Emma to come back to England for her annual visit – she procrastinated three times, even though we had all been looking forward to a family reunion to celebrate my son Johnny's twenty-first birthday. In the end, she never came, and we celebrated without her. We were sorry that Emma couldn't be with us, and further disappointed when Jennie disappeared on her travels abroad again. I remember standing on the fringes of the party, watching Johnny dancing with his friends, and Erica in the arms of her new boyfriend Hugh, and feeling sad that my other two children had missed another happy occasion.

It is probably an individual quirk of mine, but I am always very disconcerted to receive private phone calls when I'm at work. This is partly because my mind is almost certainly going to be locked onto some purely practical and impersonal matter, from which I have to, as it were, put another head on my shoulders before I can begin to understand what it might be about. And on that June afternoon, it was compounded by the fact that I was working in an open-plan office at Bear Stearns, with at least five potential eavesdroppers, who would probably have found great sport in trying to reconstruct the whole telephone conversation based on the words spoken from my end.

There was a long-distance call for me. It was Emma.

'Mum, it's me. Listen, I'd better be quick. I've got some news for you.' The pause in her sentence made my heart beat suddenly faster.

'Oh . . . well. You'd better say – is it good or bad?' I asked in some confusion.

'It's definitely good for me,' she answered, and I could tell from her voice that she was smiling her most mischievous smile. 'But it may not be so good for you.'

I waited.

'The fact is, I've got married.'

I remembered my vow, when my mother was being so difficult about my own marriage. I promised myself then that I would never, ever behave the way she had to any daughter of mine. I vowed that I would let her marry the man she wanted, when and where she wanted, and in any way she liked.

After a few stunned seconds, I managed a feeble reply.

'Oh, congratulations,' I said, followed by a rather overly casual: 'Well, so who did you marry?'

'A Sudanese.' In the light of what I was later to discover, her answer seemed so simplistic, so understated. But in my state of numb shock, I couldn't think of anything other than monosyllabic questions.

'When?' I asked, my voice catching. Any hopes and dreams I had ever entertained of watching proudly as Emma walked down the aisle, on the arm of her brother in lieu of Bunny, of hosting a reception and waving her off on her honeymoon amid a shower of confetti while I wept into a lace handkerchief all vaporised.

'Oh, not long ago.' She seemed reluctant to give me anything but the most basic details.

'But *where?*' My heartbeat was by now pounding in my ears. I felt unbearably hot, as my colleagues' eyes watched me across the room and I reached for a glass of water.

'We had a Presbyterian service in Sudan,' Emma said, simply.

Disbelief evolved into a numbing realisation that what Emma was telling me was perfectly true. The crackling silence on the line between us was palpable.

'Then I wish you every happiness,' I managed to say, though it came out with a ludicrous ring of formality. For God's sake, I sounded like my mother, I chided myself, but I was a long way from putting any sensible thoughts together. Trying to assemble my feelings, I asked: 'But I mean . . . have any of your friends met this man?'

'Oh yes,' Emma gushed. 'Willie's met him.'

The mention of Willie's name shook me further. Poor Willie, I knew how much he loved Emma and hoped that she might one day marry him. The last time I had heard from the pair of them, they were very much an item and I had been pleased. Now, Emma had decided on a sudden and radical change of tack. Willie was history, and this Sudanese man was her betrothed instead.

'So what's he like – your husband?' I asked, my knees feeling so wobbly, I had to sit down.

'Speak to Willie,' Emma said brusquely. 'He'll tell you. Look, I really must dash, Mum. I'll try to get through soon. Bye.'

With that the line went dead and she was gone.

My eldest daughter. The baby I had held proudly in my arms in the Assam tea garden hospital, and had told Bunny how I felt she was really going to make something of her life. She had stepped into another world from anything I knew. I accepted that Africa was her passion; I knew she was committed to her work there, but I think, secretly, I always believed that it was something she would grow out of: that one day she would simply announce that she had had enough and was coming home: to marry Willie or someone like him; that she'd have a traditional English wedding and live back in this country and settle down. But, instead, she had made her own choice. A choice which would take her away from me, and from her family, forever. I felt shattered.

Some moments are virtually obliterated by shock. I probably rose as steadily as I could to my feet, muttering something about fetching myself a cup of tea, under the frowning scrutiny of my eavesdropping colleagues. I suppose I eventually came back to my desk, to look uncomprehendingly (and therefore unconvincingly) at documents dealing with matters that suddenly held no interest for me. Even after I had left the office that evening, I was still in such a trance I can't remember driving back to Surrey. What woke me from that strange dream, not long after I'd reached the sanctuary of home, made everything more curious.

The telephone rang. When I answered, I heard Willie's voice. This was pure coincidence: unknown to me, he had come over to England for a brief stay. He'd been out of touch with Emma for quite some time – so he had no idea of what had happened – and he'd rung simply to find out how she was, where she was.

'Emma's fine, I *think*,' I told him falteringly. 'Look, Willie, I'm rather at a loss for words.'

I could sense the growing anxiety in his voice. 'But why? Where is she?'

'She's in Nairobi,' I answered, cursing Emma silently for leaving me to break the news to Willie in this way.

'But – has anything happened to her?' Sweet Willie, always so concerned.

'Yes,' I replied, taking a deep breath. 'You see, Willie, she rang me today to tell me that she's married.'

There was an agonising delay. Then the outburst. 'Married! Who's she married?' I could sense the hurt in his voice.

'He's Sudanese,' I replied. Still that awkward pause, filled only with the sound of Willie's breath. 'Apparently you know him . . .'

There was an even longer silence. Then a sharp intake of breath followed by a groan. 'Oh no . . . oh God,' he started, as my own pulse increased. 'She's married Riek.'

'Riek?' I echoed, my anxiety mounting. 'Well, who is this Riek character?'

Willie had a voice like lead. 'Riek's a commander of the Sudan People's Liberation Army. He's fighting a guerrilla war out there,' he said, adding flatly: 'Maggie, he's a war lord.'

Still reeling from the shock of Emma's news, I was now so winded that my knees gave way completely and I sank back into an armchair, unable to speak. A war lord? My new son-in-law was a guerrilla leader? How could that be? How could Emma be so stupid? What about the dangers to her? My mind swam with all the dreadful possibilities, the risks she was taking. Suddenly overwhelmed, I muttered something to Willie, replaced the receiver and burst into tears. How could she do this to me?

In the following days, weeks and finally months, I tried to reason out the conundrum of Emma's decision. Unable to contact her, to put any more questions to her, to glean any more information from any quarter, I was left to flounder in the waves of fear and worry and anger. I didn't know what to make of the news. I had heard people refer to 'African madness' – had Emma gone mad? Was she just being naive? Or politically ambitious, simply setting a stage for herself which would bring her publicity? She had loved to be at the centre of attention ever since she was a child. Was this one more manifestation of that desire, and, perhaps, a fatal one? Or did she merely want to push unconventionality to its limits? In time, I could see that all these elements played a part.

I agonised night after sleepless night over how I was going to tell our friends and relatives the news – dear Aunt Margot, my father, and others from a generation where it would all seem so strange. But I finally found my courage and I began to break the news to all those who needed to know. To be fair, the vast majority responded magnificently, trying to bolster my spirits and joking with me that at least she had saved me the cost of a big English wedding.

And, on reflection, I realised that I did trust Emma's judgement and that I'd give her all the love and support I could. She was an exceptional young woman, she had always been so, and whereas before it had made her seem endearingly adventurous, if it now made her appear foolhardy or if her actions frightened the living daylights out of me, then I would just have to deal with that. It was my problem not hers. She hadn't changed a bit; she was being true to her spirit, the spirit I had nurtured, and I could hardly now complain just because it didn't suit my overly conventional plans for her.

Also, Emma cared passionately about the people of southern Sudan, and she lived to prove that devotion, by helping them and risking her life for them. And, much more importantly, I came to realise that she was deeply and immovably in love with Riek.

And so, in due course, I arrived at a state of calm acceptance, a level of peace with what had happened, and even an ability to revel in Emma's 'spirit of enterprise'. Besides, there were other puzzles for me to ponder. I wondered what on earth I was going to do with the thirty-four long horned cows which had apparently been offered to me by Riek's family as the bride price.

The war and Emma's work went on. Death and the fear of it were never far away, but Emma remained stoically at her new husband's side. The villagers welcomed her as their own, and built a special mud hut for her and Riek in Nasir, daubing the walls inside and out with pretty hand-painted motifs. She had a new home.

By this time the SPLA had reached the height of its power, capturing almost all the south, and was well placed to begin a push towards the territories held by the Khartoum government. It was clear to everyone who knew about the polarised politics of the region that Emma's influence over Riek was considerable. She had already tried to bring in a code of conduct for his men, to prevent some of the more barbaric practices such as rape, pillage and the recruitment of child soldiers, and had many long and heated discussions with him late into the night about the consequences of his war on the ordinary people – those she had come so far to help.

She continued to lobby for the projects closest to her heart – educational and medical facilities, and funding for small industries and agricultural programmes. She set about developing a women's project, to give Sudanese women a greater say in matters of importance. This became the Southern Sudan Women's Association (SSWA). It was the women, Emma always argued, who were left to struggle with life and death once the boys with the Kalashnikovs had marched on. Emma assumed that her work with SKI could carry on unaffected by her change of marital status, and she ploughed straight back into the schools programme on the morning after her marriage. A few days after the wedding, she left Riek's side to fly to Nairobi and order more supplies. From there, she sent Peter Dalglish, SKI's director, a regular field report, updating him on the latest developments. The typewritten report had a small addendum: 'PS. I married Riek Machar in a short ceremony in his community.'

The news came as a tremendous shock in Toronto. Nobody could believe that someone of Emma's experience, hired by an apolitical organisation which was having problems enough getting aid to the war zone, could have done anything so foolish as to ally herself, so permanently and irrefutably, with one side of the fighting. Peter was stunned, and so were his board, who voiced their disapproval in no uncertain terms. Reluctant to act in haste, and still impressed by Emma's achievements so far, Peter advised caution and persuaded his team to wait and see what it all meant.

For the newly-weds, still in the first flush of their love, the war and the internal politics of aid agencies were all but forgotten for a while. Riek pined for his new bride when she flew to Nairobi. He bombarded her with letters and radio messages, professing his love. In one, dated two weeks after their wedding, he thanked her for the Tolstoy novel and love letter she had sent him and added:

'Since I got your first letter I did not know how to reply to it. I was overwhelmed with joy but I know very well that I love you and I am in love with you. Before I received your letter I was waiting expectantly. I read it over many times and kept it in my pocket, afraid of losing it, and eager to snatch a few moments alone to read it again, even at the airstrip. All these days, my thoughts and feelings are on and about you.

By day, when I am awake, I keep touching the wedding ring you gave me, probably to feel you and to kiss you even if you are far away. By night, when I am in bed, memories of our love focus so strongly that I keep awake for long hours on the bed in our love nest. When I am not asleep I think about you and what you might be doing at that time, and many times I spend hours lying on the bed trying to reach out to you by telepathy.

There are moments when your sweet, lovely voice wakes me up from a deep sleep . . . I am so proud that I am married to you. You can see how much I miss you: very much. No siestas any more, no lovely private talks. Emma, if wishes were horses, beggars would ride – your people's saying. It is my wish that you come back to me in Nasir before you leave for England. Tom Jones' greatest hit: "If loving you is wrong, I don't want to be right. For being right means being without you." I

*love you. Come. I am in love with you. I like surprises, do not tell me
the date of your arrival, but only the week. Bye, bye, I love you a lot.
Riek.'*

Hardly able to believe that such an outpouring of emotion came from a
man who had spent most of his life ordering bombing raids and military
attacks, Emma felt honour-bound to comply with his wishes. She did
indeed return to Nasir to spend a few snatched moments with her new
husband, this time taking Sally with her, who could hardly believe what
her best friend had done and was determined to meet this man for
herself. Strolling arm in arm with Emma around the village and the
garrison, being introduced to everyone and joining in with their simple
activities, she found it difficult to accept that Emma had given up her
vibrant life in Nairobi for the naked austerity of life with the forgotten
people of southern Sudan. But, in Goethe's words, 'Boldness has genius,
power and magic in it.'

On 17 July 1991, Emma returned to Britain as planned, only this
time as a bride. It was the first time I had seen her in seven months and
I was more than a little apprehensive about our meeting. It was, after all,
her first visit home since the wedding. She arrived with Sally at Heathrow, exactly a month after the marriage ceremony, and, I could tell
immediately, she was completely happy.

She soon threw herself back into English life, making a mess of my
little house and completely taking everything over. I came home one
evening to find floury footprints down the hall, up the stairs and in just
about every room. She'd been baking.

'Oh, Mum, don't tell me off,' she said, flour and pastry all over her
face, her hair and her clothes. 'I don't get a chance to do this at home.'

How could I chide her?

Apart from wrecking my kitchen, she also spent her time feeding
her mind with visits to the theatre, cinema and art galleries. She
embraced her western life; so very different from the one she now lived.
Friends spoke of her that summer looking stunning, chic 'in a twenties
way', vivacious to the point of exuberance, and obviously very much in
love.

It was one afternoon in my garden during that trip, while she was in her usual relaxed pose on my bench as I weeded the flowerbeds amid the bees, that she casually dropped into the conversation the fact that she was Riek's second wife.

'Oh,' I answered innocently, looking up, 'I didn't think they had much divorce in the Nuer tribe.'

Emma grinned impishly at me over her designer sunglasses.

'They don't,' she said, as I sat back on my heels suddenly and wondered what she meant.

Not only had my daughter married a war lord, but she had married a polygamist. She was the second of two wives, but there was nothing to stop Riek taking three or even four wives – as many as he could afford. His father had had five. Despite my attempts not to be, I was shocked. Emma revelled in her shock value.

'Imagine what the nuns at the Convent of the Assumption would say if they knew I'd entered a polygamous marriage,' she giggled. 'But then they do say convent girls are the worst.'

Riek's first wife was called Angelina and was the daughter of a Nuer politician who had been one of Riek's teachers at school. They were childhood sweethearts and had married in 1981, when she was only eighteen, and she now lived alone and on the dole in west London with their three children; a fact I found ironic – that his Sudanese wife should be living in Britain, while his British wife lived in a mud hut in Sudan. Although Emma had tried to make contact with her to pay her respects, Angelina, as Wife Number One, was apparently furious that Riek hadn't asked her permission to marry again, and she refused to see her new rival.

Emma was ebullient to the point of irritation about Riek's polygamy. She explained that the system had come about in answer to the war – so many women were left widowed or fatherless that unless they could be taken in by another man as his new wife, they would die. She bragged that if such a system was set up in western society, there would be no marriage breakdown.

'Look how much divorce there is in Britain,' she would say, 'and how many people commit adultery. Nearly everyone. You don't get that in Sudan because of the polygamous system.'

Privately, I wholeheartedly disagreed. There would have been no way I could have stayed with Bunny and his mistress under the same roof. I knew that, despite her protestations, Emma couldn't have borne it either. I secretly wondered if she was truly at ease with her enforced unconventionality. One thing, however, remained frighteningly real: the war. Despite personal happiness in Emma's life, the political situation in southern Sudan began to deteriorate to a dangerous degree in her absence. Growing differences of political belief and strategy between Riek and Garang emerged, and darkness and danger loomed. The more I read of the war, the more I began to feel a sense of impending doom. Was it a 'just' war? Was any war just? I couldn't help but wonder if Riek was – as Emma always claimed – blameless in his actions.

Emma was an invaluable asset to him in his struggle to gain recognition for his rebel faction; her commitment and loyalty to him were unswerving. She was the consummate politician, the perfect consort. She spent much of her time networking with the Sudanese community in London, meeting people at the Africa Centre in Covent Garden, and sometimes giving talks on her experiences in Eastern Equatoria. She desperately wanted Riek to come to England and meet her family, she longed to parade him for all to see, but it was not to be.

In a letter to Emma in early August, Riek wrote:

'I will not be coming to England though I would love to do so while you are there. My presence in the field at this time is crucial. I am nervous about writing a letter to your Mum now. I will do so when you return, after you have briefed me of her reaction to our marriage. I do not like hitting the wrong note since I am ignorant of her views about us. I would really love to drop her a line, but I think I will wait until you are back.

I have missed you so much. I dream every night of you. I wish you'd come back sooner to Nasir. Life here without you is empty . . . I want you in Nasir. I hope you are enjoying all the razzmatazz and the extravaganza of the modern world. Don't be excessive. A million kisses, Riek.'

The letter, on green notepaper, was adorned with tiny hand-drawn hearts.

Emma didn't always heed her new husband's advice and continued to undertake a dizzy round of social engagements, travelling to Yorkshire, Shropshire and the West Country to visit friends and relatives. With spontaneous generosity, she paid for Yo to fly with her to Spain for a week to stay with friends, a holiday which they both enjoyed and which helped to heal the rift between them which had started to emerge in childhood and which had widened since Emma's marriage. They flew home on 19 August, tanned and relaxed, before Emma took the train to London to stay with friends and engage in some more serious partying.

Little did she know what astonishing, historic events were going on in Sudan in her absence, nor how much they would come to affect her life.

11

Emma had just returned from her holiday in Spain and was oblivious to what was happening in Sudan when Riek chose to challenge Garang's autocratic leadership, accusing him of human rights abuses, of using child soldiers, allowing his men to commit atrocities and of imprisoning his critics. Garang threatened to strip Riek of his authority, a situation which would have been unthinkable for Emma's husband, so long at the top of the tree of power.

FURIOUS, HE AND HIS CO-COMMANDER, DR LAM AKOL, ANNOUNCED A COUP ON WEDNESDAY 28 AUGUST 1991, IN A BID TO REMOVE JOHN GARANG FROM POWER. They claimed a platform for greater democracy, promised respect for human rights and declared their aim for an independent southern Sudan, rather than a secular united Sudan. Emma was staying in London with John Ryle at the time, an old friend and the man who had delivered Riek's first-ever love note to her. She was staggered to hear the news on the BBC in a report by Colin Blane when she got in from a shopping expedition at six o'clock that night.

The telephone didn't stop ringing all evening and all night, as she and John and all her Sudanese contacts in both Britain and Kenya tried to find out what was going on. Angelina, Riek's wife, unexpectedly made contact with Emma and expressed her shock and disappointment at the news. Emma was inundated with people arriving on the doorstep, telephone calls and faxes. She called SPLA contacts in Kenya and was told nothing. They said it was a rumour, that Riek would not be so stupid and not to worry. But, in her next phone call, another contact would say that it was true and that Riek and Lam had asked Garang to resign and that he had been detained by Riek's men.

Over the next few days, Emma stayed at John Ryle's anxiously waiting for news. I fielded calls at home in Surrey and passed Emma's contact number on. She desperately wanted to speak to Riek, to find out what he was up to, to see if the BBC reports were true, to find out whether he had taken a major, probably dangerous, political move in her absence and completely without her knowledge. To compound her problems, by the Sunday, Angelina was on the doorstep, wanting to know more. It was a difficult meeting for the two women as each waited for reports of the man they loved. They were further frustrated by a misinformation programme started by Garang's supporters in Nairobi, which meant that all the news they received thereafter was either false or second-hand speculation.

Emma, smoking cigarettes and drinking endless cups of coffee, was at her wits' end, especially when (unconfirmed) reports began to circulate that Riek and Lam had been arrested by Garang's men and executed. Garang certainly made a declaration to the BBC that night that he was 'still in charge' and claimed to have the support of nine members of his High Command. Emma didn't sleep a wink that night, waiting for news of her beloved husband. They had been married just ten weeks.

The next day, Monday, Emma discovered that Garang was spreading rumours that she was a spy for MI5 and had orchestrated the SPLA split. He claimed that she had gone to Europe at such a critical time to gain foreign support. How little did he know – she had been sunning herself in Spain with her sister, shopping and eating out with friends, and sitting at home with me in Surrey, gossiping into the night. Foreign support indeed. In the face of such vitriolic opposition, Angelina became an unlikely ally, in that people automatically assumed that she still hated Riek for marrying Emma, and so they confided information in her which they would not have shared with Riek's second wife. Garang's wife, Rebecca, spoke to Angelina and told her: 'Don't worry, it's all the white girl's doing.' To her credit, Angelina reported straight back to Emma, although the news obviously distressed my daughter greatly.

In her diary for that Monday, Emma scribbled: 'I was upset. It never crossed my mind that I would be implicated. They thought our marriage was purely political.' Later that night, drained and distraught, Emma took a train to Surrey and came back to stay with me. We sat at the kitchen table, talking late into the night over numerous mugs of black coffee. Emma smoked and smoked, played with her wedding ring and was obviously extremely upset. The calls kept coming for her, with more and more news, and each one only served to distress her more.

Garang had now dubbed the split 'Emma's War' and continued to circulate rumours that she was behind the whole scheme. He said she wanted to be the 'First Lady' of a new united southern Sudan and that she was a spy in the pay of the British government who had been sent to inveigle her way into Riek's heart. In the paranoid culture of the war-ravaged region, and within two months of her wedding, Emma now found herself at the centre of a vicious tribal war. She had somehow become Sudan's Public Enemy Number One, and the realisation that Garang was using her as a political weapon left her totally ill-prepared to handle his accusations. It also left her the most distressed I had ever seen her.

Sitting in the kitchen, I let her just talk and talk as she poured out her hurt and concern.

'What if Riek's been killed, Mummy?' she asked me, her eyes wide with fear. 'What will I do then?' At another point, she turned to me, wiping her tears, and said: 'Mummy, you and I are very similar, we are both very brave, and we both have courage.' I patted her hand and gave her what counsel I could. She was caught up in the middle of something over which she had no control. She had no choice but to wait for fate to deal her a hand.

The news from Sudan got worse. The Nuer and Dinka tribes were obviously split by the in-fighting, but the Dinka chose to side with Garang, and the Nuer with Riek. Within weeks, Riek's soldiers – including the White Army, which was led by a provocative 'prophet' – had swept into Garang's hometown of Bor and massacred some 2,000

Dinka civilians. It was a vicious and brutal attack. Women were disembowelled, children were tied up and shot, old men were hung from the trees. Thousands more men, women and children fled to the swamps, where many died of hunger and malaria.

Riek always denied any involvement with the attack on Bor, and said his men had acted without his authority and had gone out of his control, incited by the White Prophet with false promises of Dinka booty. But he was, undoubtedly, seriously discredited by the event. There were rumours that he had consorted with the enemy, received military supplies from the government in Khartoum secretly, to help the Arab Muslims reclaim the Dinka heartland. Whatever the truth, the ever-increasing aftershocks continued to cause death and destruction for many years to come. Bitter tribal wrangling worsened the conflict in the south and the Khartoum government exploited the situation to seize back many key areas. Once, when Emma challenged Riek over the massacre, he admitted to her that he had underestimated the Dinka nationalism.

Garang was incensed – quite apart from the personal affront of Riek's mutiny, and the attack on Bor, the SPLA had been as close as they had ever been to seizing back lands from Khartoum. Now they had played straight into enemy hands by dividing into two bitter factions. United We Stand, Divided We Fall had been their motto and yet they had divided in the worst way possible. He made it clear to all around him that he held Riek Machar and his English wife personally responsible for this disastrous new turn in Sudan's war-ravaged history. Such a declaration could only mean one thing. Emma's life was now in extreme danger.

It was never my business to persuade my daughter out of returning to Africa. I knew that her heart was set on going back to her husband and there was nothing I could or would do to stop her. But plenty of others tried. Even Angelina, when Emma went to say goodbye to her and the children and to videotape them all for Riek, warned her against it. But on 4 September 1991, exactly a week after she first heard of the split, Mrs Riek Machar caught a flight to Nairobi from London's Heathrow. I waved her goodbye with my heart in my mouth and wondered if I would ever see my daughter again.

Emma was followed all the way to Africa by one of Garang's men, whom she first spotted at Heathrow. In Nairobi, she stayed with friends for a while and tried to find out more about the political situation in Sudan, after confirming that Riek was still alive. Many friends begged her not to go back, but her mind was made up. On Monday 23 September, she flew to Nasir to be with Riek. Half-way through the journey, at the Sudanese border with Kenya, she was pulled off the plane and questioned by a belligerent UN official and faced hostility from all quarters. By the time she eventually reached Nasir and Riek, she was ready for a fight.

Steaming with fury, she marched into his tukul almost as soon as she arrived and laid into him verbally in such a way that the seven-foot giant was visibly shaken by her anger.

'What the hell do you think you've been playing at?' she screamed at him, backing him into a corner and almost overturning the table at which he had been sitting, writing. 'This marriage is meant to be a partnership, right?'

Riek nodded sheepishly, amazed to see her and further astonished by her fury. Bowing his head, he looked genuinely contrite. Emma, relieved and secretly delighted to see him again, refused to show any signs of softening.

'Do you have any idea what I have been through in England?' she asked, her eyes flashing. 'I didn't even know if you were alive or dead. My poor mother has had to put up with me sobbing at her kitchen table, while I waited for news.'

Riek's head remained bowed. His huge hands rested on the table in front of him, as he resisted the urge to reach out and pull his bride towards him, and into their marital bed.

Emma wouldn't let it go. 'I can't begin to tell you how angry I am with you for doing this, Riek. What on earth were you thinking? Have you gone mad?' She continued to let him know in no uncertain terms that she was livid with him for not confiding in her and not sharing his plans. It was their first big row, or would have been, had he responded in any way. Seeing that she wasn't going to get any answers, she swept out of his hut in a huff and stalked through the garrison, her eyes blazing with fury.

Spin a coin, spin a coin, all fall down;
Queen Nefertiti stalks through the town.
Over the pavements her feet go clack.
Her legs are as tall as a chimney stack;
Her fingers flicker like snakes in the air,
The walls split open at her green-eyed stare . . .

from 'Queen Nefertiti', Anon

It was a long time before Emma forgave Riek for what she saw as a personal betrayal. His actions marked a turning point in their young relationship. This was the first time she had realised that he could be duplicitous and deliberately keep things from her. Although he had always been happy to seek her advice and accept her help in writing up his reports, she realised now that the very nature of African politics and the culture she had married into was such that it was unlikely she would ever be fully included or confided in. It made her wonder what other decisions had been made or would be made in the future without her knowledge.

That view was worsened by her discovery that the plans to split from Garang had been afoot long before she and Riek married. Riek's partner in the split, Dr Lam Akol – who had never approved of the marriage and told Riek he was a fool for weakening their cause – was the prime mover. He needed Riek alongside him to keep the support of the thousands of Nuer loyal to their movement, but it was he who orchestrated the split and who pushed Riek into it that August. The two men had been plotting for months and decided to enact their plans while Emma was safely out of the country. Riek had foolishly not considered that she might be implicated in the move, he just wanted her out of the way if and when Garang's troops arrived. His attitude had always been that it was nobody else's business who he married and when, and that Emma had nothing to do with the split.

Now that Emma had been so blatantly implicated, however, he realised he had badly misjudged the situation, and he was genuinely sorry. Listening to his wife as she vented her anger, he wished things could have been different, that he could turn back the clock. Emma made Riek promise that he would never treat her so badly again, and would include her in all decisions that affected both her and their people. If Riek had not realised it before, he now knew that his new wife was a force to be reckoned with. He was amazed she had come back to him at all in the circumstances, and he recognised her return as an act of extreme courage.

Emma set to work immediately, doing all she could to rally support for Riek. She helped him to draw up draft resolutions, contact support-ers in Ethiopia and Kenya and arrange for Lam Akol to go to Nairobi to meet a delegation, to see if some sort of SPLA reconciliation could be effected. Riek listened to her counsel and advice, her views mattered enormously to him now, because he realised they reflected the way that other outsiders would perceive the situation. Somehow in the middle of all the muddle, four months into their marriage, Riek found the time to write his first letter to me, his new mother-in-law, introducing himself formally and thanking me for my support. He wrote:

'We are both fine. It is terribly humid but we are not complaining . . . I am aware of the fact that we deprived you of some of your motherly rights in the marriage ceremony – we risked and gambled on your support. I was relieved when Emma came back with your complete support.

The main reason we married in Africa is because I was not sure when I would travel to England because I am tied down by a lot of work in the field. I love Emma very much and that is why I married her. I will try my best to be a good husband to her. I anticipated problems would crop up . . . and we are in the middle of another political crisis within our movement at the moment. She has been supportive and understanding in all these difficulties. I assure you that Emma and I are happy together and will continue to be. She is a courageous woman. I adore her.'

Emma also wrote to me, her first letter since she got back:

'Dearest Mum, What can I say? A huge thank you for putting up with me over the summer, supporting me, advising me and giving me such *fun. I did so enjoy my holiday – a little marred at the end by the political situation in Sudan. But now that I am back in Nasir with Riek, I am happy and relaxed. The simplicity of life has returned.*

Riek is well and, as I imagined, as "cool as a cucumber". The response is positive from the army and the population to their declaration to reject John Garang as leader of the SPLA. They are expecting a "creeping revolution". My fellow expatriate staff have been very supportive and welcoming, especially my office. We are sitting under a waxing African moon, the mosquitoes are out in force. The various night sounds chirrup, the fireflies flash.

The Sobat River which runs through Nasir is rising fast. The other day a rather large fish jumped into the boat as we were motoring along. We ate it the next day. The water hyacinths, introduced from South America by a priest, clog up the river. They adapted rather too easily to the climate and have caused huge logistical problems to boats. Outside a leopard skin dries. It apparently mauled eight people before it was killed. The weaver birds are busy making their nests in a nearby tree, chatting furiously – probably gossiping. See you soon, Emma xxx'

Emma stayed with Riek for a month, and a great deal of her energy was spent helping her husband to try to effect reconciliation talks with Garang, hiring planes and arranging international delegates' accommodation, so that Riek would be able to put his side of the story about the split and the attack on Bor. Sadly, the talks came to nothing and the split remained a bitter one, exacerbating the age-old rivalry between the Nuers and the Dinkas. Garang sent his men to Riek's home town of Leer twice, to stage a revenge attack for Bor, but were successfully fought off each time.

On 19 October, Emma flew to Nairobi to resume her duties and commitments with SKI and to do some shopping for necessary supplies. Her hastily scrawled shopping list in her diary included a screw injection pump, five cassette head cleaners, batteries for her Sony Walkman, photocopying paper, Tippex, an eraser and staples. She also had more important things on her mind. Two days earlier, she had been very alarmed to hear rumours that she was about to be dismissed from her job because of her allegiance to Riek and his latest move, and she wanted to speak to Peter Dalglish, personally, in Toronto to confirm that this wasn't true.

Sick with the flu by the time she arrived at Sally's, she couldn't sleep that first night, for worrying about her job. She left several late-night messages on Peter's answering machine to no avail. She was concerned for the future of the project should she be dismissed. The need for her presence was even greater since the SPLA split – with renewed fighting in the south and thousands more families displaced, any education the children had been receiving would be once again disrupted. She was determined to keep the systems running as long as possible.

Emma had always been so moved by the keenness of the young Sudanese to learn. She once told me how children, who had walked hundreds of miles through the bush after being made homeless, would arrive somewhere like Nasir and the first thing they would ask for was a book and a pencil, rather than food.

'Without education, there is no future,' she would say, over and over, like a mantra. Her bodyguards learned that as their first sentence of English. I often wondered whether Emma remembered the struggle I had to educate my children, and my determination that, whatever else went, their education was paramount. I suspected she did remember.

A few days after arriving in Nairobi, Emma finally got hold of Peter Dalglish and had a long telephone conversation with him. It was true, he confirmed, he had been considering her future in the light of the SPLA split. She urged him not to make any hasty decisions, claiming that the situation could change any day. Using the charm that had first beguiled him, she managed to persuade him to come to Africa and discuss matters with her, face to face. She knew that once she had him in her clutches, she would almost certainly get her own way.

Fearless as ever about the continuing danger to her life, she returned to Nasir after a tense and exhausting trip in the city, and waited for word from Peter. Acknowledging that the Upper Nile was hot and inhospitable and among the most unhealthy of African environments, she was nonetheless happier there than anywhere else. She loved the people and had begun to understand their culture. Africa was becoming her life and she realised that the important thing about the continent was not its landscapes or animals, but the politics of human relationships; and that change had to come from within.

Insightful as she might have been with people whose skin colour was different from her own, she seemed not always to have the same clarity of mind when it came to relationships with others. On 1 November 1991 Peter Dalglish officially sacked Emma from SKI because he considered her to be no longer impartial to both factions. In retrospect, he probably had no choice. She had compromised her position, he said, and that of SKI. Emma was deeply hurt at the news and the manner in which Peter Dalglish's letter came to her – by fax from Nairobi. He wrote:

'After much deliberation we have come to the conclusion that we must ask you to relinquish your responsibilities as co-ordinator of the Street Kids International School Programme in southern Sudan. The programme is ambitious in scope, covering a large part of Eastern Equatoria, most of which is under the control of the SPLA. The co-ordinator must be someone who has free and unlimited access to as much of this region as possible. In addition, as the SRRA [the Sudan Relief and Rehabilitation Association – the relief wing of the SPLA] remains the implementing partner for the programme, the co-ordinator must be someone whom they are comfortable working with on a day-to-day basis.

We are not carrying out the programme in isolation . . . We must ensure that the programme continues without interruption, and hope that you will assist us in identifying a possible successor for your position, and in handing over your responsibilities in an orderly manner by 1 January 1992 . . . We acknowledge that you have made an extraordinary contribution to the lives of the thousands of children who have attended programme-assisted schools. I know that your priority is the welfare of these children. I admire your dedication and your energy. Let's hope that the school programme can continue for many years, no matter how difficult the circumstances, Yours sincerely, Peter Dalglish.'

In a separate letter to Alastair Scott-Villiers at UNICEF, Dalglish admitted that 'Most of the success of the programme was due to the extraordinary commitment of Emma McCune, who made the children her life.' But he added that Emma's association with Riek and the Lam Akol faction 'complicated matters' and told Alastair of her sacking. He proposed that Emma now work with UNICEF and the ICRC (the International Committee of the Red Cross) to continue helping the schools programme – by then reaching approximately 20,000 children – as she 'knows the region well and has strong local contacts'.

Years later, he wrote:

> 'Emma's very public relationship with Riek put us in a bind . . . Emma was labelled the Yoko Ono of southern Sudan . . . questions were being asked about the role of Street Kids International. In the end I had to fire Emma. I had to ask her to step aside, and to serve only as an informal advisor to the education programme, but I knew that she would refuse my request. She was never one for compromise. When she received my termination letter by fax, she called me from Wilson Airport in Nairobi. The conversation was short and painful. "You're punishing me because I fell in love," she accused me. I told her that I was firing her for the sake of the 20,000 children involved in our schools programme, that we could not get caught up in the internal politics of the SPLA. But she wouldn't listen to me, and she hung up the phone. It was the last time we spoke.'

Peter was right about one thing. Emma was indeed furious with him for firing her. She spent days drafting and redrafting a two-page acerbic response in her defence. In it, she said:

> 'I understand your reservations about employing me as the SKI co-ordinator while the present political crisis is happening in southern Sudan. I advised you not to make a hasty decision as the situation is uncertain at present, and a decision at this time may be seen as political and exploited by both sides of the SPLA faction. Obviously, this advice has not been heeded. As I told you over the phone, I married a man that I love who happens to be a Sudanese and a high-ranking SPLA commander. I knew that my marriage would not be easy, but what to do? You can't go around looking for an ideal situation and then say "Now I want to fall in love". Unfortunately, life is not like that.'

She accused him of being unnecessarily unkind in his tone, and pointed out that were it not for her fund-raising abilities, the SKI project would not have been able to function at all for the previous six months. It is clear from her letter and phone call that she was mortified by her sacking, but her entreaties were to no avail. Peter Dalglish was upset by her anger and wrote her a poem about 'the moving hand of time'. But, on the instructions of his board, he had made his mind up and a successor for Emma was quickly chosen.

Emma was devastated. Quite apart from the fact that she loved her job and relied on the US$12,000 annual salary to feed and clothe herself (when the money arrived on time) her lifeline in and out of southern Sudan had been unexpectedly severed. In the light of her sacking, the UN had likewise accused her of losing her neutrality and instructed its staff to ostracise her, forbidding her to fly on any of its aid planes in and out of Kenya. It even banned its pilots from carrying any of her mail or supplies.

With no source of income, she was virtually trapped in the south. Without access to Kenya, her official educational work had come to an end. Almost as distressing, she was boycotted by people she had previously considered friends, banned from flying with pilots who knew her so well that they had shown her photographs of their children, and mocked by some of the very aid workers she had spent so much time with, setting up vital projects for the rural communities. One former colleague even commented to her:

'What do you expect if you marry a nigger?'

It was an extremely tough time for Emma. All her life, she had been the centre of attention, the striking-looking woman people wanted to see, to meet and to talk to. She liked to fascinate and to fire imaginations, flirt and toy with the men in her company, galvanise people into action and titillate with her tales from the bush. There had never been a truer test of her love for the rebel commander she had vowed to spend the rest of her days with, as she was abandoned by many she knew, forsaken in the wilderness without money, status or the companionship which had previously been her life's blood.

There was only one thing to do, as far as she could see. Make Riek's plan work, enable and ennoble him. If he were to win in the battle for

Emma and Riek's wedding on 17 June 1991 in Ketbek, Southern Sudan, was presided over by Riek's adjutant resplendent in pink quilted dressing-gown

Emma on the Sobat river (*Richard Ellis/The Sunday Times*)

Riek and Emma photographed for a television documentary about their lives in Sudan (*Wildcat Films*)

Emma with Riek and his bodyguards in Nasir, Southern Sudan (*Peter Moszynski*)

Outside Emma and Riek's home – a tukul in Nasir (*Peter Moszynski*)

. . . and its beautifully decorated interior (*Peter Moszynski*)

Emma and Riek walked for five days to reach Ayod to celebrate the hallowed Leopard Skin Ceremony

Soldiers of the Sudan People's Liberation Army at a training camp (*Peter Moszynski*)

Emma with her great friend Sally Dudmesh at a
Genesis concert in 1992 during their summer visit
home from Africa

With my sister Sue in the Brecon
Beacons in Wales in 1991

Erica, Johnny and Jennie with Riek

The plane which brought me to Sudan for Emma's funeral, surrounded by local people who had waited hours in the broiling sun (*Peter Moszynski*)

Emma's coffin is borne aloft by the people who loved her (*Peter Moszynski*)

A soldier carrying a bucket of flowers which quickly wilted in the heat (*Peter Moszynski*)

Me with Annabel Ledgard and Johnny at the burial ground

Emma's grave at Leer, Southern Sudan (*Peter Moszynski*)

Sudanese mourners (*Peter Moszynski*)

Emma's funeral service in All Saints' Cathedral, Nairobi, Kenya (*Peter Moszynski*)

Emma's legacy: Teaching Emmanuel, the refugee boy whom she helped, to use a computer

Her dog Come On being transported in great style by boat to the next village (*Heather Stewart*)

Talking to Stephen, Riek's bodyguard, during my visit to Khartoum to research this book

leadership of the SPLA, then she would be back in a position of authority too, able to command the respect and admiration of those who had rejected her, and resume her important work with the children of southern Sudan. Giving herself to Riek's cause full-time, she supported him in any way she could, advising him and guiding him, sharing his vision of a country in which there could be pluralistic politics, and they could endeavour to catch up economically with their neighbours.

She spent many hours typing up useful guidelines for visiting aid agencies (still used in the region today), encouraging communication between the villagers and the people trying to help them, and drafting constitutions and memoranda for her 'beloved husband' on their solar-powered computer. Fierce battles continued to rage between Riek and Garang's men; whole communities were wiped out and human rights abuses were rife. Death threats were made almost daily, and Emma lived in the constant knowledge that she might be dragged from her tukul and shot at any minute.

Declaring: 'I understand nothing,' and closing her eyes to the details of what was going on around her, she preferred not to know. She was in the middle of a war, people she knew and cared for in villages all around her were being killed and mutilated. Women were brutalised, children kidnapped, old men murdered. She was several hours' flight away from civilisation or any western allies, the only white woman for hundreds of miles, trapped in the centre of a bloody conflict whose origins she barely understood, listening to the gunfire in the distance. She never once complained. In the letters she was able to smuggle out, she wrote to friends of the personal empowerment she felt, climbing out of bed after lovemaking with Riek to draft some new political agenda.

In true McCune style, when in a crisis, dig. Emma turned to tilling the soil of her little vegetable garden for solace. She was determined to entice the new phalanx of heavily armed soldiers standing on permanent guard around her tukul to put down their weapons and plant. Emma's hunter-gatherer instincts surfaced and she supervised the planting of indigenous seeds that she had collected or seeds sent from England. Afraid that when she was busy or out in the swamps on patrol with Riek, her lovingly tended plants would die for lack of care, she set up a rota of watering and weeding among Riek's troops, a responsibility they carried out almost as gravely as that of saving her life if Garang's men attacked.

As befits a commander's wife, Emma often assumed some of Riek's duties as tribal chief when he was busy with affairs of war. She settled disputes, sitting in on traditional court meetings, and she monitored aid and involved herself in every kind of rehabilitation work. She cajoled people into temporarily forgetting about the conflict raging all around them, persuading unemployed carpenters into making furniture out of old ammunition crates; doling out fishing hooks, bulbs and tools she had smuggled in, forever urging the villagers to become self-sufficient, to help themselves in some small way.

Through the Southern Sudan Women's Association, she had learned a great deal about the society to which she now belonged, and she encouraged women to organise themselves into self-help groups to make anything they could sell to tourists in Kenya and which would help give them greater independence. She wanted to give them a 'voice'. In her romantic way, she believed that the women would one day control the destiny of Sudan. In return, the Nuer women adored and revered her. For hours she would lie outside her hut being waxed as they covered her in a caramelised mixture of lemon and sugar, before peeling it off. Body hair is considered freakish in Sudan and – with her lack of concern about whether her legs or armpits were shaved at any one time – she was constantly being badgered to remain hairless by her new Sudanese sisters.

Despite her fall from grace in western eyes, she still commanded the respect of many aid agencies; she had a deeper knowledge of the Upper Nile region than any other expatriate in the field, and some of the agencies harnessed that expertise secretly, asking her to use a pseudonym on her reports and updates. She thereafter used the name Alison Lewis, the two middle names Bunny and I christened her with in Assam.

When she simply had to get out to Kenya, she coaxed the UN pilots to smuggle her out as 'a spare engine' or 'tractor part'. Arriving in Nairobi, dusty and dirty, she would beg a bath and a bed for the night, borrow one of Sally's designer dresses and emerge, looking a million dollars, ready to gate-crash the next cocktail party and to shock the expatriate society, some of whom had so cruelly rebuffed her. She jokingly referred to herself as the 'First Lady-in-Waiting' and brushed off concerns for her welfare and political future.

She knew she had plenty of critics and innumerable enemies. Many considered her naive, an idealistic romantic who had probably caused more harm than good. Even her closest friends and relatives often found it difficult to reconcile her love for the people of southern Sudan with the inevitable consequences of her soldier husband's actions. How could she stand by a man whose split had caused more death and destruction in the region than even the worst famines? Erica had been against the wedding from the start and was now her most vociferous critic within our family circle, accusing her of stupidity and selfishness.

I was still divided and terribly torn. I had never met Riek, nor seen the place my daughter called home. I felt that if I could just meet him, look him in the eye and, in a way, try to peer into his soul, then my mind might be put at rest. I, of all people, knew how much Emma would be smarting from her experiences; reading between the lines of her rather too breezy letters about gardening and the weather, I knew that all was not well and I suspected that she could do with cheering up.

Putting all other matters aside, I decided to fly to Kenya for Christmas and spend time with Emma, to see how she was for myself. I arrived at dawn on 16 December 1991 so exhausted that I had to go straight to bed with an almighty migraine. I hardly saw my errant daughter at first. She had recently flown in from Sudan and was relishing the bustle and relative safety of Nairobi, rushing around gathering Christmas gifts for Riek, which she lovingly wrapped and sent to him in Nasir via a courier. She was delighted to enclose some English bars of chocolate I had brought out with me. Determined to make the most of my visit and of her brief dalliance back with civilisation, Emma had the whole trip organised. Sally threw a dinner party on my first night, at which Emma was on dazzling form. By six o'clock the following morning, we were on the road to Mombasa en route to Watamu, on the Indian Ocean coast – travelling fast and furiously in Roo and Simon's Land Cruiser so as to make it before dark.

What followed was the most magical few weeks with Emma and about six friends at Kilifi. We saw in the new year with Willie and his family and friends – including Annabel Ledgard, who had flown from England specially – on a small, remote and sparsely inhabited archipelago called Kiwaiyu. We travelled there by dhow in the middle of the night, our way lit only by a single hurricane lamp and the stars. Bobbing through the Indian Ocean, scattered with fluorescence, the crest of each wave catching the light, we were led by a school of dolphins. Blown by the warm night winds, we camped in the sand dunes under a tamarind tree overlooking a vast area of mangroves. It left an indelible mark on me as an utterly enchanted time with my daughter.

It was also, I think, the moment I truly fell in love with what Emma called the 'magic of Africa' and started to understand its special hold on her heart. Sunbathing side by side on the beach, we talked and talked, getting to know each other once again, and catching up where we had left off. Relaxing into the holiday, she did eventually let her guard down and confided in me her deep concerns for the future. Overall, though, I was encouraged. She was obviously still very much in love with Riek and never spoke of a future that did not include him. I gave her what advice I could, encouraged her to be brave and wished her every happiness. Lying under the stars, deep in conversation, we became best friends again, as well as mother and daughter. I am so grateful for the time we had.

Willie, understandably, did not think the holiday was quite so magical. He had not yet forgiven Emma for her past misdemeanours, and was resentful at her brazenness in joining his family's new year party. I thought it more than a little naughty of her to have imposed herself upon him when he was still hurting, but I honestly don't think she even noticed. Willie never allowed his underlying feelings to mar our holiday, however. It was, in every way, a great gathering of the Knocker family and friends; a holiday to cherish in the memory for each and every one of us.

Returning to Nairobi, Emma did everything within her power to get me to Sudan to meet my new son-in-law, but it was impossible. I wanted to meet Riek, especially after all she had told me, but the agencies had cold-shouldered Emma even more and refused point-blank to carry a relation of Riek's, claiming that I would have constituted a threat to their flights. We tried every trick in the book, changing my name, reverting to my maiden name of Bruce, considering bribing the pilots, but to no avail. So it was with tremendous sadness that I flew home early in 1992 having never met him, or seen my daughter's home. For Emma, it was one more stab in the back.

A letter arrived from her shortly after I returned to Surrey, echoing my sentiments. She wrote:

'I did so enjoy Christmas and new year. It was rather deflating to wave everyone off at the airport . . . It was all very disappointing that you were unable to travel to Sudan. Riek was very upset. He had built you a special hut in the compound. Anyway, next time you will be able to languish in it.

Our compound is getting established. My banana trees are doing exceedingly well, all the tree seeds I planted have germinated, although the rose cuttings and jasmine did not survive the journey from Nairobi to Lodwar, courtesy of ICRC, the Red Cross. Unfortunately the dill got eaten by ants. My vegetable garden is flourishing, mainly because a team of soldiers toil in it every day. The weather is rather pleasant at present, cool in the evenings and no mosquitoes, although the flies have replaced them somewhat. The full moon is up and we even played chess by moonlight last night. I was thrashed three times by Riek's radio operator.'

A few weeks after I had gone, Annabel did manage to visit Nasir under the guise of a journalist, claiming that her intention was to write a proposal on education in a war zone. I felt hurt and jealous that she could visit and I couldn't. But she did very kindly take some photographs of Emma's surroundings which consoled me no end as I was now able to picture her in her home and garden, as I pottered around mine.

I could see from the photographs that my daughter's life was very basic. The garrison compound was not large and she was the only woman allowed inside an area peopled by a militia of giants, on average six-and-a-half feet tall. She had her pet dog, 'Come On' – so called because she used to call out 'come on' to her and the soldiers believed that to be the dog's name – and several cats which she acquired to chase the rats, but which she was now afraid would be killed by either the local medicine man for their fur, or by the soldiers who were fed up with them eating their chickens. Inside her tukul, the furniture was extremely basic. There was a table made from a long piece of wood, balanced on bricks, some chairs made out of old ammunition boxes, some bookcases made from the same source, a bed, and a mosquito net. Local women had hand-painted murals and Nuer symbols on the mud walls, both inside and out, and there was a small pit latrine in the corner, but no running water or stove. She lived in constant dust and dirt, sweat and heat, and was rarely able to wash herself properly, brush her teeth or clean her clothes. She had virtually no privacy – her hidden supply of tampons, for example, became the subject of much local fascination when they were eventually discovered. Her 'wardrobe' consisted of a small bag tucked under her bed, in which she would keep her range of extraordinary outfits, mixing and matching hues and styles with the panache of a true bohemian.

Everything had to be cooked over wood fires, and Emma was rarely allowed to prepare a meal in her position as the commander's wife. The women of the garrison spent much time pounding the sorghum (sugar cane) into a thick brown paste, then spreading it thinly over a piece of metal heating on an open fire. Forming it into the dry pancake called kisra, it was then folded up like a pocket handkerchief and used to dip into goat stew or rice cooked in goat fat, or scoop up chunks of the bony Nile perch. Sometimes, if Emma's vegetable garden had been well tended by the soldiers in her absence, she could add the occasional tomato or piece of okra to their meals for a touch of western-style variety.

She longed for herbs and old English roses – she loved the way I had created an old-fashioned cottage garden at Little Farthings (based on memories of my grandmother's romantic garden in Scotland), and she often floated around her own little garden dressed like a latter-day Gertrude Jekyll in an absurdly incongruous Victorian period costume, consisting of her floppy felt hat, blue Hush Puppies with psychedelic pink socks, flower-print skirt and blouse, carrying a parasol. The only items that gave her away were a necklace made from indigenous seeds and the ever-present colourful beads and bangles, made of ostrich shells.

All her crops had been planted neatly in little circles edged with red half-bricks, laid out in a fan pattern more usually seen in the Home

Counties than in the dust of Sudan. Together in Kenya, we had gathered seeds for her to plant in Nasir, and she had ambitions of growing all sorts of prolific and unusual specimens, although Riek's bodyguards advised her strongly against planting shrubs close to her tukul for fear of attracting snakes.

I was glad she had settled into her home in Nasir, and refreshed from my visit to see her. Between us, we had decided that, from that year on, I would fly out every winter and she would come back to England every summer. That way, we would always see each other at least twice a year – even if we missed some important celebrations in between. The first for me was in March 1992, when I reached the ripe age of fifty. I was proud to have reached my half century and we had a tea party for a few friends and family at Springwood to celebrate. A friend, Guy Davenport, made me a chocolate cake in the shape of a tukul, with a tiny Union Jack made from rice paper fluttering at the top. Ever since discovering that Emma was married to – as he put it – the unofficial 'king' of southern Sudan, he dubbed me the 'Queen Mother' and I became the butt of many a joke. Among them was a mock official invitation to a soiree in my honour, at which the menu was to include mud pies, spear-mint cake, dessert rat, bombe surprise and kalashnakoffee.

Later that month it was my father's eightieth birthday. By now widowed for the second time, after a brief, but happy, marriage to a lovely lady called Polly, Daddy was living in Shropshire and in excellent health and spirits. He wore his red Bruce tartan kilt for the lunch party we hosted for family and friends. It was a month I wished Emma could have been home to share, but I understood and accepted why she couldn't. In April, she wrote a letter to us all from Nasir.

'The rains have started, an event everyone looks forward to. Thus the cultivation season has arrived. People are busy pounding the hard, but fertile soil. Before an impending rainstorm, the air is still, the humidity high – one waits, sweating, for the refreshing rain. I have been a little cut off from the outside world for the last two months as there have been no UN flights to Nasir – hence no letters.

I only received Mum's letter, written in February, two weeks ago, plus all our Guardian weeklies. Nevertheless, we followed the British *elections, the Royal scandals, tabloid gossip and world news via the BBC. Today, I heard that Francis Bacon, British painter, had died . . . The aid circus, as I call it, comes to town, leaves and returns again. Tonight, all the expatriates in Nasir are coming to supper. They will be sampling some of the produce from my vegetable garden which has proved successful. I tried my hand at hard labour the other day and am now suffering from numerous blisters – a sure sign that they see very little manual work. I now do weeding, a little less taxing than ploughing. We have grown tomatoes, lettuce, courgettes, papayas, mangoes, water melon, lady's fingers – in fact this land will grow anything.'*

Four months later, in July, she returned to Britain for her annual visit. I so looked forward to seeing her and the times we spent together were precious. Still working at Bear Stearns, I booked some holiday to coincide with hers and excitedly prepared for her visit. She would use my house as her base to take off to London to meet friends to catch up on the latest exhibition at the Tate or the National Gallery, and then we'd travel around the country visiting. Although it was a little like having a whirlwind arrive in the ordered solitude of my home, I loved it.

Collecting her at Heathrow, I was surprised by her appearance – she looked frail and painfully thin, and told me she had recently suffered from typhoid malaria. Sally had been nursing her in Nairobi until she was well enough to fly, and until I could take over. She was dreadfully gaunt and I was worried about her. She languished in bed for almost a week, sleeping most of the time, and gradually regained her strength. After plenty of rest, relaxation and good food, Emma was set to enjoy her home visit and – with her usual flair – started with three weddings in one weekend, Annabel Ledgard's on the Friday afternoon in London, followed by Madeleine Bunting, an old school friend and a journalist, on the Saturday morning in Wiltshire and Jo Mostyn, an old childhood friend, the same evening in Oxford.

Determined to make an entrance, Emma treated herself to a gorgeous mint green designer outfit in which she knew she looked stunning and attended all three, arriving fashionably late and making everybody's head turn. She was the life and soul at each event, on what was to be her last trip to England. I accompanied her to the first two weddings, giving us prime time together, an opportunity to catch up and to see many old friends. Emma clearly revelled in her novelty value, and soaked up the attention. She loved to tell people where she was living and who she had married. She boasted she could make a fortune out of secretly videotaping people's different reactions to her news.

'I'm living in southern Sudan, married to an African guerrilla chief in a "Flip-Flop" Army,' she told one British army officer's wife, her eyes bright in anticipation of the response.

The woman smiled politely and nodded as she sipped from her champagne flute and fiddled with her pearls.

'How *fascinating*,' she said, absent-mindedly. 'Which regiment?'

Emma had always loved parties, from the grand old days of Cowling Hall, and that last summer in England was no exception. She would dance and drink, flirt and flutter, reminding all the men who had ever loved her what they were missing, and assuring all her girlfriends that she was truly happy, while horrifying them with stories of gnats gnawing her forehead in her sleep, puff adders under the bed and spiders the size of dinner plates.

'People ask me what it's like being married to a guerrilla leader,' she would tell them in one of her best-loved sound bites, 'but I have never known anything else. I don't know what it's like being married to a stockbroker, so I have nothing to compare it with.' With a playful shrug of her shoulder and that endearing smile, she would be off to dance another reel, have another glass of champagne, or drag the giggling bride aside for a good old gossip.

When all the confetti had settled, she continued to party in one way or another, joining me, Sally, and the family, to see the band Genesis play at Knebworth among other events. In between the dizzy social whirl, she would come home to Little Farthings and take her familiar place on my garden bench while I weeded, making me rock back on my heels with laughter as she shared her jokes and reminiscences.

Not long before she was due to fly back to Africa, she confided in me that she desperately wanted to have Riek's baby but that they had been having some problems getting her pregnant. I was more than a little taken aback; I had only just reached fifty and I wasn't remotely prepared to be a grandmother. Nonetheless, I made all the right noises and offered what advice I could. I told her I thought that her illness couldn't have helped, not to mention the fact that she was so thin, and advised her to go and see someone. Thus began a whole host of medical tests, which found her to have a slight hormone imbalance. Armed with the fertility drugs the doctors gave her, she couldn't wait to get back to Riek and start making a baby.

In between her shopping expeditions for clothes and other creature comforts to take back with her, Emma told me she was keeping a journal and planned to write a book of her experiences one day. I remember commenting:

'For God's sake, don't mention me.'

Her reply was: 'Of course not, Mum . . . I'm saving your life story for the second instalment.'

On 12 September 1992, a week before her departure, we once again held a very happy party for her at my sister Sue's home, Springwood. It was a warm gathering of Emma's English friends, her family and a few of my closest friends in Surrey. In her languid, relaxed way she made everybody laugh with her tales from Africa. It was the last time most of them would see her alive. She flew back to Nairobi on Sunday 20 September, unusually weepy at our parting. Seeing her tears, I realised how torn she was now between her two lives and how difficult it was becoming for her to transcend the barriers between the two.

From Kenya, she flew into Sudan, bearing wedding gifts including a visitors' book and spotted handkerchief for Riek from the family, and a new computer for them both. While Riek pored over his manuals and instruction books, learning the Windows computer program, Emma launched herself back into her work and started to write her book with focus and determination. It kept her mind occupied and free of the fears which had begun to haunt her.

Within days of her return, however, she was reminded of her vulnerability when the shattering news came that Maung, the Burmese UN Resident Project Officer who had nearly killed her once in a car accident on her first trip to southern Sudan, had been shot along with a Norwegian journalist. She wrote in her diary: 'Maung, dear Mynt

Maung – the last person to deserve a bullet from a southern Sudanese gun, he had served them faithfully the last three years.' Two expatriate aid workers, Wilmer Gomez and Francis Ngure, both friends, had also been pulled from their cars, stripped of their clothes and shot by Garang's troops. A further two had been injured. Emma was deeply shocked by the incident, which she first heard about on the BBC, via the new radio given to her and Riek as a wedding present.

She was also very upset to learn of the death of James Chany Reer, the Sudanese Education Co-ordinator who had wiped away her tears with his fingers after the first air-raid she had ever experienced in Leer. Fleeing Garang's men and walking through the swamps to the town of Waat, he had fallen ill and died from kala azar, a parasitic disease transmitted from the bite of a sandfly, which had swept through southern Sudan that year, killing thousands. In her first letter home, she wrote: 'Mum, thank you so much for making my trip to the UK so enjoyable. I have so many happy memories and I feel fresh and ready to cope with Sudan.' But she described the deaths as a 'terrible tragedy'.

After the murder of the aid workers, Emma knew that, more than ever, her own life was in constant danger. She could have been kidnapped or assassinated at any time, such was the hatred Garang's men had for her. And the danger didn't necessarily have to come from outside. For all she knew, an infiltrator among Riek's men could be the one hired to pull the trigger. There was also the constant threat of government raids on civilian targets as the Khartoum government wrestled for control.

Riek, as concerned as she was, doubled the number of bodyguards and told her that they were going to have to move for a while, to Waat, nearly 200 miles west of Nasir. Apart from the benefits to their security of keeping mobile, Riek wanted to devote some of his time to the people of a different region, the Lou tribe, an ancient subdivision of the Nuer. Within a few days of arriving in Waat they were invited to the remote town of Ayod, sixty miles further west, to celebrate their arrival with a hallowed 'Leopard Skin Ceremony', welcoming their leader and his bride. The journey to Ayod was long and tortuous and could only be done on foot. It was October, the peak of the rainy season and extremely wet. Water had accumulated everywhere and the swamps were flooded and muddy.

Riek wrote later that Emma was amazing, coping with disease and bad food, even hunger.

'She marched with me in the rainy season in mud up to her knees through swamps infested with bilharzia [a blood disease caused by parasitic worms]. It took five days each way. She joked that she had never properly used her muscles before, they were aching so much . . . I had never walked such a long distance before and I found it a struggle. It was such hard work walking through water below the knees, because it created added pressure against your lower leg each time you bent your knee to take a step forward.'

By the halfway point of Pathai, Emma was so weak, so ill, that a meal of couscous and milk could not revive her. Riek radioed back to Waat for a plane to come and collect Emma and fly her on to Ayod. He and his men made a makeshift runway between the mangrove trees and, when the terrified pilot refused to land because it was too dangerous, a passenger who knew how to fly a plane took over the controls. They carried Emma on to the plane and took off, but reappeared within the hour because both pilots were too nervous to land at Ayod, where the runway was short and had been shot to pieces by government attacks. There was no choice left to Emma but to continue their journey on foot through what Riek called 'the swamps of hell'.

The mosquitoes were unbearable, the poisoned thorn trees extremely hazardous, the uncharted route covered in muddy water with the very real possibility of treading on an unsuspecting snake. They were attacked by a swarm of bees during which the soldiers all panicked and ran. Riek said: 'I held Emma's hand and said: "Don't run or you will be stung." She kept still and we were the only ones not stung.' As they neared Ayod, Emma was in a state of near collapse, leaning heavily on Riek's arm, tearful with exhaustion, overcome with emotion.

'I whispered to her "Don't collapse, please don't collapse. You must keep standing, you simply have to."

The soldiers offered to carry Emma, but she refused, she was a strong woman. Summoning up all her strength and courage she managed to complete the journey on foot, and even gave a smile when she saw the tumultuous welcome waiting for her – thousands upon thousands of people had travelled for days to greet us, all of whom were hugely impressed by her resilience.'

Emma wrote:

'The women sang and danced, the church groups waved their banners. The whole town reverberated with excitement. We were wet up to our waists, muddy and tired. I was brought near to tears by their welcome. The chiefs sang their deep, throaty chorus. I slumped into bed and slept and slept.'

Riek and Emma spent four days in Ayod, the reception they received was astonishing in its warmth, and the local Nuer government had gathered everyone to welcome them. On the second day the crowds were even larger, as more and more people filtered in from the bush. Riek communed with the men, while Emma spent time with the women, who presented her with her own cow, a fine beast with pale brown and white markings, and they called Emma 'Yan', the name for the colour of their palest, creamiest cows. Thereafter Emma was known by that name in Ayod.

Two days later the leopard-skin chiefs (sacred men without political authority, similar to a clan chief in Scotland) assembled to confer on Riek the powers of the leopard-skin chief or 'Earth Chief'. The skin of a leopard was presented to him by a delegation from Ayod. This cere-mony was an ancient Nuer tradition to transfer the powers of the leopard to Riek, who would then have the authority to perform special rites within the society such as absolving men of murder and settling blood feuds. It was a very great honour to be chosen – the mantle was normally handed down through the same family over generations – and conferred on Riek special status and power. Emma wrote to me that morning, 13 October 1992.

'Ayod is a rather beautiful place. Large ancient fig trees provide deep

shade while the birds chatter and coo. The ground is sandy, Ayod is
surrounded by swamps . . . I couldn't face the walk back through them.
I was so stiff I felt like a cripple, unable to stand up straight or bend
over. Wading through water knee deep for hours on end tests the thigh
muscles. We were greeted by the people of Ayod so warmly, the pain of
walking seemed to be worth it. Today, Riek is being honoured. The
leopard-skin chiefs are anointing him. It is a very rare ceremony and I
am looking forward to it.'

Wearing his leopard-skin draped across him throughout the ceremony, Riek was afforded the greatest honour of all, by being allowed to have Emma at his side – it was normally a ritual strictly for the men of the tribe only, and no western woman had ever taken part before. One of Riek's aides took photographs, which Emma later sent to me. In her floppy brown hat, Ray Ban sunglasses and best floral cotton dress, she could have been at Wimbledon or Ascot rather than breaking taboos in southern Sudan, but she carried the responsibility well. Riek had explained to her that any son she might bear him would now automatically become a leopard-skin chief.

Emma wrote of the ceremony:

'Riek and I were asked to stand on a leopard skin, Riek was then
draped in a leopard skin, then the skin from under our feet was taken
and given to Riek to wear. Then all the Kuaar Muon, Nuer Earth
Masters, spat into our hands; one put the tail of his leopard skin (the
emblem of office) to my lips. Young bulls were brought forth, four in all,
to be slaughtered by one piercing jab of a spear through the heart. The
way in which they fell was interpreted as a future of peace, as the bulls
died quietly.'

More cattle were slaughtered throughout the day with each chief presenting one of his own best bulls for sacrifice. As the evening wore on, so the celebrations went on, lasting long into the night, with seven-foot giants, nearly naked, dancing till dawn to the sounds of throbbing drums. The crowds feasted on the slaughtered cattle.

After a final day recovering, and helping out with the relief situation, the long journey home began, although this time it was not quite as arduous as they could retrace their steps, recognise the landmarks and did not have to cut their way through the swamps. She wrote of her bodyguards:

> 'Peter chanted: "Good morning, water," Chol replied: "Hello, mud." Trousers were rolled up, sticks given out and in we plunged into mud and water, at times waist deep, for two-and-a-half hours. My groin muscles began to ache and the thought of rest beckoned . . . Each footprint embedded in the mud had been used by every soldier in front of us. Forty-Six picked a white lily and handed it to me as a gift of solidarity . . . I was totally humbled by a little Nuer girl, aged about nine, walking on her way to Waat to sell milk.'

They rested in Pathai and stayed there for a few days because they could hear fighting in the distance. Carrying on with the journey, Emma fell ill and found the walking exhausting.

> 'All energy is sucked out of you just by the effort of pulling one's self out of the mud. Kuac Kang kindly offered to carry me, but the indignity of failing to walk forced me to refuse this kind and tempting gesture. The sun was merciless, the lack of food, sleep and dehydration led me almost to break down and weep. It was a very hard day.'

Arriving back at Riek's military headquarters in Waat, their bags carried before them on bobbing children's heads, they rested solidly for three days and nights in their beautiful new tukul, lovingly built for them by the local women. Emma wrote.

> 'Our new house – beautifully decorated with hippos, lions, crocodiles, leopards, a rhino chasing a man, swirling around the tukul. Two tukuls joined together by a verandah. At the entrance a painted SPLA soldier salutes us, next door to a message inscribed: "Wel Come to Lou Nuer." Mosquito nets soaked in gentian violets add colour, and flowers are pressed into the chalk dust paint, and there are hand prints on the walls.'

Not long after arriving back at Waat, however, severely malnourished women and children began filtering into the town from the Dinka and Nuer areas around Ayod. The crops had failed and tribal fighting had exacerbated their problems. Emma wrote:

'This is the time of the harvests when people should have plenty. A woman thrust her skinny little baby into my arms, but what could I do? I knew what she was asking.'

She did what she could for them and helped Riek try to solve some of the underlying problems behind the enforced famine – the abuse of military rations by the soldiers, unnecessary seizure of people's cows, the abduction and rape of women and girls.

Within weeks, Emma was in need of help herself, felled by hepatitis. Riek arranged for her to be flown to Nairobi for treatment. By the time she got to the city's tropical diseases unit, she was desperately ill. Doctors said she was presenting them with a new and previously unknown strain of hepatitis and began her on a course of treatment which would last months. She recuperated with Sally, and then with Willie's mother Jeannie, resting and trying to return her skin to its normal colour, from yellow, before flying back to Waat to spend Christmas 1992 with Riek – the only one they would spend together, and their last.

In a Christmas card from the son-in-law I had yet to meet, Riek wrote:

'Maggie, merry Christmas and happy new year. I was hoping that we might meet during this Christmas, but this is not going to be . . . I will be exercising my muscles walking in the bushes of southern Sudan. This is a normal way of celebrating Christmas in the war-ravaged southern Sudan. I am looking forward to meeting you in the coming year. Happy Christmas. Riek.'

In her letter to me that Christmas, Emma wrote:

'I am longing to see you, Mum. Good luck with your plans for 1993. I do hope it is a good year for you.'

12

Christmas 1992 and the new year were spent at home in Surrey, with my father, my remaining children and close friends, while Sue and Martin went to the Far East for a holiday. My trip to Nairobi was postponed until February 1993 and, even after I had booked the ticket, I didn't know if Emma would be there when I arrived. She had anticipated my winter visit but, with typical capriciousness, she then warned me that she might not even be in Kenya. So as I touched down at Kenyatta Airport early that February morning – once again seeing the giant African sun resting on the cusp of the horizon, greeting me – I wondered if I would manage to meet up with her.

I WAS DELIGHTED TO FIND THAT SHE WAS WAITING FOR ME, AND THAT DAVID MARRIAN, A FRIEND OF EMMA'S AND AN ARTIST, WAS AT HER SIDE. David is a white Kenyan, blond, tall and handsome, a lot of fun and very charming. I had met him before and was very glad to see him again. To my surprise and delight, Emma told me that she had arranged for me to stay with David at his beautiful house in the middle of the Nairobi Game Park, at a place called Kitingella. David's wife, Emma, was abroad and had left him in charge of their three young sons, Jack, Hunter and Finlay. But my daughter had a hidden agenda. She knew I liked David and she was no doubt using him as a 'front', to soften the bombshell she had in store – Emmanuel.

Emmanuel was a Sudanese boy, a refugee she had somehow managed to smuggle into Kenya earlier that week. It did not take long for me to realise that this eleven-year-old child was completely out of control. We got off to a bad start. From the moment he met me, he called me Granny, which absolutely incensed me, because I knew that he must have been primed to do so by Emma. She and I had previously discussed my reticence about becoming a grandmother, and she was playing on my vanity.

Although Emmanuel was still very young, he believed himself to be eighteen years old. He was bright, but intensely wilful. He had never sat on a chair, or eaten from a plate with a knife and fork. When he first saw a telescope set up on its stand on David's verandah, he told us he knew what it was. Then he went into an elaborate mime, picking up imaginary objects, placing them just so, turning his back and covering his ears, with a shout of 'Bang!' He thought the telescope was a mortar rocket launcher.

He doted on Emma, slept in the same bed as her and was prone to provoking ferocious arguments between them. When locked in conflict with her, he had an unnerving habit of rolling his eyes in opposite directions. She was very good to him, she treated him as an equal, like a younger brother, and took him everywhere she went – game drives in the park, the Hurlingham Club in Nairobi to play shove half-penny, and to lunches and suppers with friends. She spoilt him rotten and he asked her for everything he set his eyes on, aiming and firing an imaginary gun at her and anything that moved.

On one occasion Emma had to go to a wedding and left him overnight in my care. I fully anticipated twenty-four hours of absolute mayhem, but in fact he toned down his wild behaviour, perhaps cowed by my seniority. Sometimes Emma would have to leave him with friends. He would instantly escape from their houses, walking home for three or four miles in the heat of the day. Then he would be taken back, only to escape again to announce: 'I have come by feet.'

At a dinner party at Sally's one night, he threw a chicken bone over his shoulder onto the carpet. Sally and Emma decided there and then they should teach him some table manners before taking him to Willie's mother at the coast. Between them, they taught him how to use a knife and fork, how to eat with his mouth closed, how to sit in a chair and other basic essentials for polite company. And Emmanuel had never seen the sea. When we arrived at the coast, he stared out from the shore and asked where the other bank was, assuming it to be a broad river. I was suddenly reminded of Emma on the banks of the Brahmaputra River, asking if this was the sea.

Much of Emmanuel's behaviour seemed comical, though tragedy lay behind it. Emmanuel had been trained as a child soldier by Garang's ironically named Foundation for African Children's Education. Like the rest of the children who had enrolled, he hardly ever saw a book, but he learned how to fire guns and rockets. He learned how to kill people. After months of fighting and abuse, and a particularly violent battle, he and scores of others decided to desert and to join Riek's rival army. Conditions there were better, they had heard. Riek Machar was said to be a kinder man. He was also a distant cousin. They walked for days across some of the most hostile terrain, the roughest wilderness in Africa, fighting off wild animals, foraging for food, lying low to keep out of sight of the soldiers. Many of the weakest and youngest died from hunger and disease, after collapsing, without hope, and ignoring the pleas of their brothers and friends to get up again. Only twelve of them finally reached Riek's military headquarters. Emmanuel was one of them, carrying a gun which was taller than himself.

In her indomitable way, Emma had smuggled him out of Sudan as 'a spare part for an aircraft engine' and found a sponsor for his education. She badgered people into becoming sponsors, playing on their guilt, and when that didn't work, she applied to all the charitable trusts she could think of for money – sending off Emmanuel's vital statistics and filling in endless forms. I was, once again, reminded of my own struggle to pay for Emma's education, and that of the other children. Until the necessary funds materialised, Emmanuel became her responsibility and – with my arrival – mine. She ended up paying for his schooling, his clothes and his accommodation, for which she received little thanks. Emmanuel was, and still is, a wild child; a law unto himself. A nomad by birth and a nomad by nature, he knows how to draw the emotions out of people, and to manipulate a situation to his own advantage. He is a true survivor.

I resented his presence more than I can say. I so wanted to spend time alone with my daughter and not have to babysit for some precocious 'grandson' I didn't want or expect. It was not the best of holidays and Emma and I had several run-ins. Even Sally said she thought Emma had been a little unkind to me. Sensing the tensions mounting, I took myself off on a three-day walking camel safari at Laikipia just to get away. By the time I returned Emma had got the message and Emmanuel had been despatched to school.

On the last day of my holiday, 2 March, my birthday – which Emma completely forgot – we had a huge row over something quite trivial and it tainted the trip even more. Sue's son Peter, Emma's cousin, had run a marathon to raise money for southern Sudan. Emma had suggested the cash raised should be used to buy footballs for the children in some of the poorest villages, to bring some fun into their otherwise drab and dangerous lives.

One of Peter's sponsors had told him: 'I don't mind sponsoring you, as long as the money doesn't go towards guns.' Bearing in mind who Emma was married to, it was not an outrageous comment to make, but I foolishly passed it on. On the day I was due to leave, we were driving into town from Langata, to price up footballs in a sports shop, Emma at the wheel, and I stupidly blurted it out. She stopped the car and stared at me, aghast. She was furious, terribly hurt by it, and angry as hell – first with the sponsor, then with Peter, and finally with me. We never reached the sports shop. We drove in stony silence thereafter. By the time she dropped me off at the airport to fly home later that evening, there was still an atmosphere between us. It was not the most harmonious of partings, least of all on my birthday, although Emma did mellow right at the end and, I think, realised that the message I passed on was not me speaking.

'Bye, Mum,' she said, hugging me to her at the departure gate. 'See you soon.' There were no tears this time, I was late, and we both felt slightly harassed. As I turned to go, she called after me, almost as an afterthought: 'Oh, Mum, I've forgotten your birthday!' Her expression was one of pure mortification. I smiled and told her not to worry, that it didn't matter.

Standing there in a grey silky skirt, black T-shirt, tie-dye blue and white cotton jacket and desert boots, her belt made of cowry shells, she beamed at me from over the top of her sunglasses. We were friends again at last. 'Love you,' she called. I turned back to her and smiled, glad that we had cleared the air. Unbeknown to us both, it was the last time I would ever see her alive.

Later that month, Emma returned to Waat, to their new home, to find that the tension between the Dinkas and the Nuers had reached an all-time high. Confusion and suspicion were rife and there were several ugly incidents where Riek's men – some of them loyal Dinkas – ended up shooting each other dead during fierce arguments. Riek was still hopeful of effecting some sort of reconciliation between the two tribes, but in some of the more remote areas his men were out of control and the killings went on.

Talk of atrocities and murder was to continue to mar the final months of Emma's life. She had remained ferociously loyal to Riek, insisting that he was not responsible for any of the killings, but not long after her return, she found herself pleading unsuccessfully for an officer's life when Riek's men dragged him off in her presence to be shot. The officer was called Hakim Gabriel Aluong and he had apparently been accused of plotting against Riek and feuding with his fellow officers. He was executed and Emma could no longer pretend that the people she was close to were not responsible – although it was Riek's men, not him, whom she blamed.

Continuing to devote her time to promoting his cause further and to wooing press interest, she went all out in her media campaign, faxing and calling as many people as she could to achieve some coverage. She was tempting bait, an easy human-interest story for the journalists to lighten the bleak landscape of fighting and starvation, and she knew how to use the press. The media were hooked.

Early in 1993, a British television crew flew out and filmed her at home with Riek in a documentary called *The Warlord's Wife*, broadcast that spring, in which she was filmed swanning around their garrison serenely on Riek's arm, smiling and clasping his hand, looking like a model for *Vogue*. In the background, the armed giants who protected them stood in full battle fatigues, their Kalashnikovs at the ready. Before long she had been featured in the *Sunday Times*, the *Mail on Sunday*, women's magazines and even *Hello!*. Emma was increasingly becoming a public figure, entering onto the world's stage and excelling as a manipulator of the press – a skill she had first learned during her flight to Australia with Bill Hall. But then it had been purely selfish, for her own pleasure and profit. Now, it seemed to me, she was unwittingly evolving more and more into an instrument of Riek's personal interests and I feared where it might lead.

One such instance was when a CNN film crew flew out to Waat to report on a 'famine situation' only to find to their dismay that there were not that many desperate, hungry people there after all. Pressed for time and determined to get some footage, they asked for Emma's help and she, it seemed, willingly gave it. Spreading the word around the surrounding villages that there was going to be a 'food drop' at a specific place, hundreds of hungry people flocked in from the bush, eager for aid. When they arrived at the appointed 'drop-off' point within the walls of the garrison, they found only a film crew and had to go home empty-handed. When challenged about what she had done later by an aid-worker colleague, Emma shrugged her shoulders and smiled.

'Bad news is better than no news at all,' she said, simply. 'At least we got Waat on the world stage.' There was always some convincing logic to her motives, but I wondered sometimes how far she would go for her ideals.

And all the while, her life was still in constant danger. Rumours abounded that Garang had put a price on her head; she scribbled as much on the corner of a page in her diary and told friends:

'There are some people out there who would gladly put a bullet through my head.' But still, she remained at Riek's side, knowing that death was stalking her at every turn. In April 1993 Riek organised a high-level meeting in Kongor, a town his men had captured from Garang. Emma travelled with him and they rested overnight in a tukul in preparation for the conference the following day. But at dawn their garrison compound was attacked by Garang's men and their defences overrun in minutes. She and Riek had to run for their lives in the middle of a terrifying battle. In the following extract from her diary, Emma described what happened:

'Gunfire pierced the new day. Startled, I looked at Riek across the table over our cups of steaming, sweet black tea. We stared at each other in

silence, ignoring the sound of the radio on the table and listening intently to the noises from outside, to the crackle of AK-47s, the thud of feet, a whistle, shouts and orders. I glanced out of the door frame – there was no door – to see our soldiers run for their guns and take up defensive positions.

"There is going to be a battle," Riek said as he got up from his chair and moved towards the paneless window of our home of the last two days, a shell of a house that had never been completed. The floor was earth, dried cement oozed out from between the breeze-blocks and bats lived in the eaves.

Riek was already dressed in his fatigues. He peered out and saw our attackers emerge from the cover of the acacia forest to the south and streak across the airstrip. He turned quickly, took my hand and led me into our bedroom to take cover. Anger was in his eyes. We didn't speak. He stooped to pick up his gun, which leaned against the wall behind our bed, still tightly clutching my hand. I felt a cloak of protection being wrapped around me. I didn't feel fear. I just did as I was told.

The sound of heavy artillery and mortars echoed. The gunfire moved closer. We could hear the ping of bullets hitting the metal roof above us. Gatnoor, a bodyguard, ran into the room, an AK-47 slung over his shoulder.

"Get down!" He had to shout to be heard. He fumbled with Riek's red epaulettes, unbuttoning the straps and sliding off the symbols of military rank, stuffing them into his pockets. Forty-Six, another bodyguard, appeared.

"They're coming, commander. We have to leave."

As we were pulled from the bedroom by those whose job it was to protect us, I turned and shouted, "My boots, my boots!" But there was no time and my plea was drowned by the crescendo of the now raging battle. I was wearing flip-flops. Outside our house the noise of war was deafening. Thousands of bullets raced through the air, but I never saw our attackers because I never looked back.

Gently Riek told me to keep my head down, as he led me past other houses and small huts, built by the Jonglei Canal Commission in 1982, but never finished because of the war. Lines of people streamed out from behind the buildings, carrying whatever they could – children, ammunition, mosquito nets, pots and blankets, running for the cover of the forest, running for their lives. We reached a road. I looked up. I had no idea where we were running. I was just being led. We were heading for the protection of an acacia forest, about half a kilometre away. But first, open land had to be crossed, an area that is bog in the wet season, but dry now, cracked and uneven – a difficult surface to run across. I discarded my flip-flops. It was easier to run in bare feet. Still the unrelenting sound of gunfire filled the air.

My hand was taken by Forty-Six. I was split from Riek and we ran ahead, leaving him behind. I never questioned that I should leave my husband. I knew we were too obvious together.

"Run, Emma, run!" Forty-Six urged, pulling me along in the grip of his huge hand.

Forty-Six is seven feet tall. His face is scarred with traditional Nuer markings, patterns of dots around the eyes and mouth, and six lines cut deep across his forehead. He was trained in Cuba and was formerly the bodyguard of John Garang – the very man who was now trying to kill us. Gunfire still taunted us.

"Run faster, Emma. You must run faster!" Forty-Six pleaded, dragging me behind him, as I panted and gasped for breath. Our feet followed a path which led into a thicket of thorny, red-barked acacia trees, their leaves shrivelled for lack of rain. The path meandered through the trees, like a tiny stream ground to dust. Ahead I could see a single line of fleeing people snaking through the forest, their heads bobbing as they ran. We followed them. My throat was dry. I could hear the rasp of my breathing. My ears popped and my legs stubbornly refused to increase their speed. Thorns clawed and tore at our clothes, as we ducked to avoid the arms of trees that blocked our path. Occasionally a thorny branch would spring back, whipping me across the face as the person in front ploughed through the undergrowth.

A clearing exposed a luak, a large thatched hut on a little rise. Three old women and some children sat outside, their legs outstretched on the ground, watching as the running feet flew past. I wondered what they were thinking, why they were not seeking safety, why they were just sitting there watching. Perhaps they had simply despaired at their sons' failure to live in peace together.

For the first time that morning I felt afraid. I could feel the beating of my racing heart and the ache of fear deep in my belly. I knew that I could easily be seen from afar – I was wearing an orange skirt and a blue shirt. I was white. I was the wife of Riek Machar, John Garang's arch-enemy. I knew there would be no mercy. If they caught me, I would be killed.

"Run, Emma, run!" Forty-Six shouted angrily, as I paused to catch my breath. My mouth had filled with saliva. I spat it out, so that I could breathe more easily. My shirt was clinging to my body, soaked with sweat. My cheeks were burning. I had been sapped of energy. I had only just recovered from a bout of hepatitis. I ran on, but I seemed to be running in slow motion.

Another luak appeared ahead. We looked in to find no one there. A gourd of water stood at the entrance to its darkened interior. Forty-Six grabbed it and lifted it to my mouth so that I could gulp a few mouthfuls. The water spilled down my chin and onto my shirt. But before I had a chance to quench my thirst the gourd was pulled away.

"Enough," Forty-Six grunted, as he grasped my hand again and dragged me onwards.

They were pursuing us. We overtook Marco, another of our bodyguards. His khaki trousers were stained with blood. Though a bullet had penetrated his back, he carried on walking. Forty-Six muttered a few words of encouragement to him, but we didn't stop to help him. We had to leave a wounded hero behind.

The trees started to thin out and soon we emerged onto an open plain. The elephant grass had been burnt to encourage new growth when the first rains came. But now there was only charred earth and blackened stumps. It felt as if we were running on a bed of nails. My mouth was parched again, but Forty-Six insisted that I must run faster. Now we were in even greater danger. In this open space where there was no cover; we could be shot like dogs.

The snaking line of bobbing heads vanished behind a barrier of unburnt elephant grass. The fire had not reached this patch, and so we, too, plunged into the tall, reed-like grass. I found Omai, our cook, at my side, also urging me on.

"Keep going! It's not far to the trucks!"

I thought that this was a Nilotic trick – to lie about the nearness of a destination in order to give one renewed strength and courage. For as I looked up, I could see no sign of them. And now Forty-Six had disappeared: he had gone back to look for Riek. I prayed that Riek was safe, that the invaders would be more tempted by the prospect of looting our camp. That the shooting had stopped gave me heart. But still voices were urging me to run.

"Please, I can't, I can't any more!" I wailed. "My feet," I gasped. They were swollen, covered in blood. A soldier nearby offered his shoes, sandals made from old tyres.

"Look, there are the trucks just ahead!" Omai cried triumphantly. It was true; it wasn't a trick. I could see their camouflaged shapes through the veil of grass. It took the last of my strength to stumble on to the sanctuary of the trucks. Then I heard the roar of an engine firing into life and saw the blue smoke spew from its exhaust. People dragged themselves wearily aboard, collapsing in the back, all energy gone. Omai steered me to the passenger door of the cab, pushed me inside, slammed the door and then jumped on the running board.

Sitting in the driver's seat, I found the commander of the forces which had been the first to retreat. In effect he was taking the truck without bothering to stop to help his colleagues further behind. But I was too tired to confront him with his cowardice. Now I began to fear for Riek. As if he had read my thoughts, Omai pointed towards the second truck, shouting.

"Look, there's the commander! He's safe!"

The reek of sweat filled the cab. For a moment my attention wandered to the flies which were bouncing on and off the windscreen. Then I looked down at my bruised and bleeding feet. But there was a pool of congealed blood – not my blood – in the well beneath my passenger seat. I guessed that someone had been wounded; I wondered what had happened to him.

The driver, with a lighted cigarette protruding from his lips, spun the wheel and we began to bump over the gnarled, dry landscape, swishing through the grass and small shrubs on our way to rendezvous with the other vehicle. The plain was dotted with figures running to meet us. As we drew closer to the second lorry, I caught sight of Riek in *the cab, his red beret cocked to one side of his head, the head that I loved. I knew he was unharmed, but I could tell from his expression that he was angry that his troops had not put up more of a resistance to our attackers.*

I opened my door. Riek sprinted from his truck, to climb in beside me. I felt the great relief of his presence. At once his elegant, long fingers – which can curve upwards at their tips – threaded themselves through mine. His hand was warm, wet with perspiration. We looked at each other, but didn't speak a word. Words, after all, were unnecessary.'

Emma went on to describe the events that followed with the same sort of graphic detail. The little group of survivors headed for a muddy water hole to quench their thirst and attend to their wounded:

'*Dr Ochan, our physician, went about examining the wounded, comforting them with words of encouragement. I noticed that his feet, like mine, were severely scratched and cut, though he paid no heed to himself. It was grotesque to see the avidness of the flies, which pestered the open wounds, the flesh ripped apart by our enemies' bullets. There was not much that our doctor could do, stranded out here in the bush, bereft of clean water and medical supplies.*

We passed around a cup of grey mud, sparing ourselves only a sip. We drank it through a piece of cloth. That the water might have harboured deadly parasites seemed, at that moment, not to matter at all. One of our soldiers came over to me. I was astonished to see him present me with the flip-flops which I had discarded during the flight from our encampment. Running behind me, he had gathered them up and secured them to his belt.

It is these small things that stand out in the memory: that a man from a different race from me would, in the path of the bullets, instead of thinking only of his own life, have the care and the courage to stoop down to pick up some worthless items which happened to belong to me. This is what makes us human; what makes life worth living. I very badly wanted to cry. But I checked the tears. Instead, I smiled. Because a smile is an affirmation.

Riek had meanwhile gathered together with his council of war, to discuss a strategy for a counterattack. I happened to glance at my watch. It was almost noon. The time took me by surprise: it meant we had been running away from our attackers for two hours. The midday sun flamed in a cloudless, cobalt-blue sky. But a cooling breeze stirred the leaves of the nime trees and passed like a sweep of a hand across the grasslands. The area in which we had found ourselves is famous for its lack of features. You can focus on your destination as you walk for at least two hours before you arrive at it.

The Dinka, who are indigenous to this land, migrate with their cattle to reach the toich, the swampy grasslands by the River Nile. They graze their cattle, take the fruits of the great river, until the rains come and they return to their point of departure, the lands they cultivate. In the warm, painted vista before me were the subtlest shades of auburn, brown and ochre. Yet soon the impending rains would come, and this world would turn to vibrant greenness under charcoal skies. The scarcity of water would turn to abundance.

I stared at all the forlorn people around me: women cradling their children in their arms; soldiers inclining their heads, as they discussed the gravity of the day's brutal events. But I also saw figures curled up fast asleep, oblivious, the inhospitable reality annihilated by their dreams. I watched. And I envied them.

Two geckos scramble up a tree trunk, one chasing the other's tail. Tomorrow it may be the other way round: the pursued become the pursuer. I wonder what has happened to all the people in the town – the malnourished children in the feeding centre; the skeletal old men and women. Lives on the point of ebbing away. Where had they run? This renewed conflict in Panyagor had summarily brought to a halt the relief supply of food for the local population. I thought to myself:

"Isn't this enough after two years? Does there have to be more suffering? Will we never be able to stop the war between the forces loyal to John Garang and the forces loyal to Riek?"

Riek had come to Panyagor about a month before, with the intention of providing protection and security for the UN relief planes. Prior to this, no relief supplies whatsoever had reached this area for two years. Some efforts to make peace between the Nuer and Dinka tribes had started. A semblance of normality had returned to this shattered community: a health centre had been established; a school was about to open; a feeding centre was operational. All this would now be jeopardised. Garang did not want peace.

Only two days before, Riek and his colleagues – Kerubino Kuanyin Bol, Arok Thon Arok, Lam Akol, Uncle Joseph Oduho and William Nyuon – had held a public meeting with the local civilians. The people had danced and sung their traditional songs. They had not had many opportunities to celebrate during the past two years. Arok Thon Arok had returned after spending five years in detention for criticising John Garang's style of leadership. Kerubino, who had fired the first shot of the war in 1983, had been arrested and detained for six years, Uncle Oduho for seven.

"I hope Uncle Oduho managed to hide in the forest," I said. He was a sick man of sixty-five and would not have been able to run. Then I saw his relative Ben sitting a few feet away. "Do you know what happened to Uncle?" I asked him.

"No, I was not with him at the time of the attack," Ben replied despondently. I knew that everyone feared the worst and was blaming himself for the chaotic retreat.

"SPLA Oyea. SPLA Oyea. Wa, wa, wa, wa . . ." chanted the troops who were preparing for battle, thrusting their guns into the air as they ran around us in a circle. The trucks revved their engines, whilst the soldiers clambered aboard. We watched as the trucks lurched forward and roared off in a cloud of dust. We were left to sit in the shade, to wait for the return of our warriors, victorious we prayed.

Some blankets were found and we spread them on the ground so that we could lie down and rest. I could now take stock of what we had lost, the things that had been left behind in our house – private letters, which Garang would most certainly publish, Riek's briefcase containing valuable documents, my radio and binoculars, gifts from my mother, my money, the list went on.

"Are you all right? I expect your feet are very sore?" Riek asked me.

"Don't worry. I'm okay. I'm just a bit stiff." I could sense that Riek was angry with himself for having put me in so dangerous a predicament. Yet if he had not felt compelled to ensure my safety, he *would almost certainly have stayed behind to fight and would probably have been killed. I knew how stubborn he could be, how unnecessarily brave.*

"Do you think Come On and the puppy survived?" I asked. Come On was Riek's dog. She was no stranger to the front line and had recently given birth to a puppy. That was why she would have stayed behind.

"They were probably shot," Riek replied rather distantly.'

Emma and her husband waited for news of the garrison and the scene of the ambush after the attack. Some soldiers who had returned had managed to retrieve a rucksack and two pairs of boots from their bedroom. At least the bag was full of clothes, even the red and white spotted handkerchief which I had sent Riek from England. Emma told me later that Riek had scolded his guards for considering clothes to be more important than his briefcase which was full of important military documents.

Emma prayed that a survival pack and medical kit she had bought at a shop near Euston station before she left England was in the bag, but it had gone. Instead, all she found was a packet of hot lemon sachets, for soothing sore throats. Undaunted, water was put to boil in a pot and they were soon drinking hot lemon instead of tea.

The sun was sinking; the shadows of the nime trees lengthened as the evening peace descended. As the truck carrying the returning soldiers drew closer, they could hear the men singing, proclaiming their good news. They climbed aboard and Emma cradled a four-year-old boy in her lap, his limbs tense, his face still startled from his first day of war. Soldiers sat on the roof of the cab, their legs dangling in front of the windscreen. She wrote:

'As we approached Pangayor, we saw the vultures. As the truck moved closer they withdrew, watching us, waiting for us to pass on our way, so that they could resume their feasting. The first body had been stripped of all clothing and was already severely mutilated. The skull was eyeless. A walking stick lay beside the corpse. He was an old Dinka man, mown down as he tried to hurry away from the fighting. We got

out of the truck to inspect the other bodies which lay in our path, but none bore any resemblance to Uncle. It was difficult to comprehend the fact that these corpses had been living beings only a few hours previously. They had suffered the terrible indignity of being stripped of their clothes and then devoured.

We observed all this, but nobody showed any emotion. We passed a lone woman sitting outside her luak, staring into the distance. Ben went over to ask her if she had seen Uncle. In a faraway voice she told him she had not. Suddenly a single shot rang out, shattering the deathly calm of the evening. The bodyguards leapt from the truck, hitting the ground, rifles in hand, searching the rim of the forest. My heart began to race. This must be another ambush. Then shouts of fury were heard from the back of the truck. It was a mistake: a soldier had accidentally let off his gun. Relieved but shaken, we climbed back on board, with the adrenaline still pumping in our blood.

Soon the few buildings of Pangayor came into sight and we drew to a halt outside the UN compound. The place was eerily quiet, with not a soul to be seen except for the armed soldiers who were patrolling the town. The civilians had all fled, abandoning jerry cans, pots, firewood beneath the trees. The UN camp had been devastated, the canvas torn from the tents to reveal their skeletal metal frames. The ground was littered with high-energy biscuit packets and papers and files were being scattered by the evening breeze. The pale UN flag no longer flapped; it had been ripped down and only a bent flagpole remained. As I turned to walk back to our compound, I passed two little malnourished children, who were crouched under a thorn bush. They must have come in the morning to attend the feeding centre. Instead of being fed, they had witnessed the whole day's carnage.

I took the path which led to our house. Come On, Riek's dog, suddenly emerged, tail wagging, to greet us as though nothing had happened. Her puppy scampered about, unaffected by the day's events. We guessed that they had hidden under our bed, the base of which was an upturned cupboard with a hole in one side. Outside our front door, a dead body lay face down, naked except for his underpants. It was the flies, not the vultures, which swarmed upon him here. I did not recognise him.

Men brought chairs for us, so that we could sit down and rest. I slumped exhaustedly into mine and closed my eyes for a few seconds. When I opened them again, the dead body had disappeared. The soldiers told me that they had discovered four bodies in our bedroom. Some were relatives of Arok Thon; the others seemed to have killed each other in a frenzy of looting. Papers were littered all over the floor. We gathered up the letters and vital documents. Our collection of Guardian weeklies was retrieved virtually page by page.

I picked up one of our books, The Arctic Desert. It had a bullet hole right through it. A broken briefcase lay on the ground. It had been forced open and then discarded. Then Forty-Six appeared with a look of triumph on his face, giving me back my black handbag, which had been found near the airstrip. I expected it to be empty, but was amazed to find that it contained my radio and binoculars, a hat, a letter from Riek, a pair of scissors from Riek's washbag, my cheque book and bank card, coins in a plastic bag and various other bits and pieces. But the visitors' book we had been given as a wedding present had gone. It was full of the names of those who'd stayed with us and so it was, I suddenly realised, useful in terms of our political affiliations. It had never occurred to me before that a simple visitors' book could become a weapon of war.

I got up from my chair, feeling the pain in my limbs, and wandered over to the pit latrine. It was the only place that had remained completely intact. I peered through the window to our bedroom. The bodies had been removed, but the floor was strewn with my supply of Lillets and Tampax. Many had been broken open to their cotton core, in an attempt to fathom what this unknown contraption could possibly be.

A cup of hot tea was brought by Omai and also a packet of cigarettes which had been rescued from the debris. I lit one to calm my nerves. Riek stared at me.

"Why don't you give up smoking?"

"Riek, this is emphatically not the right moment."

From behind the house emerged a biblical figure, dressed in a torn purple shirt and white underpants. He stooped over a walking stick. His long, spindly legs were burnt dark red from the sun; his uncombed blond hair stuck out from his skull like a scarecrow's. His feet had also been torn to pieces by the African bush. His name was Jean Francois and he was the UN representative for Panyagor.

"Jean Francois!" I exclaimed. "Come and sit down. What on earth happened? We were so worried about you." Forty-Six helped lower him gently into his seat.

"They tried to kill me. They shot at me eight times, eight times would you believe and missed every single time. Which shows what lousy shots they are!" he exclaimed in his thick French accent. "I was confronted by a soldier, who was shouting at me, asking me questions. I backed away, saying I knew nothing. Then he raised the gun. I was so close I saw the fire leave the gun, like in a bad movie. So I ran away, jumping and hopping like – I don't know – like a rabbit, shouting, non, non, non!" he said animatedly, gesticulating all the while.

He went on telling us the story of his survival with breathless excitement. He had escaped into the forest, hiding in a thorn bush. Some of Garang's soldiers passed close by. The last soldier passed within four feet of him. Their eyes met for a fraction of a second, but the soldier ran on. Then all of a sudden more soldiers appeared, but Jean Francois realised they were Riek's troops and his salvation.

"But what was that soldier asking you, before you escaped into the forest?"

Jean Francois looked at me gravely.

"He was asking about you, Emma. He kept asking 'Where's Emma?' I said I didn't know, which was true. I didn't know. He said you worked for the CIA. He said the UN was supplying ammunition to Riek."

We talked for hours. It was very dark and quiet, with a young moon above the silhouettes of the trees. We drank tea with sugar and ate biscuits. Somehow the sugar and the biscuits had been overlooked in the looting spree. Out of the darkness Arok Thon Arok appeared and sat down with us. He had been to talk with some of his relatives.

"Listen," he whispered, "it seems our attackers were scheduled to appear last night, but they got lost. But there is bad news. Very bad news. They will be coming with a bigger force, tonight or tomorrow morning. They are coming to finish us off."

My whole body started to shake upon hearing this news. The prospect of repeating the same experience terrified me. I wouldn't be able to run this time. Up to this point, I hadn't experienced any emotions, but by now I knew Uncle was dead. His body had been found. I didn't want anyone to see me with terror in my eyes. Nervousness is infectious. I wouldn't be able to run this time . . . That night I slept in my shoes, just in case.'

Riek arranged for Emma, Jean-Francois and the wounded to be flown out to Lokichoggio, a UN base, but the emergency airlift had to be delayed three times as the fighting continued all around them. Finally, it was safe for the plane to land, and Emma kissed her husband goodbye, wondering if she would ever see him again.

'I looked down and saw Riek and his men watch us go until they became mere dots on the earth's surface. Part of my heart remained behind with Riek. As we soared up, magically lifted from hell, the vastness of the great flat land overwhelmed me . . . It was not until we saw Lokichoggio that the strings that held me together throughout the last two days broke. Unstoppable tears poured down my cheeks, washing away all the shock, the fear and the grief. I grieved for those who had died and who would die in this endless struggle – Uncle – I couldn't believe that this old man of whom I'd grown so fond, who was alive yesterday, was now dead. He didn't deserve to die like that. He had served southern Sudan all his life, to die in the end at the hands of his own people.'

Emma spent much of the summer of 1993 flitting to and from Sudan, as the situation improved and then deteriorated alternately. Death threats and rumours of Riek's involvement with Khartoum continued, and they were often deeply concerned for each other's safety.

Whenever she was with him, Emma would try and snatch a few sacred days alone together – alone, that is, except for the constant presence of bodyguards, a full army and the myriad camp followers. But they were able to have some time together. With Come On and her puppy Freedom Fighter, they went for long walks in the bush, spent time by the river and enjoyed intimate nights together in their tukul, although not always alone – one night they heard a strange noise and found a deadly red cobra under their bed, and geckos clung nightly to their mosquito net, silhouetted against the moonlit sky, waiting for their supper – the only creatures in southern Sudan assured of a regular meal.

In June and early July – instead of being home with us as normal – Emma spent six whole weeks with Riek, travelling with him to Nasir, their old home, and her first visit back there in a year. She wrote to me on her return.

'I enjoyed the trip despite the stresses and strains of war. We travelled along the Sobat River by boat to Ulang, a tiny settlement between Nasir and Malakal. The local people had recently quarrelled over fishing rights and raided each other's cows. Riek had to settle the dispute by organising the return of raided cows. The rains have not come properly yet, however the landscape has been painted green, a change from the autumnal colours of the dry season. From Ulang we crossed the river and travelled overland towards Waat until we got stuck in the mud, three hours from our destination. We abandoned our trucks and struck out on foot through the mud, arriving at Waat as the moon rose.

I have made an effort this time to learn Nuer, the local language, with some success. I can now chat with the ladies and even translate for the aid workers . . . Mum, I plan to return to the UK around September when air fares are a little cheaper. We thought of you a lot as we listened to the Wimbledon highlights on the BBC radio in southern Sudan. They said that the weather was fine and not a drop of rain fell for two whole weeks. Please send my love to everyone. Lots of love as always, Em XXX'

When she was back in Nairobi, she and Riek communicated by letter or radio. Their messages to each other were often openly affectionate but always sent using code names – she was Nefertiti, the beautiful fourteenth-century Egyptian queen; he was Sennar, named after an old province of Sudan. In one letter to her that summer, Riek wrote:

'At times I am lonely. My thoughts would quickly drift to you and a lot *of things would come back to my mind. Building a farm and a ranch somewhere and having kids with you are among the conspicuous day and night dreams I have. Love, next time why don't we have a baby?'*

Emma continued to be gravely disappointed by the reaction of some of those within southern Sudan, and the SPLA, to Riek's choice of wife. Sending Riek a radio message, she said:

'I have been very upset by the behaviour of Lam Akol, John Luke and Taban. When I asked them if I could go on a plane carrying journalists to Kongor to see you for one night, they refused, saying I would be interfering with your work. They went on to say that I was a political liability to you and I should get used to not seeing you, maybe for years; that it is dangerous for journalists to see me next to you and that I should go and find a job instead of sitting idle in Nairobi. In fact, they were advocating that I leave you alone and go away.'

Riek responded in a letter, expressing his anger at the attitude of his senior aides and urging her not to be upset. He wrote:

'They have no authority to talk to you like that. I want you to fight. They are trying to harass you and humiliate me. They must be designing ways to frustrate you and make you quit. This must never happen. My love for you will never falter because of such political blackmail. I love you and will ever love you. You must not listen to such nonsense. If you want to come to where I am, nobody will prevent you.'

On 23 July, Emma decided to try and redress the question of her popularity by flying in to Leer, Riek's home town, with her husband's Dinka colleague Kerubino, to meet her new extended family and villagers in an attempt to win them over. She needn't have worried. In her diary, she recorded the extraordinary welcome that was awaiting her as she emerged from the plane:

'I was greeted by many hands, a sea of unknown faces. I heard in the distance the approach of women. I felt out of place among the soldiers

without Riek. The women brought comfort and I wanted to be with them. I rose and went to greet them outside. They picked me up and carried me to where, I knew not, across the fields of durrah, past luaks. One woman slipped and fell, others came to take her place. They sang and ululated, chatted to each other, shouting instructions. They struggled to carry me, sweat poured down their faces. I pleaded with them that there was no need to carry me, but they said I couldn't walk to Leer until I had set foot in my luak.

I was placed gently on the ground outside a large luak, amongst a little homestead flanked by two samml mud huts. The women crowded round to see me, hands from every direction thrust forward in greeting. A group sang and danced, waving nime branches, using rhythmical footwork. A chair made of branches and covered in hide, rough stitches holding it together, was placed for me to sit on. I couldn't see what was happening. They said I had to wait. Suddenly the crowd fanned out. In front of me was a black and white cow, already down on the ground, its legs and head held down by men, their muscles flexing as they struggled to control the beast as it kicked and attempted to get up. They held its head back and the spear went into the throat. Blood spurted out, frothy, and oozed into the dusty ground. When it was proclaimed dead, I was pushed forward by the throng. I knew what I had to do, step over the slaughtered animal to be blessed. As I stepped over the stomach, onto the bloodstained ground, the women cried and ululated. My hand was held and I was led towards the dark entrance of the luak. As we stooped to enter there was a contrast from the brightness outside to the dark within. I couldn't see for a few seconds. Led to the centre, I saw a pile of ash and the red glow of the embers – the source of the family fire. As my eyes adjusted, I followed the gnarled branches that supported the huge hut up to the ceiling. I could see the dark faces near me and feel the presence of many silent people. This was my new family.'

Introduced to Riek's relatives – many of whom looked like him, tall with high cheek bones and deep set eyes, Emma was surprised to find so many of them wearing woolly bobble hats in stifling heat – they were gifts sent from a foreign church, she was told, and only the most senior tribesmen wore them. One gap-toothed elder wore a captured Arab general's hat, a white polo necked jumper and a blue blazer. She thought he looked like a member of the Royal Yacht Club.

She told them a little about herself and her family through an interpreter. She mentioned Yorkshire, her childhood at Cowling, me and Bunny, and her brothers and sisters. She was greatly touched by their warm welcome and their unquestioning acceptance of her into their family. She wondered how we would all cope if the tables were turned. They fed her on goat stew, peanut butter, a vegetable similar to spinach and another stew made from goat's stomach and intestines. They let her sit with them, eat with them, be with them. And all the while, just like her, they kept smiling.

To her very great surprise, Riek arrived unannounced, and the festivities began all over again. It was his first trip home to Leer in four years and the crowd mobbed him, going wild. More cows were slaughtered, and four young bulls lined up in a row, each one calmly watching the one before it die. Emma had to turn her eyes away so as not to see the death throes.

Riek led her to Kuduk, a village five miles east of Leer. After walking the distance in the incredible heat, with nothing yet to eat, Emma was finally introduced to her parents-in-law, including Riek's father who had five wives, and his birth mother, who was the third wife. She wrote:

'Riek was quite emotional about being back. He was close to his mother. She was a strong woman who had rebelled against tradition and pushed her two youngest sons through education. "This is my wife, mother," Riek said in the dark, "I love her and I have brought her to you." '

Riek had already told Emma how his mother had been determined to send her two sons to school ever since a cousin of hers became one of the first Nuer to attend university. She had them baptised as Presbyterians to quality them for the local missionary school, and then went to Khartoum, brewing beer on the streets, to earn enough to pay for the school fees. Riek ended up with a PhD in engineering and his brother became a professor of veterinary medicine. They were the only two, among thirty-one children sired by Riek's father, who went to school. Because of their educational achievements and absence from Leer during their teenage years, neither one of them had the traditional manhood markings carved onto their foreheads. As the Nuer prophecy had predicted: 'An unmarked left-handed Nuer chief will one day marry a white woman.'

The following day, Emma was able to look around the village before yet another ceremony, yet another slaughtering of cattle. She wrote:

'There was a maize garden surrounded by a fence constructed of doun palm branches tied together. Kong, one of Riek's brothers, patted his cows as they were milked and cleaned beside the luak. Children gathered the dung for drying and its musty smell filled the air. There were wood hoopoes. The date palm stood majestically, its unripe dates plentiful in bunches. People folded their bedding and chatted to friends and family they had not seen for some time. We ate kobɛnup (a local cereal) for breakfast. It was going to be another hot and humid day.'

At the ceremony which followed in the oppressive heat, the elders called on the prophet Teny, Riek's ancestor, for peace and unity. Emma wrote:

'They rubbed ash on our feet and threw tobacco, spat on our heads and chest. They asked Teny to give Riek a son from me, chanting: "Tut, Tut, a son, a son, we want a son from your marriage who will help us in the future." '

Little did they – or Emma – know that she was, by that time, four weeks pregnant with Riek's child.

13

Emma had long been desperate to have Riek's child, but after several unsuccessful attempts, she was downcast. I had always fallen pregnant so effortlessly, and I think she believed that she would fall the same. Asking her physician's advice on one of her return trips to Nairobi, he had suggested that she spend at least part of her life in a less tense environment.

'WAR ZONES ARE NOT GENERALLY CONDUCIVE TO SUCCESSFUL CONCEPTION,' HE ADVISED.

Emma laughed his suggestion off, claiming she had seen hundreds of Nuer women give birth in the middle of armed attacks and bombing raids, and told him she had work to do.

Despite her positive mental outlook, however, physically things were not going quite so well as planned. She suspected that she was not conceiving because she had not yet fully recovered from previous illnesses: hepatitis and bouts of malaria. On returning to Leer on her previous trip, she fell ill once again. It was the night of the ceremony to pray for a baby. She wrote:

'I had a thundering headache. A cold shiver clawed up my back and I knew I had malaria. Malaria in this part of the world is considered a common cold. We reached home and Riek ordered me to have a shower to take down my temperature.

"It is so cold," I said, "I don't want to," but he told me I must. He said I would feel much better.

I ran to the shower just as the storm broke. I couldn't close the door, it was buffeted and flung open by the rain and wind. I ran back draped in a kanga; there was no point putting on any clothes, I was already drenched by the time I reached the door. Shivering, my teeth chattering, I had aching joints. I warmed myself beside Riek's body, the shivering subsided and I relaxed and lay on our bed wrapped in an Ethiopian cotton jabi.

That night the fever came and went. My knee joints ached. I lay, and sat, next to Riek's cool, relaxed body. I had goose pimples, it was a fretful night.

"You're pregnant," Riek said. "Your breasts are getting bigger, I can feel it." '

Emma took the new wonder drug, Halfan, for three days but the malaria came back. Concerned now, she asked Riek to arrange for a plane to fly her to Nairobi for medical treatment. He wanted her to stay, assured her she would be all right, but – as always – Emma won in the end. Seriously unwell on the flight, she was admitted to the casualty department of Nairobi Hospital and tested positive for malaria. She wrote:

'The charming, grey-haired Dr Saio appeared and asked where I had been. Italian-born and a world expert on malaria, he is only interested in you when you are sick. When I told him I thought I might be pregnant he said he would do a test. If it was positive, there were certain drugs he couldn't give me.

"Even Halfan is dangerous," he added. "In my experience it either kills the foetus or leaves it unharmed." Seeing the look of horror on my face, he added, in an attempt at reassurance: "Of course, you will have to have a scan to check that you don't have a monster." '

With the pregnancy confirmed and frightened by what she might have done, Emma finally took the advice of the doctors that she take better care of herself and be grounded in Nairobi. She gave up smoking and began making plans to come back to England for Christmas 1993. She would have her baby in Surrey, and return with it to Africa the following spring. She knew that if she planned carefully, her child would qualify for a British passport – something that might not otherwise be so easy for the half-caste baby of a woman born in India, married to a Sudanese, and living in Kenya. But, first, she had to break the news to me.

In a faxed letter, dated 18 August, she wrote excitedly:

'Dear Mum, I was whisked back from southern Sudan last Monday and immediately admitted to Nairobi Hospital with malaria. Now I am fit and well and fully recovered . . . The good news is that I am pregnant – two-and-a-half months. Riek is delighted. I have decided to change my plans and come back to the UK for Christmas and stay on until the baby is born. I very much want to be near you when I give birth as I know you will have lots of good ideas and advice. What do you think? . . . Mum, if you are able, it would be lovely if you could ring me today, this afternoon. Lots and lots of love, Emma XXX'

In a letter to her Aunt Sue, explaining her plans, she added: 'It will also be nice to be with Mum, who will be very supportive.'

It is a matter of the most bitter regret to me that, sadly, my first reaction to Emma's news was unfavourable. In her usual disarming way, Emma had shocked me with the news by sending the fax to my office. To be honest, and despite the fact that I knew she had been trying for a baby for a while, I was so completely taken aback at the idea of actually becoming a grandmother that I didn't respond as fulsomely as a mother should. I called her that very afternoon, as she requested. When she asked me what I thought of her news I let my vanity get the better of me, a regret I shall live with for the rest of my days.

'Well, Mum? What do you think about being a *genuine* Granny this time?' she asked, her voice full of anticipation. Her reference to Emmanuel's nickname made me bristle slightly.

'We – ell,' I faltered, 'I – I am not sure I really like the idea, to be perfectly frank,' I said, rather frostily. 'I mean, Emma, don't you think I'm a bit young to be a grandmother?' Assuming that she had been taking the fertility drugs the doctors had given her, I had spent the morning wondering, with some trepidation, how many little Sudanese grandchildren were going to come trooping down my garden path, and what the neighbours might say. There was a cold silence down the line. I knew immediately that I had said the wrong thing. You could cut the atmosphere with a knife. Finding an excuse to finish the call, Emma rang off abruptly, leaving me feel more like a wicked stepmother than a fairy grandmother.

In any event, I now know that my reaction disappointed my daughter greatly. In a long letter sent to Riek shortly afterwards, she said: 'I told Mum about the pregnancy but she was not very pleased, although she tried to pretend. So I feel very alone and nowhere to turn to. Please, please help me.'

Fortunately, after the initial shock, my attitude softened once I grew accustomed to the idea and I resolved to make it up to Emma next time she came home, at Christmas. I had Johnny's old bedroom in my house changed into a nursery in preparation for the baby's arrival. I had already rearranged some of the furniture and unearthed some old pictures from the nursery at Cowling – little hand-painted images of the four seasons, which I had given to each of my children born at various times of the year. Emma was winter, Erica summer, Jennie autumn and Johnny spring. I planned to hang them ready for when Emma returned and looked forward to shopping with her to choose nursery furniture and baby clothes.

Emma heard of this via Johnny and was thrilled. Thereafter she couldn't wait to come home. She proudly told her friends that I was preparing the nursery. By then she was in full 'nesting mode', giving up smoking, forbidding others to smoke in her company and thriving on the early stages of motherhood. But for the moment, her most immediate problem was where to live while she stayed in Nairobi. She hated living in hotels, and didn't want to put upon friends indefinitely because of the complicated paraphernalia of her personal security, so she pleaded with Riek to help her set up a sanctuary, a home, a secure house of their own which could double up as an SPLA headquarters.

In a long letter to Riek about her hopes and dreams for the future, dated 5 September 1993, Emma wrote:

'I have already lain awake at night worrying about the future of our child and whether you will be there to help me. I wonder, will I ever

have a home to raise my children in and food to eat, and whether I am totally irresponsible in bringing a child into such an uncertain future . . . I know it is not easy for you, but you have to take a more active role in the future of your child. All the wives of your senior colleagues are not expected to live on 10,000 Kenyan shillings a month [approximately £100]. You must come to Nairobi to help me sort out this problem. Your family is just as important as the SPLA . . . When I married you I had money saved from my job and for two years I never asked you for anything, and I shared what I had with you. That money has now gone and I need your help. You know I love you very much and we have endured many difficulties together. But you cannot spend all your time sorting other people's problems out and ignoring your own . . . Your baby needs your hand to touch and feel her – I think it is going to be a girl. I went and had a scan two weeks ago when the baby was only eight weeks and I could see the little heart beat.

Riek promised faithfully to come to Nairobi later that month, his first trip out of Sudan in four years, if Emma agreed to fly up to Mankien to escort him out. He also authorised the necessary permission and finance to set her up in a safe house. In the strange and mysterious ways of Third World funding, the building, its fittings and other sundries were all willingly paid for by the Lutheran World Federation, the relief arm of the Scandinavian and German Lutheran Church, and the Lonhro organisation, headed by controversial businessman Tiny Rowland, a long-term investor in Sudan and a meddler in African politics.

Emma began house hunting, and soon found a beautiful place called the Ngong Dairy in Karen, a suburb of Nairobi. It was the house used in the film *Out of Africa* – the story of the life of Karen Blixen, the Danish novelist. Emma was entranced by the house and desperately wanted to live there, but Riek's security advisers, who went to see it with her, blocked any possibility.

'It would be a security nightmare,' one told her. 'Out in the middle of the fields; there are a hundred places an assassin could hide.' After her terrifying experience in Kongor – an event which still caused her nightmares – Emma knew that she was in danger and had to heed their advice. She was bitterly disappointed, but determined not to miss out on a good opportunity when she saw one, so she rushed round to where Sally was living in her tiny house in Langata and dragged her back to the Dairy.

'You simply must take it,' Emma insisted. 'I'll rent a room to help pay the bills and you can get a lodger.' Sally, laughing, agreed.

Emma soon found a suitable property for her, Riek and the baby, a place the security men agreed they could handle. It was a white stone house within a secure compound, in the Riverside area of Nairobi, where all the ambassadors and diplomats live. After signing the lease, she collected the keys and started the process of fitting and furnishing her first proper home. Walking Sally proudly through the grounds, she declared:

'This is going to be a happy home. I shall name it Peace House.'

For a brief period, all was complete happiness and domestic bliss; it was a far cry from the brightly painted mud huts she had been living in for the last few years. Riek returned from Sudan and she was able to introduce him to her many friends in Nairobi.

'He isn't a phantom husband after all,' she told them delightedly, clutching him to her side.

Riek swung into high-level peace talks in Nairobi, before flying on to Washington and Atlanta, Georgia, at the instigation of former US President Jimmy Carter, to meet the Presidents of Kenya, Uganda, Ethiopia and Eritrea and to take part in UN-brokered talks. Emma enlisted her friends around the world to ensure that he wear a suit and not his battle fatigues. In October, after those talks collapsed, he flew into London for more meetings, his first visit to Britain in many years and a chance for him to see Angelina and his three children. It was also our first chance to meet.

Emma rang Johnny from Nairobi to say Riek was arriving and asked him to arrange a supper party with as many of the family as possible. My lovely, happy-go-lucky son did all he was asked and duly hosted the meal in the house he shared with a friend, inviting as many of us as he could muster. My sister Sue and her son Peter travelled up with me from Surrey, and Johnny's friend Clare was also there, along with Riek's two burly bodyguards and a Sudanese colleague called Majok. Jennie was living in Egypt and couldn't make it. It was midweek and Erica felt unable to travel from Bristol to London to meet her new brother-in-law. Johnny thought Riek might be a little nervous because he had violated the strict English custom of asking the bride's family for permission to marry first. He wanted to reassure Riek right from the start that we weren't too concerned by that.

'We come from a pretty liberal family,' he said not long after his brother-in-law walked in. 'If Emma is happy, we're happy.' Riek smiled and patted Johnny fondly on the shoulder.

My first impression of my son-in-law, then forty-one, was how big and black he was. Standing seven feet tall – eighteen inches taller than me – and dressed in a smart suit, when he opened his mouth to smile, his teeth positively dazzled with their whiteness. He was extremely charismatic and confident, with warm dark brown eyes, and long eyelashes which he often fluttered as he spoke. His head and neck were thickset and he had a broad nose and a round face. And then there was his velvet voice, with its lilting, melodic tone.

'Maggie, how good to meet you at last,' he said courteously, taking my hand and squeezing it. 'I feel I know you already from your letters.' His gap-toothed grin engulfed me. I could see what Emma found so attractive. Unless I was mistaken, he was almost flirting with me and I actually felt myself blush. This was a man who knew how to handle a woman, I thought. Even my daughter.

There was no hint in his eyes of nervousness, no suggestion that meeting his wife's family for the first time was an ordeal. Just the cool, calm presence of a man in charge, someone completely at ease with westerners, and willing to answer any questions we had for him. When I did ask a few pertinent questions about the current political situation in Sudan, he was charming and polite, but he gave away only as much as he wanted to. He was a natural war lord and a consummate politician, as his wife had also become.

Johnny cooked a delicious chicken casserole, and Sue brought a plum crumble with almonds. We sat around the candlelit table in an informal, convivial atmosphere, not unlike any normal family dinner party. The difference was that this time we had a rebel commander with a price on his head among us, and his bodyguards stood rather menacingly by the door. Despite all of that, the evening was a great success.

Riek told us a little of his family history – we were amazed to learn he was his father's twenty-sixth child – and he reassured us of his love for Emma and his desire to keep her from harm. Shortly after supper, during a brief lull in the conversation, he stood suddenly, jolting his bodyguards into life, and announced, with firm politeness, that he had to leave. We shook hands quite formally and said our farewells.

'You are, of course, all invited to my home land when the conditions are a little less . . . hot,' he beamed, pleased with his double entendre. The bodyguards held open the door and swept him out in a single flanking movement. He was gone.

Emma was delighted when she heard how the evening had progressed, although a little disappointed that Erica and Jennie couldn't have been there. She was excited by the idea of us all being together in the same room in west London, thrilled that I had met him at last and relieved that it had passed without incident. Her only wish was that she could have been there to share the moment. Riek left London for Europe, visiting France, Germany and Norway to further the peace talks, while Emma, in Nairobi, orchestrated his schedule, telephoning ahead, booking hotel rooms and faxing him and his delegates with the latest information from Sudan. He was due to fly back to Kenya briefly before going on to Uganda for more talks. Then, she hoped to have him to herself for a while.

She was also extremely busy with the projects closest to her heart. From her hotel room in Nairobi, while waiting for Peace House to be ready, she was busy setting up a new non-government organisation to be called Woman Aid, to be registered in Nairobi. This evolved from the Southern Sudan Women's Association (SSWA). She drew up the registration documents and outline manifesto, claiming that few international organisations were directly assisting the women of southern Sudan. She wrote:

'Women have been left by their husbands, children by their fathers and brothers to fight the war. Women have had to take over the responsibility of the households, building houses, finding food and looking after the livestock. Thousands have been forced to flee to refugee camps. Women Aid wishes to help women displaced by war and famine to help

themselves and their families. Women Aid will specialise in small income-generating projects which will enable women inside and outside Sudan to better their lives.'

It was pioneering stuff and Emma hoped to attract international funding, particularly from the UN. She was also involved with curriculum development projects for educational-based charities, an expanded programme of immunisation through UNICEF, and self-sufficiency projects for the Southern Sudan Women's Association, and help for the war wounded.

Emma furnished Peace House in a matter of a few weeks, buying bargain furniture from auction houses, and arranging brightly coloured sofas, scatter cushions and curtains to fill the airy rooms of her new home. She had commissioned a huge metal bed for her and Riek from the artist David Marrian. In short, she was making a nest. She also had great plans for the grounds and garden, planting her beloved vegetables and fruit between the sprawling bougainvillea and lush bedding plants, brimming with blue agapanthus. There would be an English feel to her garden, she boasted, with roses and herbs. It would be a place of tranquillity and calm for her and her baby.

Emma was happy, she had her best friends around her and she was in a place of safety, after Sudan. She would have loved to have seen more of Riek, could well have done without the security circus that surrounded her, and wished I could have been with her, but generally, she was content. She was further uplifted by the news that her brother Johnny had decided to visit her in Kenya with a close friend. Their youngest sister Jennie had decided to join them, flying in from Egypt, where she was a cook on a dive-boat. And Johnny brought the footballs – bought with money raised by Emma's cousin's marathon – out with him. They were swiftly despatched to southern Sudan and distributed to the children. With Jennie and Johnny's help, Emma finally moved in on 1 November 1993. In those last three weeks of her life, Peace House was where she truly did find sanctuary. With a child on the way, something she had longed for and a responsibility she felt deeply, she knew she had to relinquish her peripatetic and spontaneous existence. She needed a life which was safe and secure, a place with doctors and all those things which are important for a family. Although she had dreamed of having her child grow up happily in Leer, playing in the dust with the other children, for the first few years of her baby's life at least, she wanted the safer option. She was painfully aware – after her years in southern Sudan – of how lucky she was to have the choice.

Reading her letters and listening to her on the telephone as she told me all about her new home, I was greatly relieved that she was away from the immediate physical danger of southern Sudan, even though I could tell she was still very fragile emotionally. Although she sometimes seemed like a cat with nine lives, she had gambled so nonchalantly with her life in the past that I was worried that she was somehow becoming immunised to death. At least in Nairobi, I thought, she would be safe.

> *Stay with me, God: The night is dark,*
> *The night is cold: my little spark*
> *Of courage dies. The night is long;*
> *Be with me, God, and make me strong.*

from 'A Soldier – His Prayer', Anon

I was alone in my house in Surrey. It was early – 5.27 am on Thursday 25 November 1993. The telephone by my bedside rang, rousing me from a deep sleep. I reached out to answer it, but was far from being fully awake, and I had no premonition of bad news. It was a call from Kenya. It was Johnny.

'Where are you?' I asked in confusion, surprised to hear his voice, but pleased nonetheless. Silly Johnny, I thought, must have got his time zones muddled up.

'At the coast,' he replied. I remembered that he was staying with Willie Knocker's family in Watamu for a few days, while Emma remained in Nairobi. Fond memories of my holiday there earlier that year filtered slowly into my sleepy brain. Johnny began to speak calmly and clearly.

'Mum, there has been an accident, a fatal accident.'

I heard him say the words and yet nothing seemed real. All of a sudden my mind jerked alert, racing ahead of him to my first thought, that something had happened to Jennie. I sat bolt upright in bed, my heart pounding as the idea flashed through my mind that she had drowned, because I knew she was a great diving enthusiast.

'Jennie,' I gasped, my throat tightening by the second.

'No,' Johnny said firmly. 'It is not Jennie.'

My mind raced on. Who then? Not, not . . . Before I could continue with the dreadful process of elimination, he ended my agony.

'Emma . . . It's Emma,' he finally blurted out. 'She has been killed.'

The burden of having to break this terrible news to me suddenly overwhelmed him, and I could hear him fighting for breath.

Emma. Emma. I am being told that my eldest daughter, my first-born child, my crazy, zany girl, the one who has been my closest friend since Bunny died, has gone forever.

Ever since she had first started to flirt with Africa, and to become interested in their politics, I had had a nagging fear that Emma was putting herself in danger. In recent months, before she moved to Nairobi, I had lived in fear for her life, thinking that she might succumb to some fatal tropical disease or fall victim to an assassin's bullet. Yet now I was stunned into silence because – so far as I understood it – she was somewhere safe, away from the malaria and the bullets of the southern Sudanese war zone.

'How did she die?' I whispered, my throat suddenly dry. Images of a bloody assassination flooded my brain.

'In a car accident.'

I almost laughed. A cruel twist of fate after all the bombs and bullets and disease. I had to force myself to believe that it was true.

Poor Johnny could only bear to speak in short bursts, for the waves of unspeakable pain and sadness, and the last time I had received such news, I ran, like some cornered animal, howling at the moon. Now, I did the same thing. I dropped the receiver to run and wail and groan out my grief.

I didn't cry at first, I didn't weep tears. There were no racking sobs. Just the cry of an animal in the most extreme form of pain – that of bereavement. I can't remember what I did next, I only know that I wandered downstairs for something, the strange howling still coming from my lips. My son, only twenty-three, still hanging on the end of the line, was shouting into the telephone receiver more than four thousand miles away, calling for his mother.

I wandered back, picked up the dangling receiver and listened to his anxious calls. Falteringly, I tried to finish our conversation. He was imploring me to telephone my sister Sue, who lived close by, so that I wouldn't be on my own. Calmer now, and settling into the numb state that descended, I insisted that it was too early.

'I'm all right,' I lied. 'I'll wait for an hour or so until people start to stir.' There was silence between us, an echoing empty silence. 'Where was the accident?' I asked feebly.

'In Nairobi . . . last night,' Johnny replied, his voice choked with tears. 'Mum, I'm so, so sorry.'

More silence, a huge chasm between us – impossible to fill. Finally, I stuttered: 'I – I'll be on a plane to Nairobi later today. I – I'll let you know when.' There was no reply, just a muffled sobbing. 'Goodbye,' I ended and carefully, oh so carefully, lowered the receiver into its cradle.

Slowly my disbelief turned to belief. It is true. My Emma is dead.

I began to cry uncontrollably. The grief overwhelmed and engulfed me. Unable to see for the tears, unable to speak for the great sobs that shook my body, I lay on my bed and cried my heart out. Then – almost as abruptly as it had begun – it stopped. Somehow, automatically, I dressed and made myself a mug of tea – the first of many that morning. I realised that a mountain had risen up before me and I had no alternative but to climb it. And yet, though I felt paralysed, something was already beginning to drive me, some primal need.

The doorbell rang, shaking me from my reverie. It was Sue; Jennie had telephoned her immediately after her brother's call to me. There wasn't a great deal to say, my head was still reeling from the news, spinning with the information that had so badly winded me. With one look at Sue's tears, the emotions erupted again, and we clung together, rocking each other in our grief. Sitting at my dining-room table by six o'clock, Sue with her coffee, and me with my tea, we slowly gathered ourselves together and drew up a plan of action. There was so much that had to be done.

266

Even though only a short time had passed since I heard the news, I started to feel amazingly clear-headed, totally focused on what I had to do: to get to Nairobi as soon as possible. Sue drew up a list of all the people we had to call, the arrangements we had to make, and the essential things I would need to take with me for the journey. By seven o'clock, I was ready to start putting the plan into action. My priority was to speak to Erica at her home in Bristol. Johnny and Jennie knew, I knew, Sue knew, but poor Yo had no idea as yet. She was probably deeply asleep in her bed, expecting nothing more than another normal Thursday at work. Checking my watch, I saw that it wasn't even half-past seven.

'Let's wait a little longer, and allow her to wake up naturally,' I pleaded with Sue, who nodded her agreement.

We resolved instead to concentrate on organising my flight to Nairobi. I called James Basnett, a friend of Johnny's who is an international airline pilot. I thought he might be able to secure me a flight to Nairobi later that day. I literally begged him to fix a booking for me.

I had been procrastinating about calling Erica, knowing what a wave of grief the call would bring for her – and for me. Afraid of it almost. But, with Sue's gentle urging, the number was dialled. Fortunately, Hugh, her lovely boyfriend, answered and I was able to warn him of what was to come. Yo came to the phone, a tremulous note to her voice, afraid of the look in Hugh's eyes. I broke her the news and there was a long silence. She seemed to take it calmly at first, though she was obviously finding it hard to rally her thoughts so early in the morning.

'I am flying out to Nairobi,' I said, flatly. 'Do you want to come with me?'

There was more silence. 'I'll come to Surrey, and then decide, if that's okay, Mum,' she said softly.

As the clock ticked and dawn began to break, Sue dashed home to sort out her children on the morning school run, leaving me alone in the house. I sat silently in the sitting-room for over an hour, my mind clicking forward in perfect synchronisation with the second hand of the clock.

Stop all the clocks, cut off the telephone,
Prevent the dog from barking with a juicy bone,
Silence the pianos and with muffled drum
Bring out the coffin, let the mourners come.

from 'Funeral Blues' by W. H. Auden

When Sue returned, and with a fresh mug of tea cupped in my hands, we set about telephoning close relatives, friends and godparents to break the news. Some couldn't begin to accept what I was telling them. We would end the conversation and then they would ring back seconds later, simply unable to believe it was true. In the case of Emma's closest friends I spoke to their parents first, asking them to break the news for me. As soon as I put the phone down, another call came in as the news got around. My father, by then aged eighty-one, was naturally stunned by the news. He listened and appeared to take on board what I was saying and was even more staggered by the concept of me jumping on a plane to Africa that evening.

'I'm so very sorry, Rabbit,' he told me and put the phone down.

Wendy Burton, Emma's godmother, was also amazed at my sudden departure and asked: 'Well, what are you going to do when you get there?'

'I don't know,' I replied.

Truly I didn't have any clear idea of what would happen or what I could even achieve by going. I just knew I had to get to Africa. It was an animal instinct. The pace became increasingly frenetic. The phone calls kept coming. Sue took them while I packed and organised the details of the trip. I tried to remain focused on what I needed to do. There were my employers to be notified, money to arrange, booster inoculations and malaria tablets to collect from the surgery, and things to pack. I remember walking into the waiting room at the doctor's surgery and staring at the only other patient, a man in his fifties. I wasn't crying, I sat still, very still, waiting. As my name was called, he spoke to me as I stepped past him.

'The heart speaks loudly,' he said softly. He knew.

At first I felt as if I was in control, but soon afterwards I felt as if I was walking along a conveyor belt, going through a process of coping, as events unfolded with increasing momentum. I realised I had to let the physical and practical demands take their course, otherwise I was in danger of falling off the conveyor belt altogether.

I returned home to find that Erica and Hugh had already arrived and were waiting for me, red-eyed and sniffing, but there was little time for any communal keening. By this time, we were being bombarded with calls – newspaper reporters from around the globe had heard of Emma's death on a BBC World Service newsflash and were asking me for details of her life. The police rang and then the Foreign Office. All was confusion, as we had no clear information about what had happened, or how. But still the calls kept coming.

A reporter from one of the tabloid newspapers started to hammer on the front door. Yo opened it and heard him telling her that he was sorry to intrude but he was looking for the 'human aspect' of the story. Erica drew herself up to her full height and told him, rather imperiously:

'I don't think we want a story in the *Express*,' before sending him packing. To deter any more similar visits, we contacted Madeleine Bunting, an old schoolfriend of Emma's and a journalist, to take on the task of briefing the press – including the man on the doorstep – on Emma's background.

At last the call that I had been waiting for came. It was James Basnett. I was booked on a Kenyan Airways flight departing from Heathrow later that evening with no idea of what to expect when I arrived at my destination. I flew alone, as on so many other journeys in my life.

Erica was still in a state of shock and needed a bit more time to gather her thoughts together. She had left her home in Bristol that morning with only the clothes she was wearing and her passport. It had somehow never occurred to her that she might not be returning to work the next day. Even in the hour of tragedy, the routines of life go on. Sue, with three small children and a home to run, could also not drop everything. Erica promised me she would join me in Africa later, and as Sue kissed me goodbye she pressed two poetry books into my hand for the journey.

Call her once before you go –
Call once yet!
In a voice that she will know:
'Margaret! Margaret!'
Children's voices should be dear
(Call once more) to a mother's ear . . .

from 'The Forsaken Merman' by Matthew Arnold

Erica, Hugh and I sat in a bar at Heathrow after I had checked in. The time had come for me to switch from cups of tea to a shot or two of neat whisky and the transition felt good. Erica walked to the airport bookshop to buy me a thriller for the journey – *The Firm* – thinking, I suppose, that I needed some escapism. But I never opened it. I fumbled in my luggage for the poetry books Sue had given me, chose one, and handed the other to Hugh to return to Sue. We abandoned the empty glasses at the bar when my flight was called and made our way to the departure gate. They kissed me goodbye, their tears wet on my cheeks, and I disappeared.

On board the aircraft, I had the curious feeling that somehow I was the possessor of a closely guarded secret. Though many people had, by now, heard about Emma's death, no one knew who I was, or why I was on this flight to Kenya. I was alone for the next eight hours, with thoughts racing round my head, thoughts of the past rather than of the future – the future didn't exist for me, not then. In the pressurised cabin, my mind floated freely; I reflected on life, on my life and Emma's. Now death had snatched her life away from me, rousing me from sleep at dawn, to bring me the worst of all waking nightmares – the loss of my child.

I was drifting, drifting backwards in time. I could only focus my mind on Emma and her life. I saw the naked toddler dancing and giggling on the grass in Assam. I saw her cluttered bedroom at Cowling, filled with gymkhana rosettes and the paraphernalia of childhood. I saw her riding out with the West of Yore hunt, her hair flying in the wind, her eyes wide at the stirring sound of the hunting horn; and I saw her on her return from Australia, her face tanned, her head thrown back laughing, as she presented me with the length of beautiful blue silk from a foreign land.

I thought about the last time we spoke, a brief telephone conversation ten days earlier, discussing the fun she would have with Johnny and Jennie during their holiday to Kenya. The scratchy notes I'd made as I doodled through our conversation were still clipped to the notice board in my kitchen. There had been something in her voice that had bothered me. She hadn't yet moved into Peace House and was calling from her hotel room. She sounded like a caged animal with no privacy, she was constantly surrounded by Sudanese, and her bodyguards, and was impatient to get into a place of her own.

'I'm feeling okay, just a little tired,' she said wistfully. I could tell that there was something else, she was perhaps a little weepy, a little hormonal, and probably feeling a little down. It was understandable, she was twenty-nine, five months pregnant with her first child, trapped in a hotel room without her husband or her mother, unable to walk freely for security reasons.

'Well, do you want me to fly out, and spend some time with you?' I asked.

There was a pause. I could tell she was seriously considering it, momentarily lifted by the idea. But then she sighed; she knew it wasn't the best time either for her or for me. I had recently started in my new job as a secretary at St Paul's Cathedral, I couldn't just up and leave. She was due to come home in a few weeks anyway – she had already checked out her last possible flying date – and Johnny and Jennie were about to fly in.

'No . . . it's okay, Mum,' she said, slowly. 'Thanks for the offer, I really appreciate it, but . . . I'm okay.' That tone again, a flatness in her voice. I was starting to get worried. She must have been able to tell, because she suddenly brightened, ever the one to hide her deeper feelings.

'Don't worry,' she added. 'I'll be fine once I get into the new house and have something to do . . . Really, I will.'

I told her to take care of herself and that I loved her. Putting down the telephone, I mentally placed myself on red alert. I felt instinctively that I might need to make a sudden journey.

I remember crying on the plane, shedding so many silent tears. But in the subdued light of the aircraft, no one could see me wipe them away. I was isolated in my grief, and I couldn't order my thoughts clearly. I read some poetry and short pieces of prose – lines that didn't require too much concentration, where the words now took on poignant new meanings. They applied to me, to my situation. And all this did was to make me cry even more.

When I am dead, cry for me a little, but not too much. Think of me now and then, as I was in life. At some moments it is pleasant to recall, but not for long. Leave me in peace and I shall leave you in peace. And while you live, let your thoughts be with the living.

from 'Indian Prayer', Anon

It was an endless journey in some ways, but in other ways it wasn't. Lulled by the pulsing motion of the plane as it flew through the air to a darker continent, fortified by a few drinks along the way, I was able to suspend time for those eight hours, to stop and start it and rewind it to wherever I wanted it to pause. It gave me the courage I needed for my heart to handle my soul. It was *my* time to be alone with my thoughts in the dark, to hurtle inexorably towards my daughter, to where she lay in peace.

Dawn was breaking as the plane landed and taxied off the runway at Kenyatta Airport. It wasn't a particularly sunny morning, though hot and humid, and I queued, exhausted, with other passengers, waiting at the various desks to have my documents stamped and authorised. And still I had not talked to anyone; no one knew why I had come from there to here.

'What is the purpose of your visit? Business or pleasure?' the officials asked wearily, barely looking up as the queue of people behind me waited.

Without emotion, I replied: 'I am here to bury my daughter.' I watched for their reaction. Once they realised my mission, they regarded me with sincere sadness and waved me through. Moving along the conveyor belt, on automatic pilot, to the baggage reclaim area, I stood for what seemed like an age waiting for my luggage. The carousel went round and round as I stood alone, the last remaining passenger, waiting for my case to appear. Eventually it came, crashing through a square hole in the wall, and I grabbed it before making my way towards the area where Emma had met me on so many occasions before.

I passed through customs with nothing to declare and wandered through a maze, a haze of people, not knowing where I was heading. Then thankfully, two faces emerged from the crowd that I recognised – Johnny and Jennie appeared, walking ashen-faced towards me. We hugged each other in silence, unable to speak. We found a seat in the chaos and sat down heavily. Jennie put an arm around my shoulder; with the other she held my hand. Johnny was at my shoulder; and for a few silent minutes we hung our heads together in grief. Accompanying them was Sally, Emma's closest friend. I always thought of them as being like sisters. Seeing the sorrow etched on her face now as she hovered in the background, I knew that – in their souls – they were. We tried our best, but our conversation was stilted. No one could find the appropriate words, because there were none.

It was a silent journey into the city, as Sally drove us towards Riverside. The world outside was all noise and mayhem as we drove through the dust and the morning rush hour traffic: horns honked in furious impatience, *matatus* – overcrowded, badly driven minibuses without indicators – lurched into our path unpredictably, or slammed to a stop without warning, as people leapt on and off in front of our car. This hardly helped to ease the fragile state of our nerves.

I had been inundated with offers of places to stay, but I knew where I wanted to go. To Roo and Simon's, the last people my daughter had been with before she died. We arrived and I was given a warm welcome. Each meeting replicated the last, as people were lost for words, shocked, dismayed, unable to believe what had happened. After a few more tears, we had some breakfast, all of us stifling our emotions once more. Still more friends arrived and were ushered in to meet me as I sat, exhausted, on a sofa in the guest wing.

You would know the secret of death.
But how shall you find it unless you seek it in the heart of life . . . ?
If you would indeed behold the spirit of death, open your heart wide
*   unto the body of life.*
For life and death are one, even as the river and the sea are one.

from *The Prophet* by Kahlil Gibran

It was during those first few hours that I learned the details of my daughter's final days. Johnny and Jennie had been with her for a week and said she was very happy. Johnny had brought her the three things she asked for from England – salt and pepper grinders, the new Delia Smith *Summer Cooking* cookbook and a telephone answering machine. Leaving her to unpack, plump up the cushions and enjoy a few days alone with Riek, recently returned from his world travels, Johnny and Jennie had then gone to the coast for their holiday with the Knocker family. The last time they saw her, Emma was buzzing around, her distinctive laugh echoing through Peace House, giving orders to house-boys and trying to organise her first big dinner party – for the Nairobi Cabinet, no less – complete with a live goat that had to be killed and cooked for the meal. The evening was apparently a great success and Emma shone in her new role as the diplomat's wife.

On the day she died, Riek was out at a meeting, so she worked all morning on her proposals for the Southern Sudanese Women's Associa-tion, breaking off in the afternoon to visit Roo, a short walk away from Peace House. When Emma arrived for a cup of tea and a chat, Roo was so taken aback by her beauty as she blossomed into her pregnancy that she thought she really should take a photograph of her. As Roo said afterwards:

'There was this wonderful serenity about her, a contentment within herself. She was happy, really happy, she was in love and looking forward to her baby and her future.'

The two friends quickly started talking and Roo forgot about the photograph, something she would always regret.

The telephone rang, it was Willie Knocker, recently arrived in town and on his way to the coast.

'Guess who's here?' his sister Roo teased down the phone. 'Emma.' Emma grabbed the phone and she and Willie spoke, agreeing to meet up later in the evening for drinks at Sally's, at the Ngong Dairy at Karen. Despite Emma's past treatment of Willie, there was a bond between them which had always filled a need in her. Ever since they had started dating, she had pushed him away, pulled him towards her again, then pushed him away. She needed his reassurance. In her own way, I think she probably loved him; she just didn't want to be his wife. Excited now at the prospect of seeing him later that night, and always happy to visit her best friend Sally, Emma put the phone down. It was the last time she and Willie were ever to speak.

It was late afternoon by the time Emma got up to leave, so Roo offered her the use of Simon's Land Cruiser, a common occurrence if she didn't have her own transport. Unusually, Emma wasn't accompanied by Forty-Six, her trusty bodyguard who normally would have driven her. Emma had given him some time off to go and visit his family in Waat and – glad to be free of the shackles of security that bound her – she had resisted the offer of another bodyguard in his place. Roo handed her the car keys with the words: 'See you later.' Emma promised to be back with the car around eight o'clock.

When she hadn't turned up by nine, Roo began to worry, which was unusual – she had never worried about Emma before. She telephoned the Dairy and Sally answered to say that Emma had never arrived. Simon disappeared off to bed, brushing aside his wife's concerns, and reminding her what a free spirit Emma was.

'She probably changed her mind,' he said. 'Don't worry, she'll bring the car back tomorrow.' But Roo had an uneasy feeling in the pit of her stomach and she went out in her own car, cruising the streets to look for Emma, without success. 'I had a sort of knowing, I was absolutely certain in my mind that I had to go out and look for her,' she said afterwards, 'I wasn't content to sit at home or even go to bed. I remember feeling very alone in the darkness because I felt no one else knew or understood what I was experiencing.'

Arriving back home and eventually retiring to bed, but still restless and reading into the night, she was disturbed by a tap at her window. It was her *askari* (or night watchman), to tell her that Riek was at the gate. Walking out, she took one look at Emma's husband and knew something dreadful had happened.

'I remember it clearly, it was his size, his blackness and the whites of his eyes, very wide and fearful in the night.' She led him inside and he told her what had happened as they sat and sipped a stiff whisky each.

Not long after leaving Roo and approaching a notoriously dangerous crossroads at the Gitanga Road and the James Gichuru Road with the sinking sun in her eyes, Emma had slowed her car down and then started across. There were no traffic lights and she did not have the right of way. She apparently did not see the *matatu* bus bearing down on her at full speed and she accelerated straight out into its path. She was not wearing a seat belt, she rarely did – it is not law in Kenya – and she was thrown out of the vehicle and onto a grass verge in the front garden of a house. The heavy car then rolled on top of her.

She had suffered severe internal injuries, taking the full force of the impact on her chest. Landing awkwardly, and initially trapped by the car, she had injured her leg, but her face and body were otherwise untouched and there was not a trace of blood. Emma never fully lost consciousness, and in her delirium she called out again and again:

'My baby, my baby.'

She also called the name 'SPLA, SPLA,' in an effort to identify herself and to let people know who they should contact.

The Indian lady in whose garden she had landed did all she could to make Emma comfortable, wrapping her in a blanket, but she was clearly critically injured and still in considerable distress about her baby. Because she was so tall and lean, and not obviously pregnant at five months, valuable minutes were wasted by those who had first run to her aid, looking for her 'baby' which they assumed had been thrown from the car. As more and more people stopped to scour the accident scene and search the bush for an infant, Emma's life was ebbing away.

It was only when a passing Kenyan politician stopped and realised that the main priority was being overlooked that Emma was taken to hospital. He literally lifted her, wrapped in a blanket, and laid her on the back seat of his own car. He drove to Nairobi Hospital as fast as possible. But she died before they arrived. It was too late. The doctors could do nothing to save her; she died of massive internal injuries to her chest and stomach, which had also killed her unborn child. It was a little boy.

In the immediate aftermath of Emma's death, and in the intervening years, there have been many wild rumours circulating in Nairobi and Sudan that Emma had been murdered, that her violent death was not an accident. It seemed too coincidental that she had died on the night her bodyguard was not with her and in a week when there had been death threats. The theories ranged from a paid assassin at the wheel of the *matatu*, to the suggestion that another car might have been tailing her and when she got to the crossroads it pushed her out into the path of the bus. My surviving children believe she was deliberately killed, a view not shared by the Kenyan authorities who ruled her death an accident. My own view was, and is, that, however the crash happened, speculating about it will not bring her back. She is dead and it helps nobody to think that it might have been anything other than another tragic accident.

Once Emma had been certified dead, the hospital authorities had the difficult task of finding out who she was. Going through her dirt-spattered belongings, they found her diary and a business card of a friend. Gradually, through a tortuous series of telephone calls, Riek was contacted and rushed to the hospital with his aides.

'I am here to see my wife,' he told the nurses in the casualty department, his voice almost breaking. 'She has been involved in an accident.'

The nurses looked blankly at the tall black man in front of them and told him he must be wrong, that she wasn't there. There had been no black woman brought into casualty after an accident that night, they said. Riek sighed, desperate for news.

'No, my wife is a white woman,' he explained as calmly as he could. Finally, the penny dropped and they led him gently to a side room to wait for the doctor who had certified Emma dead. Riek sat with his elbows on his knees, holding his head in his hands, sobbing silently. His huge frame shook, and when he looked up and saw Emma's sunglasses, neatly folded alongside a small bundle of her belongings, their lenses flecked with mud, he knew, in that instant, that she was dead.

> *Help me, O God, when Death is near*
> *To mock the haggard face of fear,*
> *That when I fall – if fall I must –*
> *My soul may triumph in the Dust.*

> from 'A Soldier – His Prayer', Anon

I desperately wanted to sleep, to drift off into that calming, emotion-free state where the waves of pain inside me would no longer be able to inflict their agonies. But, first, I must see Riek, my son-in-law. I had to hold his hands and see how he was bearing the loss of his wife and his comrade. Sally offered to drive me to Peace House, the house that Emma had made her home, but I declined the offer, telling her I would prefer to walk. It wasn't far, the day was warm and the exercise would do me good. Jennie, Johnny and Sally escorted me, and I summoned together all my inner strength as we reached the house and walked down the path to the front door.

Turning to savour the beauty of the white building set in its lush tropical garden, the garden she had so loved and had already told me about, I gasped when my eyes fell upon something. Tied to a tall tree in a shade-dappled corner of the plot was a wide wooden swing, just like the ones Emma had enjoyed as a child in Assam and at Cowling Hall. Instantly reminding me of how Emma always loved her swings and how she loved to go higher and higher, giggling infectiously and begging to be pushed that little bit further.

Once inside the cool building, I regained my composure. Riek appeared before me, strong and calm. We embraced briefly, but I could tell he was holding himself back, playing the role of leader in the company of so many of his followers. Leading me into a large and spacious room, I stopped myself from lovingly examining my daughter's home, and concentrated on my son-in-law instead. There were scores of people sitting and standing around, as is the custom in Africa when someone dies. I was overwhelmed by the sheer numbers. One by one they came to me and to Riek, to pay their respects, taking our hands and saying 'Paalɛ, Paalɛ' (sorry), before sitting with us in respectful silence for anything up to twenty minutes.

Once their homage had been paid, they were ushered through into the garden to a marquee which had been hastily erected with tables and chairs, and where houseboys served tea and other refreshments. Sally told me that it was customary for the communal grieving to go on for four days. Suddenly aching with tiredness, I took leave of Riek and his people and decided to go back to Roo and Simon's to have a bath and sleep.

Clearly there were many decisions to be made, but everyone was sensitive, unwilling to push me into any course of action. It was somehow touching that they waited for me to make up my mind, although they of course knew how best to make arrangements in a foreign land. On the walk home, Sally and my two youngest children tried to steer me towards deciding on a venue for a funeral service and to choose where Emma should be buried – matters I simply could not decide on a whim.

As I crawled between the sheets of my bed at the Woods' house after a bath, I could still hear people talking, arriving, telephoning, wanting to see me, to know more, to share their grief. Unable to face another soul, I closed my bedroom door, relieved at last to give way to the unconsciousness of oblivion – at least for the next few hours.

It must have been late afternoon when someone woke me. I think we had some tea before Sally began once again to coax me into going and looking at possible venues for a service. The Rev Matthews, a Nuer himself, was anxious for it to be held in the Presbyterian church in Nairobi, which was a Sudanese stronghold. Rev Matthews knew Emma, and had spent much time with her and Riek in southern Sudan; she would discuss her plans with him for the women and children of the village, and listen to his advice. I liked him, although he was a little overwhelming in presence. His church was certainly huge, but I had reservations – neither Emma nor I were Presbyterian, and I was afraid a service there might be hijacked away from us, and beyond our control.

With Sally at the wheel of her Suzuki, we went to look at Nairobi's All Saints Cathedral, and the minute I stepped into the cool through its large wooden doors, I knew this was the place. It was made of the pink-grey stone that was so familiar to me from Yorkshire. The aisle was flanked with carved wooden pews, and the gothic roof arched above it in perfect symmetry. At the far end, a single rose window in blue stained glass cast its tinted light down onto the gold cross on the high altar. The blue of the window was the same rich blue as the length of silk Emma brought me back from Australia.

There was a choir practice in progress and we lingered, listening to the beautiful music and waiting to talk to someone. Eventually the white missionary priest Andrew Gandon emerged to talk to us. He kindly agreed to come and see us later that evening in Riverside to discuss an order of service. I was hugely relieved that a decision had at last been made.

The funeral service was set for three days' time, on Monday 29 November at two o'clock. Andrew Gandon guided us through a jungle of thoughts and plans, and – with a well-thumbed Bible borrowed from the cook – we selected readings and hymns. Roo lent me her computer the following day to type up the order of service; I had never dreamed that one day I would be putting my secretarial skills to arranging my own daughter's funeral. I found it very hard to concentrate as I tried to produce something comprehensible.

Although Riek was willing and ready to be consulted, he chose to remain in the background. In retrospect I think he felt as numb as me, and was relieved that someone had arrived to cross the cultural divide and share with him what Emma might have liked.

To make decisions rapidly was difficult enough, but we were in Africa where nothing could be counted on for certain. Catherine Bond – Emma's journalist friend from Nairobi – proved to be indispensable with her local knowledge. But first I had to decide *where* Emma should be buried – England? And if so, where? Surrey or Yorkshire? In Kenya, where she was most happy and had so many friends? Or in southern Sudan, her marital home and where she lived and worked? Everybody seemed to be waiting for my answer. In the end, I made my choice.

'In southern Sudan,' I announced, and as I said the words out loud, there was suddenly no doubt in my mind.

The minute I made the decision, a whole host of problems sprang up. To bury her in southern Sudan meant that we would have to make a five-hour journey by plane into dangerous air space that we might not be allowed through. The number of people who would be able to attend would depend entirely on how many small aircraft we could charter – all an expense I knew I couldn't afford alone. But should we have the burial in Sudan first, followed by a funeral service back in Nairobi, or vice versa? Faced with these imponderables, everybody began to pull out the stops. The community spirit was incredible.

By Saturday I had typed up the service sheet, then went to the Norfolk Hotel to have a beauty treatment – a curious priority, but one which somehow seemed calming. Johnny had been in contact with friends and family back home, and Erica had arranged to fly out on the Sunday. Johnny had faxed his Aunt Sue with a note which read:

'I think you ought to come out, you played a big part in Emma's life. Do please come to her service.'

The phone rang at Roo and Simon's house immediately. It was Sue. It simply hadn't occurred to her to fly to Africa, but Johnny insisted it would be a good idea, both for her and for me. Her ticket was booked within the hour.

The following day Willie decided to take me under his wing, on safari, to get away and clear my head. I jumped at the chance. We had a picnic by a dry riverbed and talked heart to heart, frankly and openly, about Emma and their relationship. Willie was sad, defiant, but nevertheless so filled with regret for what might have been. We opened some wine only to find, as if symbolically, that it had gone sour. Instead we walked through the forest and drove home via Nairobi Game Park at dusk, to watch the wild animals grazing in the peace of the evening.

Back at Roo and Simon's house, Erica, Sue and Annabel Ledgard had arrived from England, bringing more appropriate clothes for me and a copy of Faure's *Requiem*, a piece of music I had heard once before at a memorial service and been moved by, and which I had now expressly requested in a fax. Annabel brought with her a prayer to read at the service, written by her father Frank, the family friend and vicar from Yorkshire who had led the service at Bunny's funeral all those years before. Suddenly I remembered the daffodils, clutched in my hand on that wet and sombre day.

14

*And so the day came at last, and I prepared myself for what was to come
– the funeral service for Emma and then her burial. I went to the
Cathedral early, to arrange some music to play at the beginning and the
end of the service, hoping to have some time to myself, some time with my
private thoughts, some time to gather myself in once more. But dozens of
people were already there – people who didn't know me, but who knew
and loved Emma – decking the cathedral with flowers – arranging huge,
abundant bouquets of brightly coloured and scented lilies, roses, carna-
tions and giant blue agapanthus. Sue arrived clutching bunches of
flowers she had bought from the local market and tied with kangas, the
lengths of brightly printed material the African women used as skirts or
head-dresses. We laid them around the base of the simple wooden trestle
on which Emma's coffin would shortly be rested.*

UNABLE TO FIND A WAY OF RIGGING UP THE MUSIC I WANTED
TO PLAY, I COLLARED A YOUNG AFRICAN WHO CAME TO MY
ASSISTANCE.

'Just a moment,' he promised and sprinted from the building. Twenty
minutes later, he was back with a huge chrome and black plastic ghetto
blaster, incongruous in its appearance, but perfect for the job. Somehow,
he managed to connect it to the cathedral's amplifier system and, as if
by some miracle, Faure's haunting *Requiem* echoed through the nave.

My task done, I returned to Roo and Simon's house for something
to eat and to change. I chose to wear a simple green linen skirt and

jacket, with a white blouse. It was Emma's favourite outfit of mine. As I stood in front of the mirror in my bedroom, smoothing out the wrinkles of my skirt with my hands, I caught my own reflection in the glass. I asked myself who was that pale, pinched, grey-haired woman with dark rings under her eyes? It wasn't someone I recognised. I was in a time capsule, what had to be would be. I was no longer in control.

I arrived at the Cathedral ahead of schedule and, feeling lost and unsure what to do, I waited outside until David Marrian, who was reading one of the prayers, scooped me up on his arm and escorted me down the long aisle. Seated at the front, staring at the rose window, I heard shuffling and whispering behind me as the Cathedral slowly began to fill with mourners. Unable to turn, I listened to the muffled greetings and hushed words of comfort creating a murmuring background to the organ music, as I waited for Emma.

She was carried in by Jennie, Johnny, Sally, and Kwong, Riek's aide-de-camp. Her coffin was a different shape from the ones we are used to in England, square-ended and oblong, thin and quite flat, with three ornate metal handles down each side. Some of her friends, including David Marrian, who had visited the funeral parlour where she lay the previous evening, had decided it was far too unimaginative for Emma, so they had painted the wooden exterior in dappled shades of green to make a colour-washed effect. It looked exotic. They told me tearfully afterwards that, although she had been embalmed, she looked very peaceful and had been dressed in a white Ethiopian robe similar to the one she wore on her wedding day. Her friends had also laid special grasses in her coffin, along with locks of their own hair. I could not face going to see her.

Gripping my hands together to stop them from shaking, I rose to my feet as the coffin was laid on the wooden trestle, and the flowers placed all around. It was all I could do to keep my eyes ahead. Then someone, a Sudanese man, stepped forward with an enormous framed photograph of Emma, in her favourite brown felt floppy hat, grinning from ear to ear, in the sunshine. He placed the photograph upright in front of the coffin, among the flowers. I was totally unprepared for this raw reminder of my daughter, and spent the next few minutes trembling visibly and averting my gaze. Finally, taking a deep breath, I plucked up the courage and glanced at her. She was very beautiful. Very much alive and obviously incredibly happy. It was a photograph taken at the leopard-skin ceremony in Ayod. I remembered it from the ones she had shown me. Gradually, I felt able to look at it more and more as the service went on, each time for a little longer, until I simply couldn't take my eyes off her.

The Cathedral was filled with music and the scent of a hundred blooms. Whites and blacks were crammed into the pews behind me, united in grief in an atmosphere of overwhelming love and appreciation. Emma had tied an invisible ribbon around us all, binding us together. Rev Gandon, standing at the altar in his robes, was joined by six bishops, the heads of the Anglican, Catholic and Presbyterian churches of southern Sudan, all of whom gave sermons, each one speaking fulsomely of Emma's life and work.

Willie gave an address, Annabel read her father's prayer and broke down completely, which gave others a chance to let go of their own emotions. Andrew Gandon stepped forward to squeeze Annabel's arm, and together they finished it. My heart went out to her as she struggled on, her cheeks wet with tears. I thought of poor Johnny, who was due at the lectern next. He had been determined from the start to sing for Emma *Dona Nobis Pacem* (grant us Thy peace), something he remembered from his prep-school days. Nudging him softly, I whispered:

'Are you okay? Can you do it?'

Johnny raised his head and stared directly at Emma's photograph.

'Yes, Mum,' he said firmly and rose from his seat. He had taken on the mantle of head of the family from the day Bunny died and he had no intention of letting the side down now. He stood by the lectern with two choristers singing the piece most beautifully, filling the lofty Cathedral with his tremulous voice.

David Marrian, Emma's friend and artist, he who painted the coffin, read a beautiful prayer he found somewhere, which also seemed just right:

What is dying?
I am standing on a sea shore.
A ship sails to the morning breeze and starts for the ocean. She is an
*   object of beauty and I stand watching her till at last she fades on*
*   the horizon and someone at my side says:*

'She is gone.'
Gone! Where? Gone from my sight, that is all . . .
The diminished size and total loss of sight is in me, not in her; and
just at the moment when someone at my side says:
'She is gone,' there are others who are watching her coming, and
other voices take up a glad shout,
'There she comes.' And that is dying.

from 'What is Dying?' by Bishop Brent

The service began to draw to a close and the Sudanese choir stood to sing. The rich sound of their voices, rising together in a crescendo of harmony, was spine-chillingly beautiful. At that precise moment, a shaft of sunlight broke into the Cathedral through the blue rose window, illuminating them, as if by a divine order.

The formalities over, Emma was borne aloft once more and carried out of the Cathedral into the gardens outside, where she was laid on another wooden trestle. I followed on Riek's arm, my eyes dry, my heart beating so loudly in my ears I almost failed to hear the music I had specifically wanted to hear. I had been warned what was about to happen – in keeping with African tradition. The lid of Emma's coffin was lifted and it was my task – with Riek, to lead the mourners slowly past so that each one could see her for one last time. As Emma had once written in her own diaries about a woman she had seen dead in Bor: 'Her face was entirely unmarked; and her expression strangely peaceful. I almost had an urge to shake her gently by the shoulder, to wake her up.'

I wanted to remember her as I always knew her, so I didn't look, I couldn't. I remained at Riek's side for only a few seconds before stumbling off into some nearby bushes and slumping to the ground in tears. The distant strains of Faure's *Requiem* filtered from the Cathedral, but I could take no more. My public bravado was over. This was me, Maggie McCune, and my heart was breaking for the loss of a cherished child.

I don't remember much after that. People found me, held me, lifted me up. I was led back into the Cathedral and sat on a pew. Someone wanted to speak to me, I was told, the Indian woman who found Emma in her garden; someone else was gathering all the flowers to take with us to southern Sudan.

I can't remember being taken there, but the next thing I knew I was at the wake, held at the Ngong Dairy in Karen, twenty miles outside Nairobi. The house was lovely to behold, with a dreamlike, film-like atmosphere. Everything had been organised; Emma's friends had bedecked the house with papyrus grasses, palm fronds, flowers and candles. Tea and cakes were served to the mass gathering of Europeans and Africans in a marquee in the garden. There were rich and poor, the humble and the great, people from across the political and racial divide. There were members of Riek's SPLA movement, someone from the Sudanese government, Emma's physician Dr Saio and the woman who had comforted her in her final hour. One friend who wanted to come couldn't make it, so his driver came instead. All these people, and all these gestures, showed innumerable touches of humanity and love.

Mingling with them, listening to their words of comfort, made me begin to realise that Emma had been the author of her own destiny, that her spirit had reached so many. She had become a symbol of caring and humanity in the middle of a civil war; she had used her position as Riek's wife to try to bring change to the lives of hundreds of thousands of ordinary people. And now they were honouring her. I remembered, again, my words to Bunny when Emma was born: 'I have a feeling that one day she is really going to make something of her life.'

As the evening wore on and the light faded slowly, bathing the garden in a lavender glow, we moved into the house and gathered in the main room as, one by one, Emma's friends and closest relatives stood on the steps of the wooden staircase and read from Emma's own writings. Her colourful descriptions of the cattle camp, the birds and wildlife of the Sobat River, and her beloved vegetable garden, brought southern Sudan to life in our minds and helped to fill the void in our hearts.

Jennie, Annabel and Sally spoke of their memories and the Sudanese choir interspersed these with their lilting songs. We clung to each other, like survivors of a shipwreck, waiting for help to come. I knew that I had to say something, I wanted to, and I slipped from the room for a quiet moment to compose my thoughts before speaking. Standing at the foot of the wide wooden staircase, I thanked Emma's friends and family for all they had done, and for helping to make her service so special. In her five years in Africa, I said, I had no idea that she had touched the lives of so many.

'When Emma was a little girl, one of her pastimes was to fly kites,' I told the hushed gathering. And in my mind's eye I saw her just as I'd seen her then, her face tilted to the heavens in an expression of pure joy and delight, as a captive red kite dangled and danced at the far end of her string. 'Emma has so many friends,' I said, 'who truly truly love her. And we must all go on flying her kites in her memory. We must fly those kites high in the sky. It is what she would have wanted.'

The words over, we were served the most delicious supper, a delicately spiced Swahili dish, prepared by some friends. It was just what we all needed. Fortified with a few glasses of wine or whisky, and relieved that the service was over, we relaxed – so much so that (to the horror of Riek's bodyguards) we erupted spontaneously into two rounds of Scottish dancing, reeling and twisting around the room gaily to the incongruous sound of bagpipe music. As I took Riek's hand and pulled him onto the floor, I reflected on how extraordinary it was that our two cultures had come together in this way and – to the sound of pipes and drums – we were echoing the rituals of a traditional African wake. Emma would have been proud. I could almost hear her laugh.

When the dancing was over and the music stopped, we felt some-how cleansed and grateful for the purging. In need of sleep before our early morning flight from Wilson Airport to Leer the next day, to bury Emma, we went home to bed. Sue and I shared a room. I think I had an hour's sleep that night, lying awake alongside my sister, weeping silent tears in the dark.

And so we flew to Leer to bury my daughter.

After I'd said my final, private farewell to Emma in Leer and climbed aboard Heather Stewart's little plane back to Nairobi, there was little more to do than fly home to England. On the evening of my departure, Riek offered to take me to Kenyatta Airport and see me off. I was returning home alone – the rest of my family had either previously left or were coming on afterwards. Riek picked me up from Roo and Simon's house, arriving in a three-car convoy just as the heavens opened, bringing torrential rain, the kind you only experience in that part of the world. The windscreen wipers simply could not cope with the deluge, and I was soaked to the skin within a few seconds of standing in it.

Sitting in the back of his limousine heading for the airport, watching the water pouring down the windows, I could control myself no longer. Sobs shook my body as I laid my head in my son-in-law's lap, unashamedly weeping as he comforted me as best he could and stroked my head tenderly. It was to be my last point of contact with Emma. The thought crossed my mind that I might never return to Africa, and might never see Riek again. At that moment, speeding along in the car, the rain pounding on the roof, I simply couldn't bear the agony and pain of bereavement.

Riek was wonderful. He coped admirably with his weeping mother-in-law, whom he barely knew, as he saw me safely to the plane. We said our farewells and I disappeared from his sight, eventually slumping into my window seat, a crumpled heap, as the plane took off. It was another solitary journey, my last involving Emma, and as I sat at the back of the plane, watching as the lights of Nairobi twinkled below me and receded into the distance, I felt strangely calm and no longer afraid of travelling alone.

Arriving home in Surrey to an empty house, and closing the door behind me, I dropped my bags, and wandered around the house, now decked out with flowers from friends, which helped to dispel the sensation of loneliness, and a future without Emma. On the table were a pile of letters, offering sympathy from around the world. I could not face them and pushed them to one side.

In the aftermath of her death, there was little space in my mind to deal with my grief properly. I was overwhelmed with the struggle of trying to marshal myself, my thoughts and my future into some sort of order. I was living through each day and each hour, constantly looking backwards and saying: 'This time yesterday, this time last week, this time last month,' using each and every date as a first anniversary. I was unable to think of a time before, or a time ahead, when my life would not be measured in some way by its distance from the day Emma died. The first year after losing a loved one is most definitely the worst because every gesture reminds you of your pain. I was constantly hanging on to every single thread of my memories of Emma.

The events around me didn't allow me much space either. Once the news of her death had filtered out from Africa, the obituaries filled several column inches of newsprint – some critical, but mostly fulsome in their praise of my daughter and what she had sacrificed in the name of Sudan. Peter Dalglish, her former boss at Street Kids International, said of her:

> 'No foreigner in modern times had been so completely accepted into the world of the southern Sudanese . . . In the end, when she decided to marry Riek and live among them rather than in England, people in the south understood, and few questions were asked. She had protected their children, built schools for them, and found books for them to read. She had earned their trust and their respect. The children of southern Sudan will remember Emma McCune as one of the most courageous friends they ever had.'

The avalanche of condolence letters continued to drop through the letterbox, literally hundreds. Each one I answered personally, draining my emotions, but in many ways an uplifting and cathartic experience. The words used to describe my daughter were eloquent and kind; the ones that have remained most in my memory are: compassionate, headstrong, calm, tenacious, generous, brave, energetic, free from prejudice, grace and light in an ugly situation, beautiful and fun. Almost all the letters spoke of her smile and her laughter.

The next step was to organise a memorial service in London. The theme was 'A Life Unfinished', and we organised it ourselves. Riek flew in from Africa for it, a measure of its importance to a man who rarely left his country. I was pleased to see him again. Angelina, Riek's first wife, attended, pregnant with his child, which was a complete bombshell to all of us on the day we were mourning the loss of Emma and his unborn child.

Heralded as one of Britain's largest Anglo-Sudanese gatherings, the memorial service was held on 29 January 1994 at the beautiful Wren church of St Martin's-within-Ludgate in the City of London, in the shadows of St Paul's Cathedral. The order of service was decorated with one of Emma's own drawings from her time as an art student in Oxford, an image of a woman shielding her head from the rays of what could be an African sun.

The proceedings were opened by a Sudanese choir. Frank Ledgard and Madeleine Bunting spoke, Annabel read from Emma's diary, and Frank's prayer was read by my sister Sue. Its simple words said:

We commend to your safekeeping Emma, with her love and devotion to the people of Africa and the children of Sudan. We thank God for all her many gifts, for bravery, for kindness, for generosity and the deepest care for all in need. We thank God for all that is life in her today, that cheerfulness and joy may inspire us on the way we have to go.

The service ended with lengthy eulogies delivered by Sudanese. The music ranged from hymns and psalms to a song by Van Morrison, which had somehow become Emma's song since her death.

> *Whenever God shines his light on me,*
> *Open up my eyes so I can see,*
> *When I look up in the darkest night –*
> *then I know everything is gonna be all right.*
> *In deep confusion, in great despair –*
> *when I reach out for Him, He is there.*

from 'Whenever God Shines His Light' by Van Morrison

It was an exhausting day for many reasons, not least because the mass of people crowded into that little baroque church, and thereafter in the Chapter House of St Paul's Cathedral, represented my own life and that of my daughter, now inextricably linked. Fifty years of my life flashed before my eyes in a matter of hours – faces from Assam, Yorkshire, London, Surrey, Africa. The faces of Emma's friends from those same eras, and from her time in Oxford, London and Sudan. Each one had a story to tell, a memory to rekindle, their own personal grief to share. It was a remarkable gathering of remarkable people, all united in their love of a remarkable young woman. Emma would have so loved to have been there.

But out of the darkness came light. Emma's friends resolved to channel the grief into a positive purpose. They set up the 'Emma Fund', administered by Christian Aid to help women and children in all parts of Sudan. People sent donations, and raised money through sponsored events for different projects, including sending sewing machines and 15,000 metres of cloth to make mosquito nets. There were also schemes to buy watering cans, bicycles for teachers and grinding mills for the sorghum and, most importantly, schemes for schools and education. Today, the Fund continues to help the causes which Emma pursued with such tenacity.

But, despite all the positives, all the good that had come from my daughter's death, I felt that there was more for me to do. Flicking through Emma's diaries and notes, coming across her own written accounts of her life in Africa, I felt an urge to continue writing, from where she had left off. This I felt particularly after Emma's friend, the journalist Madeleine Bunting, visited Leer. She was seized upon by the people as the new wife sent by Emma's family for Riek. Disappointed, they begged her to find a relative of Emma's, a younger sister or cousin, to give to Commander Riek. Everything had got worse since Emma had left, they said. An old woman broke into spontaneous song, praising God for Emma's life. The little town was full of people who were still cherishing the small gifts she had given them – shoes, a book, a length of cloth. When I heard of that, it seemed so unfair that someone so young, so resourceful, my daughter, had been snatched.

In the new year that followed, as I walked to and from work every day – Waterloo Station to St Paul's Cathedral and back – I would stride along the embankment on the south side of the River Thames, deep in thought, talking, talking, talking in my head . . . mostly to Emma. I found myself discussing past events with her, telling her what I was planning to do, asking her advice in a silent prayer. I would pause for a moment, listening for her answer. Sometimes I would hear it – her lovely, husky voice, that trace of a smile always in her words: 'Yes, Mum,' she would say. 'You're doing fine. Carry on.'

The more I talked to Emma and the more I thought about her life, the more I wanted to find out about the areas of her life I didn't know about. And so it was that, in July 1998, I embarked on a journey, a journey back to Africa to try to rediscover Emma.

As I flew into Kenyatta Airport on that summer dawn and saw an old friend – the vast red sun burning on the horizon – it was all I could do to stop myself from breaking down. That sun has always been a symbol of happiness to me, of hope and renewal. I always knew that seeing it out of the aircraft window as we touched down meant that my daughter was only a few minutes' hug away. This time, there was no one to hug. Emma was gone – she'd been gone for almost five years – and those joyful, tearful meetings were but a distant memory.

I was met instead by Kwong Denhier, Riek's former aide-de-camp. Emma's friend, Catherine Bond, was kind enough to put me up during my stay in central Nairobi. She had been so vital to me in my hour of need before – organising the funeral, the burial, the flights – it was good to renew my acquaintance with her. We went to the rather faded Hurlingham Club for lunch, we chatted endlessly about Emma, Sudan and Emma's life, and Catherine was once again invaluable in helping me plan my mission.

The person I wanted to see most was Riek, and I hoped he could meet me in Khartoum – a place that had, in the intervening years, become far less dangerous for him to be. But there were many others I wanted to talk to – people whose lives Emma had touched in some way, people to whom she had meant so much, and who could fill in the gaps. Kwong, now one of Riek's generals, and the man who had escorted us from the plane at Leer on Emma's burial day, had been dubbed 'Magic Kwong' by Jennie and Johnny after Emma's funeral, because he seemed to be there like magic every time we needed something. Now here he was for me again, agreeing to be my interpreter and guide for the duration of the Kenyan part of my trip. I decided that my first port of call should be to the Indian lady into whose garden Emma had been thrown after the accident. I knew she had come to the service in Nairobi Cathedral and had wanted to speak to me then, but I had been too upset to see her, and when I finally looked for her, she had gone.

We drove to the spot, on the edge of the Riverside residential area, and parked. My heart was in my mouth as we walked up her garden path in the late afternoon sun. To my dismay, we discovered that she was not home. As her gardener led Kwong, his wife Margaret and myself through the undergrowth to the spot where Emma's life ebbed away, it was all I could do to hold back the tears. Five years earlier, and almost immediately after the accident, Johnny and Jennie had planted a white moonflower tree in the garden in Emma's memory, but the gardener now told us that, sadly, it had died. However when we were led to the exact spot where Emma had lain, we saw a fig tree that Willie and Sally had planted a year later – which had survived. And to this day there remains a gap, a parched brown hole in the hedge, where Emma landed, and in which the gardener said nothing would grow.

> *Peace, Peace, she cannot hear*
> *Lyre or sonnet,*
> *All my life's buried here,*
> *Heap earth upon it.*

from 'Requiescat' by Oscar Wilde

After the disappointment of not being able to speak to the Indian lady, my quest was further blocked by frustration after frustration as I tried to make my way around Nairobi to interview those who had played a part in Emma's life. Her former SKI offices had disappeared, and the telephone system frustrated me still further – not only did I keep getting cut off, but so many of Emma's old contact numbers were no longer available.

I called in at Riek's new house – Peace House having been long relinquished – where I discovered that Angelina was now 'Number One Wife' once more. I inquired about the big wrought iron bed that Emma had had specially made for her and Riek, and the answer made me smile. It was now in the servants' quarters, I was told, where six houseboys sleep in it. Emma would have loved that.

Unable to get much further with my house calls to the various people I wanted to meet, I booked my ticket to Khartoum to see Riek instead. Our flight was delayed for three hours and I sat next to a cheerful Sudanese called Abdullah who told me he was one of thirty-nine survivors of a similar flight that had crashed earlier in the year. By the time our plane eventually touched down in Sudan in the early hours of Sunday morning, I was extremely relieved. Gathering together my thoughts and belongings, I was one of the last passengers to leave the aircraft, my head down as I negotiated the steps to the tarmac. A blast of warm night air enveloped me, bringing with it that sensation of being somewhere truly foreign. Palm trees rustled under the stars.

Looking up, I was amazed to see Riek standing on the tarmac surrounded by his bodyguards, waiting to give me VIP treatment. Considerably heavier than when I last saw him and, I thought, looking older, he welcomed me warmly with his rich smooth voice that had so often lulled me to sleep in my dreams. Much had happened in the five years since Emma died; complicated political events that she would have thought unthinkable and certainly would have sought to prevent had she still been alive. Deeply frustrated with the continuing splits between the tribal factions in the south, Riek renamed his movement the Southern Sudan Independence Movement (SSIM) and then took the extraordinary and surprising step of deciding to negotiate from within.

To cries of 'treachery' from many in the south and in Kenya, in April 1997, Riek Machar signed a peace agreement with the Islamic government in Khartoum, effectively joining forces with the enemy. His defence was, and always has been, that he had no choice. He had lost almost all of his power in the south, John Garang would have had him killed and the Khartoum government would never agree to consider his demands – to recognise the south as an independent state – unless he gave up the struggle against its forces.

I think I liked to see him rather romantically, for Emma's sake if nothing else, as a modern-day Gerry Adams or Yassir Arafat, consorting with the 'enemy' for the greater good. Whatever his intent, his actions meant that in an astonishing turnaround, the Nuer tribesmen who remained loyal to him found themselves fighting alongside their old adversaries, the Arab Muslims, against a combination of Nuer and Dinka Christians, led by the increasingly powerful Garang, the man Riek had first allied himself to in 1984.

Having helped draft a constitution for the south – a piece of paper not recognised by Garang or his allies – Riek was elevated to the lofty position of Assistant to the President of the Republic of Sudan, and Chairman of the Coordination Council of Southern Sudan. As such an honoured dignitary's mother-in-law, I was afforded every luxury, including an official welcome in the plush air-conditioned VIP lounge, and my own suite on the top floor of the Hilton Hotel. Bidding me goodnight until the following morning, Riek informed me that a car would come to collect me at eleven o'clock. And so my journey in search of my daughter had begun. I was back in Sudan and I felt strangely at home, sharing my daughter's affinity with a country she had first visited twelve years earlier.

Waking early, I pulled up the blinds, ordered some breakfast and found myself looking out across the Nile. The confluence of the White Nile and the Blue Nile is a few miles further down river, under an arched bridge referred to in Arabic poetry as 'the longest kiss in history'. I watched all the activity on the ground far below with fascination – shepherds tending their animals, people resting under the shade of a tree or in their little huts, others bathing in the wide river, some gardeners weeding the hotel compound. Two of them squatted on the hard crust of the sunburnt soil, removing some old and tired rose bushes.

Abruptly, I was woken from my trance. The telephone rang. It was seven o'clock in the morning, local time. I wondered who it could be. I recognised the voice straight away and sank onto the bed. It was Emmanuel, now living in Khartoum, saying he wanted to come and see me there and then. He was so excited and surprised to learn I was in the city that he said he couldn't wait. I had, firmly, to defer his visit until later. Riek was expecting me.

I ate some breakfast and drank some sweet-scented cardamom coffee as I prepared for the day ahead. I carefully laid out on the bed all the things I wanted to take with me – my camera, tape recorder, notes, questions, notebooks and pencils. I had brought some small gifts from England for Riek – chocolate, a couple of magazines, and some brightly coloured cotton handkerchiefs which I knew he liked. At eleven o'clock sharp, a man at hotel reception called to tell me my car had arrived.

I was duly whisked away to Riek's offices in the Presidential Palace, a grand whitewashed, three-storey, colonial-style building on the banks of the Nile. Crescent shaped and imposing, it was once the home of General Charles Gordon, the former British Governor of Sudan, murdered on the palace steps in 1885. It is now the offices of the government of Khartoum. Riek's air-conditioned office was in a separate building within the well-kept cloistered grounds filled with tall palms. It was a far cry from the cluttered little garrisons of mud huts in the swamplands of Nasir. I wondered what price he had paid to get here.

Ushered into his huge office, I could see he was in conference with some officials, but he stood up to greet me immediately and proudly introduced me to his staff. He entrusted me into the care of Helen Ashiro, the woman he had appointed to take on Emma's mantle, to co-ordinate the Southern Sudan Women's Association and the education and welfare of the children. Helen showed me photographs of the children at work and play in the Emma Secondary School in Leer, comprising five tukuls, hand-built by people who knew and loved my daughter and which had been financed by a charity based in Nairobi. Neither one of us dwelled on the fact that just a few days earlier the school had been attacked and razed to the ground – along with many other buildings and homes in the village – by militiamen opposed to Riek, who carried out two raids on consecutive days, killing many. The area was so dangerous now that my original hopes of returning to Leer to visit Emma's grave had been cruelly dashed.

Catherine Bond had already shown me BBC footage of Leer burning, with plumes of smoke rising from the military compound where Emma was buried. I had been afraid to ask if her grave had been desecrated. I suspected that even if it had, I would not be told. The thought of it was troubling, but not ultimately distressing to me, for I know that Emma's spirit roams free in Africa. We had said as much in a poem read at her London memorial service.

> Do not stand at my grave and weep;
> I am not there. I do not sleep.
> I am a thousand winds that blow.
> I am the diamond glints on snow,
> I am the sunlight on ripened grain.

I am the gentle autumn rain . . .
Do not stand at my grave and cry;
I am not there. I did not die.

from 'Do not stand at my grave and weep', Anon

What I did know was that the people of Leer were very resilient. They would soon rebuild their homes and the school. They had no alternative.

Riek also introduced me to a lovely lady called Allokiir, who was tall and plump and dressed in the most wonderful traditional African robes. Now a minister in Riek's government, Allokiir had been a friend and colleague of Emma's in the Women's Association in Nasir – Emma's Sudanese soul mate – and she sat, chatted, laughed and, with a trace of tears, told me how much she still missed her. She clearly thought Emma was wonderful and great fun and, as we parted, she made me a promise.

'I vow to remain in a position to do all I can for the women and children,' she said, solemnly. 'I owe that to Emma and all that Emma stood for.' It was my turn to choke back the tears.

Riek was obviously extremely busy and already in another meeting by the time I bade farewell to Allokiir. He introduced me to even more officials before sending me back to my hotel with Helen for lunch. Later that afternoon his driver took me to Khartoum's National Museum, where I spent the next few hours lost in time and space, strolling alone with a wizened old tour guide through dusty dimly-lit corridors, peering at the amazing artefacts – ancient relics, pottery and bracelets, ethnic jewellery that Emma would have loved. But it was the pale colour-washed stone wall frescoes rescued from the area of Faras before the building of the Aswan Dam which most impressed me. The images of those depicted were all much the same: figures from the Coptic age with richly embroidered clothes and dark eye shadow. Those faces and wide brown eyes reminded me somehow of the extraordinary images that had met me at Leer – the throng of people pressing forward, St George's flags fluttering, their arms and hands reaching out with long, bony fingers to touch my daughter's coffin.

After dark, I was driven back through the sticky evening heat to my hotel, physically and emotionally drained. Flopping onto the bed to savour the cool of my room, I stared at the ceiling and found my vision blurring suddenly. Here I was back in Sudan, back at the epicentre of my daughter's short life and all that she stood for, and I found that I had also reached the epicentre of my own emotions. The past five years had been a long journey of discovery, an exploration of my own life and Emma's.

I had never expected to be at this point, to reach the end from there to here, to accept that I was the survivor. No mother expects to outlive her children, to bury them in the earth and walk away. And it seemed to me that both Emma and I had paid a terrible price in the pursuit of happiness. Our past could never be escaped from. The tragedies of long ago made us who we were, drove us onwards. Almost at the end of my journey now and afraid of reaching that point where I would have to relinquish my hold, I wondered if I could cope.

The telephone rang, making me jump. It was Emmanuel, telling me he had called round to see me at five o'clock, as arranged, but I wasn't there. I was mortified, I had completely forgotten about his visit. Excitedly, he asked if he could see me the following day. Yes, I said, come at half-past seven, and he rang off. Utterly exhausted, I had a long shower, ate some supper and retired to bed.

The next morning I found myself unexpectedly excited about seeing Emmanuel again. He was someone Emma had cared very deeply about, someone who relied on her, and I needed this point of contact. Just after seven o'clock, I was astounded to find myself running in and out of my hotel room to check if he was coming up the passageway. When he arrived, he ran to me and hugged me with the words: 'Hello, Granny.' Now sixteen years old, he had positively sprouted both in stature and maturity to tower above me. I was tremendously impressed.

We had breakfast together, chatting animatedly, and then spent the day together with Hassa, my driver, sightseeing in Khartoum, visiting the wonderfully colourful city and *souks*, or markets, of Omduram, where I bought some exotic beads. And I remembered how much Emma had always loved her beads and bangles.

Emmanuel and I spent all day together as he filled me in on his life. When Emma had died, Emmanuel had been bereft; she was the first person in his young life to protect him. On the day of her funeral, he moped around Peace House, asking:

'Who will look after me now?' When Riek moved to Khartoum, he took Emmanuel with him, along with nine other boys, and arranged for them to be educated in Khartoum and to learn Arabic. The children all lived with Riek in his government villa and were under his protection. Emmanuel told me he hoped to do business and computer studies and travel to Britain and America one day.

'I could come and stay with you, Granny,' he said brightly, and I laughed.

Riek suddenly appeared at six o'clock, looking for me in the hotel as I sat chatting with the boy. Emmanuel scuttled from sight like greased lightning; it was clear he was terrified of Riek and his authority. I was sorry to see him go like that, not to have been able to say goodbye properly, but pleased to see my son-in-law. I desperately wanted to speak to him about his life with my daughter, Emma. We sat and talked late into the night, his soft tones recorded on my tape. He seemed immensely sad when he spoke of his young wife and how they first met, taking me through each stage of their short but remarkable partnership. I sat, transfixed, fascinated by all that he told me as he filled in the gaps I had been unable to fill in, piecing together the bits of the jigsaw until I finally had a complete picture. It was an image so clear, so true. It was a picture of a young couple deeply in love, caught up in the most extraordinary circumstances, each pulled by their own ambitions and beliefs, each one striving to achieve their goals at the same time as keeping their love alive.

Friends in Africa had kept me posted about Riek Machar in the years after Emma's death. One wrote to tell me that he had:

'lost his anchor without her and was hopelessly adrift, mentally and physically . . . His language to those around him changed dramatically, barking rather than announcing; his agenda, too, had changed, as did his capacity for the truth. Suddenly, everything could be fudged. Emma was the conscience of the movement.'

Emma had, it seems, told key friends shortly before she died:

'If anything ever happens to me, you must watch what goes on in southern Sudan and jump all over Riek if he fucks up.'

But, they said, the rebel commander had ignored their advice and gone his own, perhaps suicidal, way.

Talking to me now about happier times during his life with Emma, Riek did not cry. It was not in his tradition to do so. But his big brown eyes misted over often, and his huge hands with those long, supple fingers interlocked and entwined themselves all night long, as he recalled his vivid memories. When it was over, and we were both spent emotionally, he took my hand and thanked me.

'It would have been too painful to speak like this any sooner, Maggie,' he said. I nodded, barely able to control my emotions. 'But I am glad we did.'

I had one last day in Khartoum, spent at Riek's office and in my hotel, going through a few final points and meeting even more of his ministers, who were all dedicated to reaching a peaceful settlement for southern Sudan. I met Emma's bodyguard, Forty-Six, the seven-foot giant who had single-handedly saved her from the ambush in Kongor; I met Riek's uncle, a kindly old man who seemed rather out of place in a cosmopolitan setting; and one of Riek's ministers, a former leopard-skin chief who now spent ninety per cent of his time chatting animatedly into his mobile telephone.

On my last night, I enjoyed a quiet dinner with Riek and we sat talking again until midnight, each of us reluctant to break off.

'It is good you came,' he told me. 'It is good for me and it is good for my people. I am glad you have seen that Emma's work goes on, will always go on.'

He left my room well after midnight and told me to try and get some sleep – we were leaving for the airport, and my flight back to Kenya, before dawn.

Needless to say, I didn't sleep. I couldn't. I was too overwhelmed. Thoughts and memories flooded my brain and Emma's face drifted in and out of my mind. I packed and prepared to leave Sudan. Saying goodbye to Riek at the airport, we sat in the VIP lounge side by side, hardly speaking. There was a quiet companionship between us – two very different people from completely different cultures who might never have met but for the person we both loved. Slipping my arm through his as we stepped from the air-conditioned room into the balmy night, we strolled to the steps of the plane, I thanked him for his time, and for giving my daughter happiness.

'Goodbye, Riek, I'm so glad I came,' I told him, kissing his cheek. Leaning down to hug me, reluctant to relinquish his hold, I could see his pain; his grief was palpable, I felt that he had a long way to go. Not wanting him to see me cry, I turned and hurried up the steps and into the plane.

Once more on a solitary journey, the dim aeroplane interior blanketing me from prying eyes, I allowed the last of my tears to fall. I thought of the things Riek had told me, of the way his face lit up when he spoke of Emma. How she would always be alive in his heart. This wasn't just my loss – it was a loss for my entire family, for Riek and for the people of southern Sudan.

I wondered now about Emma, what had driven her to give such passion and dedication to the cause of southern Sudan and its people – in particular the women and children. Her youth and naivety certainly drove her on, along with her warmth and spontaneity, but she was determined from childhood, it now seems, to live life to the full. Was there something that came from within her which told her that her life might be cut short, that she had to pack it as full as possible of life's experiences? Is it possible that a feeling for danger and adventure, a zest for new horizons, had transferred itself to her in my womb, during that moment when we both nearly drowned?

It is hard not to imagine that Emma had a destiny and that all she did was part of some greater plan. All that she saw and achieved, suffered and endured, loved and adored is extraordinary. In her short life she left an indelible mark on a small corner of the globe, and a huge mark on the history of Sudan where the people gave her their unconditional love. She had planned to spend her life in Africa, to have a little farm somewhere near Riek's home town of Leer, and live a very quiet and simple life, raising their children and grandchildren, introducing a new generation of McCune-Machars to that distant corner of a foreign land. She was complete and her life ended there. She became a legend and is, I believe, more powerful in death than she was in life.

Standing at her graveside in Leer in 1993, I vowed to keep her memory alive. I have learned in the intervening years that Emma's memory will never die, not here in my heart and especially not in the place she made her home. She still holds so much influence over so many people – me for one, her own mother, who has discovered in death her magnitude in life.

Four months after she died, I awoke from a deep slumber in the middle of the night and spoke aloud to an empty room.

'Emma's baby is being born tonight,' I said, as sure as anything in my mind that it had been. The dream was exact and clear. It was 28 March 1994. Emma's child had been due on 1 April, almost a week later. There have been times since when I have thought about my little grandson, mentally ticking off the years and thinking: 'Today he would be four,' or imagining myself walking with him, hand in hand. I wondered who he would most resemble – Emma or Riek? Would there be something of her grace in him, or Bunny's smile, or would he have inherited the Nuer traits of gentleness and strength?

On 4 January 1998, my daughter Erica gave birth to her first child. It was a Sunday and a hurricane was blowing the previous night, cutting off the electricity and leaving me in candlelight. Hugh, whom Yo had married two years earlier, rang me from the hospital to tell me the good news and to invite me to come and meet my new granddaughter. I drove to the Royal Surrey Hospital in nearby Guildford with mixed feelings, hoping that I would respond correctly, that my inevitable thoughts of Emma and her child would not mar Erica and Hugh's happy day.

Reaching into the crib and holding the tiny child in my arms for the very first time, I needn't have worried. She was a tiny bundle of life, with an interesting little face. I inevitably searched for similarities between her and Erica, Emma and the other children, but here she was, this new life, an individual about to embark on her own life's adventures. I felt tremendously proud.

'What are you going to call her?' I asked Erica, sitting happily in bed, watching me as I held her new infant.

'Alexandra Margot,' she said. 'Alexandra after Gramps, and Margot after dear Aunt Margot.' I nodded my approval, blinking back the tears, thinking what a good choice they had made. My father had died three years earlier, aged eighty-five. I still missed him. I realised that nobody would ever call me Rabbit again.

When I looked up, in a book of children's names, the meaning of the name Alexandra some weeks after her birth, I absentmindedly flicked to the page that listed the names that begin with 'E'. I found Emma's name, a name I had chosen all those years ago, now to discover, with a wry smile, that it means: 'One who heals the universe. A woman of command.' Flicking back to the letter 'A' and looking up Alexandra, I discovered that it means: 'The helper of mankind.' I wondered what life would bring her.

In the ever-unwinding chain of hours, days, months and years, it is easy to lose ourselves and others in the mists of time. That is why I had to go back. In searching for Emma, I have also found myself, and have made some sense of how we got from there to here. As I come to the end of our story, there is a presence at my side, watching me, helping me, willing me on. I feel an invisible arm around my shoulder. They say that ghosts always dwell in the darkness; but now I understand that they can also live in the light.

'I will always be here,' she whispers, 'but now I must go back again, to walk in the sun.'

Index